BLACK&DECKER

The Complete Guide to

Patios

Plan, Build and Maintain

Philip Schmidt

**Creative Publishing
international**

CHANHASSEN, MINNESOTA
www.creativepub.com

Creative Publishing
international

Copyright © 2007
Creative Publishing international, Inc.
18705 Lake Drive East
Chanhassen, Minnesota 55317
1-800-328-3895
www.creativepub.com
All rights reserved

Printed at R.R. Donnelley

10 9 8 7 6 5 4 3 2 1

Library of Congress Cataloging-in-Publication Data

Schmidt, Philip.
  The complete guide to patios : plan, build & maintain / by
Philip Schmidt.
      p. cm.
  "Branded by Black & Decker."
  Summary: "A comprehensive guide that includes an
introduction to the most popular building materials: a fool-
proof method for design, planning and layout; detailed step-
by-step projects to help readers build any one of 12 different
types of patios; instructions for building popular patio
accessories and features; and tips for maintaining and
repairing all types of patios"--Provided by publisher.
  Includes bibliographical references and index.
  ISBN-13: 978-1-58923-305-8 (soft cover)
  ISBN-10: 1-58923-305-0 (soft cover)
  1. Patios. I. Black & Decker Corporation (Towson, Md.)
II. Title.
  TH4970.S36 2007
  690.1'84--dc22
                            2006036006

President/CEO: Ken Fund
VP for Sales & Marketing: Peter Ackroyd

Home Improvement Group
Publisher: Bryan Trandem
Senior Editor: Mark Johanson
Managing Editor: Tracy Stanley
Editor: Jennifer Gehlhar

Creative Director: Michele Lanci-Altomare
Senior Design Manager: Brad Springer
Design Managers: Jon Simpson, Mary Rohl

Director of Photography: Tim Himsel
Lead Photographer: Steve Galvin
Photo Coordinators: Julie Caruso, Joanne Wawra
Shop Manager: Randy Austin

Production Managers: Laura Hokkanen, Linda Halls

Author: Philip Schmidt
Page Layout Artist: Kari Johnston
Illustrator: Earl Slack
Photographer: Joel Schnell

Cover Image Photo: Steve Galvin
  The furniture was provided by Seasonal Concepts
    in Bloomington, Minnesota.
  Concrete Patio by Becker Architectural Concrete.

COMPLETE GUIDE TO PATIOS
Created by: The Editors of Creative Publishing international, Inc., in cooperation with Black & Decker.
Black & Decker® is a trademark of The Black & Decker Corporation and is used under license.

Contents

Complete Guide to Patios

INTRODUCTION 4

DESIGN 6
Patio Themes 6
Dining & Entertaining 8
Private 12
Expansive 16
Courtyard 20
Remote 24
Multipurpose 28
Welcoming 32
Elements 36
Surfaces 38
Walls & Fences 48
Paths, Walkways & Steps 50
Overheads 52
Fire & Water 54
Utilities 58
Your Patio 60
Use 62
Choosing a Site 64
Dealing with Drainage 67
Size & Layout 69
Climate Control 70
Exterior Design Style 72
Making a Plan 74

CONSTRUCTION 76
Tools & Materials 76
Masonry Tools 78
Landscaping & Specialty Tools . . 80
Power Tools 81

Mortar 82
Brick & Concrete Block
Lumber & Hardware 83
Techniques **86**
Working with Concrete 88
Working with Brick &
Concrete Block 98
Working with Stone 103
Preparing the Site **104**
Grading Soil 106
Building a Drainage Swale 108
Building a Dry Well 111
Retaining Walls & Terracing . . . 113
Laying Out & Preparing the Site . . 115

PROJECTS **120**
Patio Surfaces **120**
Sandset Brick 122
Concrete Pavers 128
Mortared Brick 130
Sandset Flagstone 132
Mortared Flagstone 134
Seeded Concrete & Wood 137
Basic Concrete Slab 140
Tile on Concrete 148
Loose Material 154
Framed Wood 156
Wood Tile 160
Installing Edging 162
Finishing Touches **168**
Raised Garden Bed 170
Fire Pit 172

Wall Fountain 176
Cobblestone Fountain 180
Brick Wall 184
Mortarless Block Wall 188
Patio Arbor 192
Trees 200
**Patio Lighting &
Outdoor Kitchens** **202**
Creating a Patio Lighting Plan . . 204
Installing Low-voltage Lighting . . 210
Planning an Outdoor Kitchen . . 212
**Cleaning & Maintaining
Patio Surfaces** **218**
Brick & Concrete Pavers 220
Concrete Slab 224
Tile 230
Flagstone 232

Resources **234**
Index **236**

Introduction

"Outdoor room" now holds a permanent place in the home designer's vocabulary. It describes a casual, open-air space tailored to the homeowners' favorite outdoor activities. A room that changes character with each hour of the day, adding a natural dimension to the home's living space. The patio, offering these benefits and more, is the definitive outdoor room.

The word patio comes from Spanish and Latin American architecture, meaning court or courtyard. In traditional homes, the patio occupied the center of the house and was the hub of family life. Today, this idea of an outdoor gathering place inspires some of the most beloved and well-used patios. Many homeowners say they are surprised by how much time they spend on their new or redesigned patios—not just for dining, barbecuing, and sunbathing, but also gardening, entertaining, and playing with the kids. An attractive patio with a convenient layout and the right feel has the power to lure you outdoors again and again.

As you'll see in photos and projects throughout this book, a patio can be so much more than a concrete slab with an umbrella table and rollaway barbecue. By virtue of being on the ground, patios offer numerous design options. While most elevated decks are made only of wood, patios can be built with brick, stone, concrete, gravel, tile, and, yes, wood. Patios can take any shape, form, and style. They can unfold before a back door or hide in a patch of trees at the corner of a lot. A patio can be sculpted with low walls or flowerbeds. And with the addition of a vine-covered pergola or outdoor fireplace, you can extend the useable hours of your patio throughout the year. Best of all, a patio is deeply rooted in the landscape, promising a unique blend of home and garden that creates an atmosphere all its own.

To guide you through your patio project, this book covers the entire creative process— from exploring ideas to perfecting the design to laying the paving and installing the lights. As you add patio features to your wish list and begin to develop a work plan, be sure to review the construction details and steps involved in each part of the project. This will help you refine your plans according to budget and time constraints, and it's invaluable for avoiding problems with the overall schedule. As an outdoor project that typically doesn't disrupt everyday life in the home, building a new patio can follow an easy pace. This makes the creative process especially satisfying.

Design:
Patio Themes

In patio design, decisions about materials, shape, style, and even size are all secondary to the theme of the space. In other words, what is the essence of your patio? What will it do for you? How will you use it, and how will it make you feel? Do you seek an intimate retreat for private relaxation or a wide-open stage for enjoying a view and backyard activities? Should your patio accommodate large parties or everyday family dining—or both? These are some of the primary questions that will help determine the function and atmosphere of your new outdoor room.

The patio themes represented in this chapter cover a range of "space" concepts, from private to expansive, remote to integrated. With any patio theme, the end use is a central consideration, but just as important is the quality of the environment. As you look through the photos, imagine yourself using each of the patios. Then, think about having a similar patio configuration on your own property. What would your view look like? Would you feel sheltered or exposed? Is the patio just a step outside the back door or at the end of a winding path? How might you use plants, walls, or an overhead to shape and enhance the space?

Of course, your patio design doesn't have to follow a specific theme and will most likely incorporate several ideas with practical features. The easiest way to find that perfect combination is to keep an open mind and work with your imagination. Don't be afraid to experiment on paper or try combinations of ideas that may seem completely odd or incongruous. If you get stuck or have trouble generating ideas, set the project aside. Often the best solutions arise when you're thinking about something else.

In This Chapter

- Dining & Entertaining
- Private
- Expansive
- Courtyard
- Remote
- Multipurpose
- Welcoming

Dining & Entertaining

If a patio is perfect for one thing it's alfresco meals. Whether at breakfast, lunch, or dinner with the family; casual weekend barbeques; or late-night hors d'oeuvre parties, food just tastes better outdoors. A patio intended for everyday meals should be casual and conveniently located. A table and chairs set up at all times lets you decide at the last minute to eat outside without much fuss. Choose lighting that is bright enough for eating comfortably but can easily be lowered for after-dinner conversation. Locating the patio just off the house kitchen makes the space convenient enough to be used as a second dining room. Of course, an outdoor kitchen brings the cooking right into the space, so the cook is never stuck inside during those precious summer evenings.

A successful entertainment patio combines indoor comforts with outdoor pleasures. The open atmosphere allows guests to lounge under the stars or take a stroll through the garden. A well designed entertainment space is roomy yet comfortable. Consider adding overheads and walls to promote a feeling of intimacy or a wide walkway or broad steps to invite guests to wander off the patio and into the yard. Furniture or more permanent features can define the "room." Consider adding a fireplace, bar, or formal dinner table.

A simple dining setup with easy access is ideal for everything from morning coffee to romantic dinners to late-afternoon cocktails.

The comfort and utility of furniture directly affects your enjoyment of a patio and should be considered carefully.

Outdoor entertaining is so much about the atmosphere. On a comfortable patio, a casual but festive arrangement is all you need to set the stage for casual summer parties.

(Above) Entertaining on a remote patio may lack convenience, but it makes up for it with drama.

(Right) Two different approaches to patio dining rooms: (A) This classic picnic table in an informal setting serves well for family meals and everyday outdoor projects. (B) A formal, partially enclosed room—complete with chandelier—feels much closer to home.

Aside from the obvious focal point created by an outdoor fireplace or other similar large structures, an open patio can be entirely defined by its furniture and can be completely rearranged to suit the occasion.

Cozy, private, yet open to the sky, an intimate outdoor room can be a perfect gathering spot for small groups.

Private

When you want to be outside but don't want to feel exposed or on display, a private patio space is the answer. Privacy can take many forms and often is as much a result of perception as it is of physical seclusion. Adding privacy might mean screening out the views of neighbors or locating the patio in a distant corner of the lot. A fountain or other water feature can provide a sense of privacy by drowning out noise and letting you dwell in your own thoughts.

Along with increased privacy comes a feeling of enclosure and shelter. In terms of layout, this creates spaces that are intimate but may have somewhat limited use. If this is not what you want for your entire patio, you can always make some parts private while leaving others open. Another option is to build a small private retreat away from the main patio. Whatever the design, a private patio should be personal and comfortable, particularly for those who will spend the most time there.

Urban patios often rely on tall fences or walls for much needed privacy. Plantings help soften the look of the barriers and add depth to the views, preventing a closed-in feeling.

(Left) **This intimate, sheltered outdoor room** stays cool thanks to the fountain and shade from the tree.

(Below) **Overheads make a strong architectural statement** while adding privacy and a sense of enclosure. This patio "building" suggests an open-air greenhouse or sunroom without window glass.

Private spaces are all about your own desires. For some, a hammock and a little shade are all that's required.

(Right) Attractive glass gates can be opened for the view or closed to accommodate privacy.

(Below) An outdoor shower is perfect for homes close to beaches. It allows you to clean off the sand on your feet before tracking it into the house.

(Above) Private doesn't have to mean small. This large patio is entirely enclosed, yet avoids a cavernous feel by breaking up the space into distinct zones, creating distinct rooms and an original landscape.

(Left) A hidden outdoor bathing area is the ultimate private luxury.

Expansive

The idea behind expansive patios is openness. Where private spaces are sanctuaries closed off from the outer world, an expansive patio unfolds into the broader landscape, often blending with its surroundings.

Wide-open patio designs are typically favored on lots that are large enough not to need privacy and in yards that offer a great view. However, creating an expansive feel is not about maximizing the patio's size. In fact, small patios can gain the most from an expansive theme—leaving patios open allows them to borrow views of the natural landscape and create the perception of increased space.

This basic concept of openness also informs the layout and decoration of expansive patios. Designs are most often simple, with no walls or large plantings that would block views or simply muddle the balance of the overall lot plan. Unobtrusive pots or shrubs placed to the side can help frame a view from the patio, but a large overhead might prove oppressive and detract from the open feeling. An expansive theme works well for remote outdoor rooms as well as patios right next to the house.

Extending from the edge of an elevated deck, this basic patio becomes an integrated part of a dynamic landscape.

The clean, open plan of this large patio makes for an easy transition onto the similarly minimal lawn. Your eye follows right through to the view beyond.

With the perfect location, all you need is a flat surface to relax and enjoy the setting. Keeping this patio simple also ensures a good view to the lake from the house.

Rather than closing off this small patio area, the soft boundaries created by the side plantings and concrete pads set into the grass add definition while linking the patio to the open lawn area. The subtle flow from patio to lawn enhances the size of both spaces.

This sprawling outdoor room maintains an expansive feel with a visual flow between levels. Accents of boulders and trees echo the view of distant mountains to blend with the natural openness of the land.

Courtyard

By design, a courtyard patio is intimately linked to the house. Typically bound by walls on three sides, courtyards tend to feel very private and secure and are often used as an extension of the indoor living space. From inside the house, views of a courtyard add a sense of spaciousness and are a constant invitation to step out and enjoy the air.

A traditional courtyard is an integral part of a home's design, with the patio nestled within a U-shaped floor plan. If you'd like a courtyard patio but don't have the right shape of house, you can improvise for a courtyard feel. Starting with an L configuration (where two exterior house walls meet), you can add on to the house to create a U or simply build fencing or a tall wall for the same effect. Anything added should blend architecturally with the house for a built-in appearance.

Water features, particularly fountains, are traditional elements in courtyards, modeled after ancient piazzas or town squares. Here, a quietly bubbling fountain creates a soothing focal point in a hot, arid setting.

The angles in this contemporary design break up an otherwise tunnel feeling in this narrow courtyard.

The courtyards of Mexico and other warm cultures offer centuries of inspiring ideas for creating a modern patio with an old-world allure.

(Right) Wall coverings and a variety of shade-tolerant plants can transform sunken or urban courtyards surrounded by solid walls.

(Below) There are many ways to style a courtyard. This contemporary space maintains a natural feel with a blend of plantings and grass.

An attractive flagstone walk passes through a garden buffer zone between this sequestered courtyard and the outside world. It is an inviting pathway into a private courtyard.

With walls as a backdrop, a courtyard patio can feel like a casual room decorated with outdoor accents.

Remote

Most patios are located right behind the house, but there's no rule saying they have to be. A freestanding or detached patio can offer added privacy or it can offer an exposed and expansive feel. For example, a comfortable perch for catching the sunset may be best left wide open to fully take in the surrounding scenery.

Making your outdoor room "out of the way" inspires creativity—being free of the style constraints set by the house, the patio can blend into the landscape or become an eye-catching art piece on its own. Detached patios are often used in addition to a patio or deck attached to a house. This arrangement offers even more freedom for designing the remote patio, since the primary outdoor activities can take place at the main patio close to the house, while the remote space can be reserved for a private retreat.

Beautiful as a composition, this remote platform is a secluded spot for peaceful contemplation.

(Left) A remote patio is ideal for private retreats. Being away from the house allows these homeowners to enjoy this secluded nook amongst the trees.

(Below) An outdoor fireplace can make a remote patio an especially cozy destination.

(Above) Detached patios offer the chance to do something different. This self-contained outdoor room serves as a dramatic focal point for the landscape.

(Right) Away from the shelter of the house, remote patios can be overly exposed. An overhead or side wall can provide shade and a barrier from strong winds, as with this gazebo-like retreat.

A vibrantly colored screen of garden plants adds privacy and an interesting backdrop to this remote dining space.

This quaint getaway is located along the back fence of a lot, creating an attractive backdrop and a stage for enjoying the garden.

Multipurpose

Indoors, people spend the most time in their multifunctional spaces—namely the kitchen and family room. The same is true for patios: When the outdoor layout and features cater to multiple activities, the space tends to be used more often. And after all, the purpose of a patio is to get you outdoors.

While a multipurpose patio requires careful planning, it doesn't have to be all about practicality.

Centering the layout around a functional dining area, for example, doesn't mean you can't include a natural garden plot, a decorative water feature, or a sequestered nook for a private reading space. The ideal plan is dynamic enough to cover your household's range of activities yet unified in design and appearance. A broad view of the patio (which is most often the view from the house) should reveal an integrated layout with a natural flow from one area to another.

On this lavish terrace patio, the clever layout accommodates distinct activity areas without interrupting the flow of the pool surround. Concrete squares form a patterned "flooring" treatment to highlight the dining area.

Linking an indoor space with a patio adds another dimension to warm-weather living.

Plants are often a welcome feature for patios. Here, the dining area is sheltered with thick plantings for an intimate setting while the sitting area is more open to accomodate those who prefer to stand and mingle.

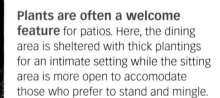

A change in level is one of the most effective ways to separate a patio. The gentle curve in these steps provides interest without busying the overall design.

Including a sheltered area adds a great deal of usefulness in many climates. This versatile patio incorporates spaces for dining and sitting.

This simple wraparound patio defines its activity spaces with specific groupings of furniture: a coffee table and chairs for coffee or tea, and a casual lounge area for reclining in the sun. Each is positioned thoughtfully to capture the best conditions of each activity.

(Left) A deck and two patios woven into this landscape result in a lot of different outdoor uses, and all locations are linked to a corner garden by the flagstone and gravel path.

(Below) This multipurpose plan serves not only as a patio but also as a common area providing access to a gazebo and hot tub for all-season recreation.

Welcoming

Not all patios are hidden behind the house. Often surrounding the front door or other main entrance, welcoming patios are a warm greeting to visitors and can provide an attractive link between the house and a driveway or public sidewalk.

The inviting appearance of an entry patio certainly adds curb appeal, but its true purpose is the same as any standard backyard space. In terms of use, the entry patio is a return to the concept of the traditional American front porch: a semiprivate space that allows homeowners to enjoy the outdoors while keeping in touch with neighbors. Being in full view, however, does place certain stylistic and architectural constraints on an entry patio. As the foreground to a home's facade, it's important that the patio complements the home's proportions and decorative scheme.

A charming walkway and casual sitting area convey a message of welcome and leisure to visitors of this house, as well as providing the perfect spot for spending warm evenings. The low gate adds a sense of privacy and closure to the patio area.

(Right) An inlay of wood decking tiles creates an area rug effect for a welcoming patio-style entrance.

(Below) Container plants and perhaps some casual furniture are great for adding a patio feel to urban entrances.

A walled courtyard is the most private of entry patios but presents an extra special welcome to all visitors admitted beyond the front gate.

Entering and exiting by this side entrance includes a pleasant stroll through a flower garden—and a constant temptation to linger in the patio areas.

This welcoming entrance has an elevated patio where visitors can relax on a bench while taking in the garden view.

Inspired by front porch designs, this entry patio has a low wall to clearly separate it from the driveway. The substantial yet airy pergola ensures a patio feel where a solid roof would seem more sheltering and porch-like.

Design: Elements

L ike any interior room, a patio is a blend of design elements—
flooring, walls, and ceiling—plus functional features and decorative
accents. And, of course, traditional decorating basics, such as texture and color, are just as important outside as they are inside the home.

The trick to successful patio design is to approach it with a decorator's eye. Start with the flooring, the most dominant element that sets
the tone for the entire space. Then move to shaping and defining the
patio space by considering walls and fences. Finally, consider overheads,
like arbors and pergolas. They are great for providing shade and a touch
of garden architecture. You can always further enhance the mood with
a bubbling fountain or cooling pool, and illuminate the night with a
fire pit or atmospheric lighting.

This chapter takes a look at these primary design elements and the
many material options available for the decorator's palette. It should help
you complete your wish list. Later, in chapter 3, you'll scrutinize the list
further and decide what does and doesn't make sense in view of practical
matters, such as zoning restrictions and seasonal weather patterns.

In This Chapter

- Surfaces
- Walls & Fences
- Paths, Walkways & Steps
- Overheads
- Fire & Water
- Utilities

Surfaces

Brick, stone, and concrete may rightly head up the list of good patio flooring options, but these materials in their basic forms are just the beginning of a much more expansive list. Brick alone comes in a huge range of colors, textures, and styles, while the availability of stone and exterior tile is constantly expanding.

After giving some thought to your preferred flooring surface, it will be well worth it to spend a few hours browsing local stone yards, landscape suppliers, building centers, or lumberyards to see what's available in your area. Ask about delivery pricing while you're there. Businesses that carry masonry paving materials are in the phone book under headings such as Stone, Brick, Rock, Landscape Equipment & Supplies, and Sand & Gravel.

An important design rule to keep in mind when choosing a surface material is that the finished pattern should fit the space: A busy or complicated design can crowd or overwhelm a small patio. Conversely, you can avoid monotony on an expansive surface with a variegated pattern or blend of materials. Choose a material with a color and texture that blends nicely with the neighboring elements, whether that's your house, garden, or significant plantings in the area.

Local brickyards, stone yards, and landscape suppliers are the best places to see a range of patio materials suitable for your location.

Made of fired clay, brick is the oldest manufactured building material and has been used for over 6,000 years. Common brick types include: (a) standard brick pavers, (b) chamfered paver, (c) concrete paver, (d) used brick, (e) fire brick.

Brick

Brick is generally considered the most classic surface material for patios—a well-deserved distinction. With its combination of warm, natural coloring and texture and orderly geometric shapes, brick is perhaps the perfect meeting point between house and garden. And with its small unit size, it's also quite versatile and can be easily applied to formal layouts or imaginative curved patterns. The standard brick patio installation consists of setting brick into a sand bed in an ordered pattern (see page 122), but it can also be mortared over a concrete slab for a highly finished appearance and a surface that won't be affected by ground movement (see page 130).

Bricks for Patios

Bricks for patio floors are called "pavers." These are flat, solid units with a rough texture that provides traction in wet weather. Other types of brick include various grades of building brick (with holes for accepting mortar), firebrick (suitable for fireplaces and barbecues), and used or salvaged brick (reclaimed from demolished buildings). For strength, safety, and long-term durability, use brick pavers for patio floors. There are also manufactured "used" bricks designed for patio surfaces, which are typically made of concrete. If you like the distressed character of aged brick, look for new natural brick that has been "tumbled" (distressed).

Brick pavers are rated for load-bearing strength and for weather resistance. Types 2 and 3 are suitable for heavy foot traffic. SX brick is for cold climates, MX brick is for warm climates without a hard frost, and NX brick is for interiors.

Things to Consider

- Natural brick is more expensive than most concrete products.
- Comparing sandset brick to poured concrete, brick requires more maintenance, such as removing weeds that grow up through the pavers (always use a barrier to inhibit weed growth) and resetting pavers that shift or become uneven with ground movement.
- Unless brick is mortared in place, it's not likely to stay perfectly flat over time; however, many people consider this to be a desirable characteristic.
- Like most solid materials, brick can become slick with algae in very damp, shaded areas.

Buying Brick

Local brickyards and brick supplier websites are great resources when buying brick. To estimate how many bricks are needed for a project, divide the total area of the patio surface (in square inches) by the surface area of the brick's face. For example:

20-ft. × 10-ft. patio = 200 sq. ft. = 28,800 sq. in. (1 sq. ft. = 144 sq. in.).

28,800 ÷ 32 (area of standard 4" × 8" brick) = 900 bricks.

Add 5 to 10% for cuts and waste, plus any extra for specific edging patterns, such as vertical soldiers (see page 165).

Some standard sizes for brick pavers include 3⅝" × 7½" × 2¼" (height × length × thickness), 3¾" × 7⅝" × 2¼", and 4" × 8" × 2¼". The easiest brick to install is twice as long as it is wide, so that two bricks laid vertically are equal to one laid horizontally.

Paving Patterns ▶

One of brick's most beloved qualities is its adaptability to custom patterns. Shown here are some of the classics that are relatively easy to create. All are suitable for a flat surface. The diagonal bond is a nice pattern for walkways. The pinwheel design looks great with a contrasting paver in the center of each section. Circular and curved patterns often require mortar between pavers, particularly near the pattern's center. When selecting a pattern, think about color and whether you'd like a subtle mixture of tones or starkly contrasting accent bricks.

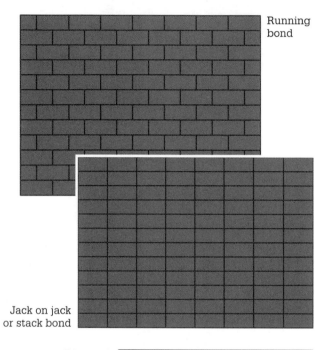

Running bond

Jack on jack or stack bond

Diagonal bond

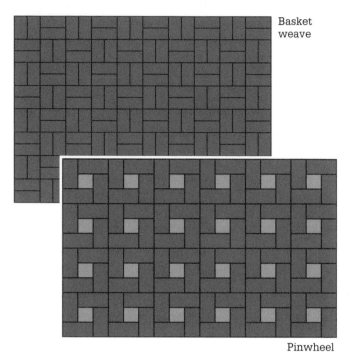

Basket weave

Pinwheel

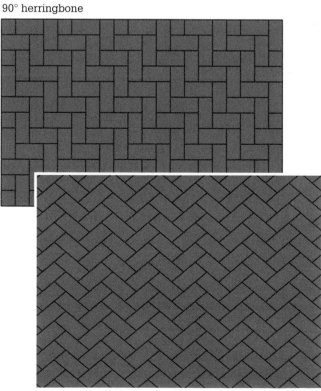

90° herringbone

Circular

45° herringbone

Stone

Natural stone has a timeless beauty that's unmatched by all other building materials. Stone paving is used the world over in grand courtyards, ancient roadways, and backyard gardens. In nature, stones form paths for crossing streams and skirting muddy fields. Little wonder why it's a popular material for patios. Stone is available in many forms, while the most commonly used types for patio surfaces are flagstone and stone tile.

Flagstone

Flagstone is the general term given to any broad, flat stone that has been split to a thickness of around 1" to 4", making it good for paving. Common species of flagstone include sandstone, limestone, bluestone, and slate. Individual stones may have cut edges for paving in linear patterns. However, stones with jagged edges and irregular shapes are most commonly used to create a patio surface with a natural, casual feel.

Flagstones can be set in sand or stable (tamped) soil or laid more permanently in mortar over a concrete slab. For an organic, stepping-stone look, you can space the stones widely and fill the spaces with gravel or ground cover plantings.

Availability of flagstone varies by region; see what's offered at some local stone yards before making a decision. For patio paving, make sure the stone is thick enough for furniture and heavy foot traffic and that the surface of the stones won't be dangerously slick when wet.

Stone delivered on a pallet close to the patio site saves your back and helps minimize breakage.

Natural flagstone is cleft into slabs with irregular shapes and an often interesting, flaky top surface. Flagstone is also available in precut tiles.

Adobe Block ▸

Traditionally made with a dried mixture of mud and straw, adobe block has a purely natural, earthen color and texture. The 4"-thick blocks have been used for centuries in wall construction and surface paving, primarily in the southwest states where the natural material can last for many years in the warm climate.

To use adobe in colder and wetter regions, some block is now fortified with asphalt or Portland cement, both of which can alter the appearance of the block. If you're interested in adobe block, first check into its availability in your area, or how much it will cost to have it shipped. Make sure any block you buy is rated to withstand local temperatures and weather. For paving, adobe is typically laid over a sand bed in the same manner as natural brick.

Slate

Granite

Quartzite

Marble

Stone tile may be thin and fairly uniform, like manufactured tile, or may vary in thickness and texture.

Stone Tile

Many types of stone are cut into flat, square, or rectangular tiles for paving. Slate, granite, marble, limestone, and quartzite are among the most commonly available species. In contrast to uncut flagstone's natural variation in thickness, shape, and texture, stone tile is more uniform and closer in appearance to manufactured tile. Its visual effect is a nice combination of natural texture and coloring with orderly geometric patterns.

Most stone tile is too thin to support foot traffic when laid over a soft base and must be installed in mortar over a concrete slab. For thicker tiles and stronger species of stone suitable for sandset paving, check with local suppliers. It's important to discuss your plans with your tile supplier, as not all tiles are suitable for all applications, especially outdoors. A local tile dealer will know what works for your climate.

Buying Stone

Flagstone is typically sold by the square yard or by the ton. Before you start shopping, calculate the area of your patio in square feet. Stone suppliers can use this amount to calculate your requirements in tons, if necessary. Buying flagstone in bulk from a stone yard is less expensive than hand-selecting individual stones, though you don't get to inspect all the pieces in advance. Also, having bulk shipments on pallets helps prevent breakage before or during delivery.

To estimate quantities of stone tile, add the face area of the tile to the thickness of the mortar joints. Your tile supplier can help with this.

Things to Consider

- The difficulty of quarrying and dressing stone makes it expensive. The more work that's done to the raw material—hand-selecting, cutting, and finishing—the higher the cost.
- When it comes to a finished patio, one of the main drawbacks of some flagstone is its uneven surface, which can lead to wobbly tables and the occasional stubbed toe. As with natural brick, many people choose stone exactly for this reason: its natural look with uneven surface is closer to the natural ground in the outdoors.
- Softer flagstone, like sandstone, can split fairly easily if not supported evenly from below.
- Sandstone is vulnerable to scratches from shovels, chair legs, and other metal objects.
- Slate and other types of flagstone and tile can be slippery when wet—an important consideration for exposed patios.

Concrete

Concrete may have a reputation as the workhorse of outdoor materials, but it's arguably the best all-around performer. Both poured concrete slabs and manufactured pavers are inexpensive and incredibly durable.

Concrete Pavers

Concrete pavers are less expensive than brick and stone; they're stronger than most natural paving materials, and they come in a wide selection of shapes, styles, and colors. They're also perfectly uniform, making installation predictable. In color and texture, most concrete pavers resemble brick. Perhaps the most convincing imitators are the small-ish, square pavers with rounded edges made to look like old-fashioned cobblestone street pavers. This effect is enhanced by color combinations in muted blues and grays.

There are two main types of concrete pavers: square-edged and interlocking. Square-edge pavers install much like brick or tile, while interlocking units have shaped edges that fit together like puzzle pieces. The interlocking pavers make for a tight assembly, with individual pavers resistant to shifting or loosening. Both types are available with specialty precut pieces for edging or creating curved patterns without having to cut the pavers.

Concrete pavers are typically installed over a sand bed and may or may not require additional sand in between units. They can also be laid in mortar over concrete. See Paving Patterns, on page 40, for installation options.

Poured Concrete

Poured concrete is clearly the default material for patios. It can be used as a foundation for other surfaces, like brick or tile, or stand on its own as a finished surface. In its liquid form, concrete follows straight lines, circles, and everything in between, making it a great medium for custom shapes. There are also numerous options for dressing up the surface of a concrete slab:

Seeded concrete is finished with a layer of fine stones for a uniform yet organic effect. This is a popular choice for patios because of its multicolored, textured appearance and its nonslip surface.

A divided concrete patio is poured with decorative wood, brick, or stone borders, separating the slab into distinct sections. This provides all the durability

Concrete pavers are available in several shapes, styles, and colors. Common concrete pavers include: (a) square, (b) keystone, (c) cobblestone, (d) rectangular.

of poured concrete without a monolithic appearance. A divided slab is a good project if concrete work is new to you, because it allows you to work in smaller sections.

Tinting or staining introduces a full range of color to the familiar cement-gray of concrete. Color is added using a variety of methods. A dry pigment can be mixed with the concrete ingredients for a consistent color throughout the slab. You can also order ready-mix concrete in a limited range of colors.

Another technique is to spread pigment over the wet concrete at specific stages of the finishing process, resulting in various handcrafted effects. On cured concrete, you can apply a permanent stain, repeating coats as desired for deeper coloring, as when staining wood. When concrete is stamped and stained, the final appearance may be hardly recognizable as concrete.

Stamping wet concrete is a popular method for adding texture and depth to a concrete surface, allowing it to mimic other materials. Often stamping in conjunction with detailed staining gives the most convincing alteration of concrete. Stamping tools are available at home centers to create the look of brick, stone, or ceramic tiles.

Embedding handpicked stones, glass beads, tiles, and other accent materials is a fun way to personalize a concrete slab.

Concrete can be used to create different shapes and can be combined with other materials to add visual interest. Here concrete square pavers lead out to the yard, and the slab is divided by brick pavers.

Buying Concrete

Estimating quantities of concrete pavers is straightforward, and you can usually follow the manufacturer's recommendations for area coverage. Buying concrete or concrete mix for a poured slab requires more calculation. For small projects, you can buy bags of concrete mix from any home center or landscape supplier. For larger projects, you might want to mix the concrete yourself, using a rented mixer, or order premixed concrete delivered by truck. See pages 89 to 91 for help with estimating concrete quantities and instructions on mixing or ordering concrete.

Things to Consider

- Concrete paver patios tend to have a monotonous, commercial look if not designed thoughtfully. Mixing complementary colors helps to give the surface visual depth. Another way to add visual interest is to use a simple layout of square-edged pavers in soft earth tones; this mimics the look of brick or adobe block.
- Poured concrete, especially uncolored concrete, can create glare in strong sunlight and can reflect a lot of heat.
- Concrete slabs are less forgiving of ground movement than pieced-in materials like pavers and are prone to cracking when laid over unstable or poorly draining soil.
- Poured concrete without staining has an unavoidably massive, manmade look that contrasts surrounding natural materials. For some, this stark contrast to the natural landscape is a desired effect.

Tile

With its clean, geometric lines and smooth finish, tile is a great choice for an elegant patio space. In warm climates, tile is a common outdoor material, often seen in courtyards and fountain plazas paved with large, handmade earthen tiles. In colder regions, outdoor tile must be nearly impervious to water to withstand winter's freeze-thaw cycles. Tile must be installed over a concrete slab, and this is one of its main uses for patios—its thin profile makes it a good material for covering a drab, old concrete surface.

Tile for Patios

Indoors, you can use just about any kind of tile. But a patio is a different matter. Patio tile must be strong enough to survive scrapes from outdoor furniture, as well as years of weather and sun exposure. More importantly, patio tile must be slip-resistant, which automatically rules out most glazed tile. The main types of suitable tile are quarry, terra-cotta, natural stone, and porcelain.

Quarry tile is a durable ceramic tile that comes unglazed in many colors. It often has a flat but slightly abrasive surface for good slip-resistance.

Terra-cotta tile has a warm, natural appearance, commonly in mottled earth tones. It looks great on patios, but because it is somewhat porous, it's not recommended for use in cold winter climates.

Saltillo tile is a dried—rather than fired—tile similar to terra-cotta but with a more imperfect, handmade character. It also is suitable only for mild climates.

Porcelain tile is the toughest, hardest, and usually most expensive tile you can buy. It is highly resistant to water and therefore a good choice for patios in most climates.

Buying Tile

When shopping for tile, be sure to explain how you plan to use it. A good tile dealer can help you choose the right type and style of tile for your climate and your specific project. They can also help you select an appropriate grout and provide maintenance tips for keeping your patio surface in shape over the years.

Things to Consider

- When choosing a tile type, consider winter freezing, durability, and slip-resistance.
- Tile often discolors (or fades) from exposure to the sun and elements over time.
- Regular maintainance requires applying commercial sealers and checking the grout. Occasionally, the joints need to be re-grouted and re-sealed.
- Sealed tile can have a shiny, shellacked appearance that darkens the tile and grout.

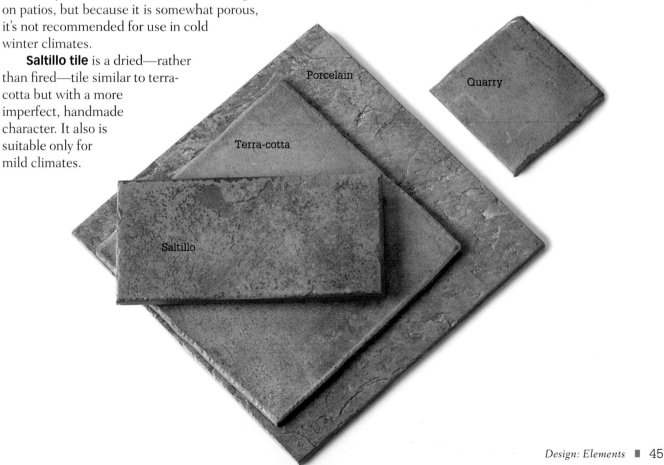

Loose Material

Loose materials can be used as filler between solid surface materials, like flagstone, or laid as the primary ground cover. A more traditional design employs loose materials as a transition between a solid patio and the yard. For a patio separated from the house, a loose material surface has an earthy quality that blends well with its surroundings.

As a primary surface, loose materials come with several practical advantages: they drain well, are forgiving of uneven ground, and can be graded with a rake for a quick face-lift. Loose materials also tend to be less expensive than other paving products and couldn't be easier to install. A typical installation starts with compacted gravel, which is followed by a weed barrier (landscape fabric), and then topped with several inches of the surface material. You can also use compactable gravel as the finish surface. Adding a border of brick, stone, or lumber helps contain the loose material and defines the patio space.

Buying Loose Materials

Standard loose materials are available by the bag, but for larger projects it's less expensive to buy in bulk. For a fee, most suppliers will deliver the product to your site. For a large bulk order, calculate quantity both in cubic feet and cubic yards, using the square footage of the patio and the desired thickness of the surface material.

For a 10-ft. × 20-ft. patio: $10 \times 20 = 200$ sq. ft.

For a 2" layer of surface material: $12" \div 2" = 6$
Then: $200 \div 6 = 33.34$ cu. ft.

For a 3" layer: $12" \div 3" = 4$
Then: $200 \div 4 = 50$ cu. ft.

To convert to cubic yards, divide by 27:
100 cu. ft. $\div 27 = 3.7$ cu. yards

Things to Consider

- The soft, mutable quality of loose paving makes it unsuitable for formal patios.
- Wood chips, sand, and some gravel create too soft a surface for supporting furniture evenly, but compactable gravels and crushed stone can be tamped into a fairly level, stable layer.
- Many loose materials aren't comfortable for bare feet—an important consideration for summertime relaxation.

River rock

Decomposed granite

Crushed stone

Wood chips

Pea gravel

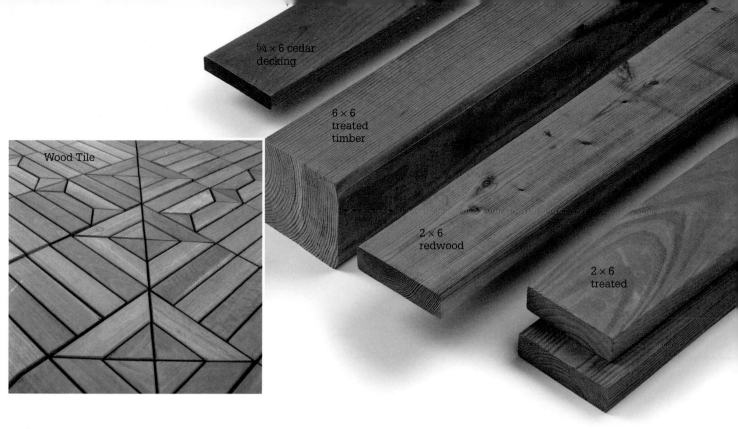

Wood Tile

⁵⁄₄ × 6 cedar decking

6 × 6 treated timber

2 × 6 redwood

2 × 6 treated

▎ Wood

Not to be overlooked as a patio surface, lumber decking offers the beauty of natural wood and a feel underfoot that's more forgiving than masonry floors. Constructing a wood patio from scratch is similar to building a standard outdoor deck, with a supporting frame of joists topped with perpendicular decking boards. Another option is to use manufactured wood tiles, which can be laid over an existing concrete slab or a bed of compacted gravel.

Wood Tiles

Wood tiles are based on the concept of parquet flooring, where uniform squares, or tiles, are set in a crosshatch pattern to form the finish surface. Individual tiles often click together and float on top of the existing patio surface.

Wood Platforms

A low, freestanding wood platform makes a great detached patio or a small patio deck set outside a bedroom or side entrance. Using precast concrete footings for the foundation, you can adjust the height of the patio surface as desired. See page 156 for complete project instructions. As an alternative to concrete footings and standard joist framing, wood decking can be installed over a foundation of treated wood timbers, or sleepers, set over a gravel bed. The timbers are leveled and spaced according to the span limits of the decking material.

(Above, left) Wood tiles are easy to install. Simply click the panels together. They can be set right on top of an existing patio to dress it up. There are also edge pieces for a finished look.

(Above) The same materials used for decks make great patio surfaces, including redwood, cedar, and pressure-treated lumber.

Buying Lumber

Wood decking is commonly available as 2 × 6 and ⁵⁄₄ × 6 (about 1" thick) lumber boards in redwood, cedar, and pressure-treated pine (and other softwoods). These wood types are rot-resistant and suitable for decking. They weather to a grayish color within a season or so if left untreated. Redwood and cedar come in several grades, ranging from all heartwood, which is the strongest and most rot-resistant, to all sapwood, which has limited rot-resistance. For framing members and sleepers, the most practical choice is pressure-treated lumber. For wood on the ground, be sure it is rated for ground contact. While not as attractive as cedar or redwood, treated lumber is much less expensive.

Things to Consider

- In most climates wood patios should be refinished every 2 years.
- New wood tiles are a simple way to dress up a drab concrete or loose material patio. They click together easily and often come pre-sealed.

Walls & Fences

Patio walls and fences can be much more than mere boundaries. They can become dramatic backdrops for water features, define intimate dining areas, provide seating for party guests, or enclose private corners for reading or sunbathing. Of course, walls and fences also make excellent barriers. By bordering and defining areas according to your needs, walls and fences promote a better sense of place, making all of your outdoor activities more comfortable.

Sometimes a patio calls for a solid barrier—to block a neighbor's view or to create an oasis by separating the patio from a street or alley. Such cases call for a tall, solid wall or fence that's at least 6 ft. high. But because you're screening off a patio, where aesthetics are important, consider a structure with some visual interest—a band of lattice along the top of a wood fence or a combination of a low masonry wall topped with an attractive cedar fence. Fast-growing ivy and other climbers help soften the hard face of a solid barrier.

Where less isolation is required, a low wall can delineate space without blocking views beyond the patio's boundaries. A perimeter wall can also serve as a safety barrier where a patio drops off onto the yard. Check the local building code for the minimum height of a safety barrier wall. For a low wall to provide seating, it must have a flat top surface that's at least 16" deep and 14" to 20" from the ground.

Retaining walls bordering a patio may allow for more living space, but they don't have to look purely functional. Terracing the wall opens up planting beds that become effective focal points when full of thriving greenery. Likewise, a bare house wall abutting a patio can be a stark backdrop, which you can soften with custom lattice panels and vines. The design goal with most patio walls is integration. The wall should contribute to the atmosphere of the space, much like interior walls do when decorated with artwork, wallpaper, and molding.

Traditional mortared stone walls now blend with modern elements in this artistic patio composition.

Enclosing a patio with attractive fencing makes it a great outdoor play area for pets or small children.

This low brick wall adds a sense of enclosure without blocking the view.

This louvered fence creates an effective yet attractive visual barrier while allowing air to flow into the patio.

Paths, Walkways & Steps

Tying the patio to home and garden is an important design consideration. Like a roadway, paths and walkways direct traffic and, to some degree, the rate of travel. These two factors must be your primary guides for planning routes to and from the patio. How and by whom the paths get used will determine their ideal shape, as well as their size and appropriate surface materials.

The first question to address is the purpose of the walkway. If it's intended to take you from the kitchen door to the patio, it will probably be used frequently. More importantly, you'll likely be carrying plates and food for outdoor meals. Such a path should follow the shortest, most comfortable route and be paved with a hard, smooth surface material so there's no risk of tripping. The same characteristics are recommended for all primary pathways that receive heavy traffic. Also keep in mind that a primary route should appear to be the path of least resistance. In other words, people tend to make their own shortcuts when paths look too complicated.

Less-traveled paths need not be so utilitarian. A small side path leading away from a patio and through a flower garden can chart a rambling course, slowing down the pace and creating natural pauses at interesting landscape features along the way. On the contrary, paths leading to less desirable destinations, such as a garbage area or storage shed, can be small and discreet.

Steps serve an obvious functional purpose, but they can also be used for dramatic effect. A set of sprawling, shallow steps make for a welcoming approach onto a patio or leading from the patio to the lawn. Steps can be made from many different materials, such as brick, flagstone or thick stone slabs, landscape timbers with brick or stone infill, and concrete with or without a decorative tile finish.

When it comes to choosing a material for your path, look to the patio surface as a starting point. A path made of the same material as the patio floor may appear to flow seamlessly from the larger area. With a change in materials, the path and patio have their own character and defined space, marking the end of one journey and the beginning of another. This also allows the patio to retain an unbroken visual line along its perimeter. In general, the same materials that work well for patio surfaces also make good walkways, with the same advantages and drawbacks for different applications.

Created with a concrete block system, this patio, stepped walkway, and retaining walls achieve stylistic and structural continuity.

A meandering path lends an air of mystery without detracting from the garden's beauty.

While two sets of steps are effective for providing easy access to this raised patio area, the side entrance is purposely smaller to serve a less traveled section of the patio.

(Above) Steps can be dressed up by adding colorful tiles or stains.

(Right) As the main route to a remote patio and well-used outbuilding, this concrete paver walkway is durable and efficient.

Overheads

A patio overhead can be anything from a simple decoration that introduces an element of architecture to a thoughtfully planned shelter for making the patio more livable. Arbors, pergolas, and pavilions are the most popular types of patio overheads; they are all relatively simple structures that lend themselves to personal creative touches.

Arbors can find a home almost anywhere in the landscape, from front entryways to secluded gardens. On a patio, an arbor can serve as a dramatic entrance portal, an ornamental frame for flowering vines, or a cozy shelter for a corner seating area. The basic design of an arbor includes two or four posts with a simple slatted roof. The sides between the posts can be left open or covered with trelliswork for supporting plants and adding privacy.

Pergolas are a step up from arbors in size and stature but are based on a similar post-and-beam construction. In its traditional form, a pergola extends from the side or roof of a building to create a semi-shaded area linking the building with the outdoor landscape (not unlike the concept behind the modern patio). Pergolas work equally well as freestanding structures, with four or more columns supporting large roof beams topped with a series of cross-beams or slats. Most often, pergolas are used to create an attractive ceiling—or the suggestion of a ceiling—over a large section of patio. Covered along the top with vines or fabric, a pergola offers an elegant solution for gaining privacy beneath the view of neighbors' upper-floor windows.

With both arbors and pergolas, careful placement of the overhead slats provide sun or shade as desired at specific times of the day. For example, if the summer sun is too hot at midday, you can angle the slats toward the morning sun while blocking out the hottest rays at midday and into the afternoon. See page 70 for more information on planning for sun and shade. Another consideration is the overhead's affect on natural lighting reaching the house.

A **pavilion** is an open-air structure with a solid roof that provides full shade as well as shelter from rain showers. Pavilions make a nice addition to large patios next to swimming pools and recreation areas, offering kids welcome refuge from the sun and a pleasant seating area for adults. A patio pavilion also makes a great stage for an outdoor kitchen or entertainment space.

This decorative arbor has turned an unused area of the patio into a cozy destination.

This playfully detailed pavilion demonstrates the essence of a casual poolside retreat.

This classic pergola does little to shade the patio below but plays a significant architectural role as both the ceiling and outside wall of the outdoor room.

Fire & Water

Nature's own elements can have a transforming effect on the atmosphere of a patio. Filling the air with soothing sounds and attracting your eye with movement, both fire and water features add a bit of life to the calm. On chilly evenings and late nights, a fire keeps you outdoors with the promise of warmth and a lively conversation piece. At the other end of the spectrum, a fountain or pool creates a "cool" feeling—an oasis for escaping the day's heat. And there's no reason why you can't have water, fireplaces, and fire pits on the same patio.

There's a range of options when it comes to adding fire to a patio. A **fireplace** is a true luxury item, offering warmth under the stars. Outdoor fireplaces are built virtually the same as indoor units, with a masonry foundation, a brick or metal firebox, and a separate flue running up through a chimney.

A less formal option is a **fire pit**. Patio fire pits are made of brick or concrete block, with noncombustible finishes and often a ring of decorative brick or stone along the top. Often circular and informal, fire pits may still be subject to strict building codes and burning restrictions. Check the codes before making any serious plans.

A more portable option is a traditional **chiminea**—an onion-shaped, terra-cotta vessel with a side opening near the base for the fire and a tapered hollow top that acts as a chimney. An ornamental metal stand keeps it off the ground. Today, chimineas are available in cast iron, aluminum, and other metals, as well as traditional clay materials. Be sure to follow the manufacturer's recommendations for safe use and proper storage of portable units during cold-weather months.

Nothing adds atmosphere to a patio like a traditional wood-burning fireplace.

Fire pits are made for gathering around. The raised sides make for nice seating or a place to rest your feet as you while away the evening.

(Above) Portable fire pits have seen a rise in popularity in recent years and are now commonly available online and at home and garden centers. Most are made of lightweight metal and can easily be carried onto a patio or lawn for an evening's fire.

(Left) With their portability and rustic styling, chimineas are uniquely suited to patios.

Water in motion has a calming effect on the mind. The sound of even a small stream splashing into a pool or over a bed of stones helps to drown out domestic noises and soothe the soul a little. Adding a **fountain** to a patio is an easy do-it-yourself project that allows for all kinds of creative touches. A simple fountain setup includes a catch basin, a submersible pump, and a fountain or spout. From there you can add your own decorative elements, such as river rocks for a natural spring or statues for a man made, sculptural theme. A shelf of metal mesh concealed inside the catch basin makes the fountain safe for young children, as it blocks access to the store of water below. See page 178 for step-by-step instructions on how to make a custom fountain.

Pumps, fountains, and other equipment for water features are available at water garden nurseries and home and garden centers. A quick shopping trip or online search will generate plenty of ideas for building your own fountain. Also available are complete fountain units that need only to be installed and plugged in. Both freestanding and wall-mounted fountains come in a range of styles and materials, including stone, copper, glass, and concrete.

Traditional courtyard fountains such as this demonstrate the beauty and drama of a centrally located water feature.

A simple fountain covered with natural flagstone enlivens a patio corner with the soothing sound of splashing water.

The contrast between hard-edged, geometric shapes and the graceful undulations of live fish is a common theme in modern-style concrete pools.

Simplicity and elegance define this sleek, modern fountain, which empties onto a grate and a hidden collection basin below.

Small **ponds and pools** are more commonly found in gardens, but can add a dramatic yet calming influence to any outdoor living space. Installation methods range from self-contained plastic pond liners to sleek masonry reflecting pools.

A popular do-it-yourself pond project starts with an excavation for a rigid or flexible liner. The liner is installed and filled with water, and then the pond's edge is dressed with stone or other material to conceal the liner and create an attractive border. A submersible pump with fountain is set in the bottom of the pond and plugged into an outdoor GFCI (ground-fault circuit interrupter) outlet. Aquatic plants and fish can be added for a natural effect.

More elaborate ponds and pools may require underground plumbing and advanced pump systems, as well as filters for maintaining water quality. Discuss water treatment and maintenance with a qualified professional, especially if you plan to grow plants and support fish in the pond.

Warning: Keep in mind that open water presents a safety concern for young children.

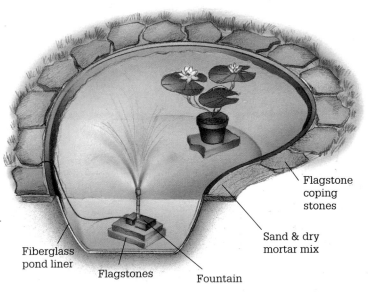

Flagstone coping stones

Sand & dry mortar mix

Fiberglass pond liner

Flagstones

Fountain

Manufactured pond liners and plug-in pumps make it easy to install a simple patio pond.

Utilities

Most patios don't require much in the way of power and gas supplies, but a few key amenities can make a big difference in the quality of your patio life, especially after the sun goes down.

Lighting

Considerable thought should be given to patio lighting. The lights chosen can affect not only the usefulness of a space but also the occupants' moods. If nighttime on a patio is for enjoying the calm of the darkness and the starry sky, the glaring light of a single 100-watt bulb in a standard outdoor fixture can completely ruin that experience. At the same time, total darkness is inconvenient and potentially hazardous. The solution is a thoughtful lighting plan with low-wattage lights in just the right places to create a comfortable, safe environment without spoiling the nighttime atmosphere.

Low-voltage outdoor lighting systems are commonly available with a range of fixtures for specific illumination effects. Most systems are designed for easy, do-it-yourself installation and are powered by plugging into a standard outdoor GFCI (ground-fault circuit interrupter) outlet. The alternative to low-voltage is standard (or "line") voltage lighting, which runs off of a 110/120-volt household circuit. Line voltage offers more power than low voltage and thus more extensive lighting capability, but most patios are better off with less light rather than more.

Electricity

Chances are good that you already have one or more outdoor electrical outlets close to your patio site. These may suffice for whatever outdoor equipment and occasional-use fixtures you use on the patio. However, if the outlets aren't GFCI-protected, have them replaced by an electrician so the circuit is safe for outdoor use. If your patio plans include an elaborate outdoor kitchen, you'll probably need an additional circuit and outdoor wiring run to the kitchen location. Make sure the circuit meets the requirements of all of the kitchen's fixtures.

Natural Gas

For anyone who does a lot of gas grilling, a plumbed gas line is a great convenience. With a dedicated gas supply, you'll never again prepare an entire cookout, fire up the grill, then realize that your propane tank is empty . . . just like the backup tank. Since most houses have some type of gas appliance (hot water heater, furnace, gas stove, etc.), it's a simple job for a professional to run an additional gas line out to your patio.

Prevent shock by making sure all outdoor receptacles are protected by a ground-fault circuit interrupter (GFCI) receptacle. A single GFCI receptacle can be wired to protect other fixtures on the circuit. Outdoor receptacles should be at least 1 ft. above ground level and enclosed in weatherproof electrical boxes with watertight covers.

(Above) A combination of lighting techniques fills this patio with low-level ambient light while highlighting distinctive features of the house and landscape

(Left) A well-equipped outdoor kitchen typically requires a dedicated gas supply for the grill and one or more outdoor electrical circuits for built-in appliances and countertop outlets. Water lines for kitchen sinks and icemakers can be branched off of household lines.

Design: Your Patio

Planning a new patio can be a lengthy process, but essentially it all comes down to a few major considerations. By answering the big questions, all of the little (and not so little) details will naturally fall into place. Try to keep these simple goals in mind to help you maintain perspective throughout the process:

Use—who will use the patio most and for what types of activities?

Site, size, and layout—where will it go, how will it be arranged, and how will you get to it?

Comfort—what are the ideal amounts of sun, shade, and privacy?

Style—how will it look?

While your decision-making needn't follow a specific order, it's important to address the most pertinent matters first. Local zoning laws, for example, may dictate the maximum size allowed for your patio, so you'll need to know the rules before breaking ground. Drainage and other potential problems also require attention before you can turn to the fun jobs of designing the floor plan and shopping for materials.

In This Chapter

- Use
- Choosing a Site
- Dealing with Drainage
- Size & Layout
- Climate Control
- Exterior Design
- Making a Plan

Use

How you plan to spend time on your patio will influence most of your design decisions. So it's best to start the planning process with a little brainstorming involving everyone in the household. What will be the primary uses for the space? Dining, entertaining, sunbathing, playing with the kids, enjoying the view? Once you establish the uses, the trick will be to accommodate all of those activities within an attractive, efficient design. For some, the solution lies simply in providing adequate space in a flexible floor plan—a quick shift in furniture, for example, can set the stage for the next activity.

Once you've settled on a site and size for the space, you can put your plans to the test by carrying out some of your primary activities within a mock-up of the patio footprint (see page 75). For now, the goal is to determine everything you hope to do on your new patio. The next step is to imagine the ideal setup for each activity. For example, if you have young children and like to spend time with them outdoors, maybe you want a comfortable sitting area near an edge of the patio that's adjacent to a sandbox. (When the youngest has grown out of it, you can turn the sandbox into a planting bed.) Or

maybe you want some space on the patio for a baby pool or a fountain for the kids to play in.

A patio for multiple uses still requires balance. Large, open areas are best for hosting parties, but they can feel empty and overly exposed for a small group of diners. To plan for both, you can separate the expansive area from the intimate with a change in floor level or maybe just tuck a furniture set into a corner under an arbor. And don't forget some personal space: the perfect spot where your favorite chair is always ready for you to read or take a quick snooze.

If your plan is to refurbish an existing patio, think hard about what you like and dislike about the current setup. A patio that's too small can be increased in size by adding to the borders or can be connected to a new, separate patio space designed for new uses. Often patios don't get used because they're uncomfortable or uninviting during the owner's usual free time. For example, if you get home from work at 5:30 p.m.—just as the western sun is blasting the area with heat—you'll probably stay inside. The solution, of course, is a shade barrier that blocks those afternoon rays. Make note of everything your current patio is not, and yet could be, and you're ready to move on to planning the changes.

With a little creative design, play areas can become an attractive feature of a patio layout. This area can easily become a flower, herb, or garden bed in the future.

(Above) This patio has been left unobstructed by walls, fences, or overheads to allow for an open view.

(Left) A patio can easily extend over to an area defined for sports.

Choosing a Site

Initially, keep your options for patio placement open for consideration. Imagine your patio in the front, sides, and back of your house. Take note of steep slopes, existing trees, and even sun and wind patterns. This is an appropriate time to consider location, patio types, and atmosphere. It's also necessary to address zoning laws, building codes, utilities, and obstacles in your yard. Let's get started!

Patio Types

For starters, not all patios have to go directly behind the house. Depending on the configuration of your lot, you might get more use from an alternative design. For example, a front entry patio may provide the best view and at the same time create a warm introduction to your home. A wraparound patio is often used to enhance a smaller home on a spacious lot—such a design expands the visual boundaries of the house and increases the perceived living space. If you're planning an addition, consider an arrangement that creates a semi-enclosed courtyard patio—the ultimate layout for privacy and shelter from wind. A detached or remote patio can take advantage of a particularly nice area of the yard or can serve as a secondary patio with its own unique feel.

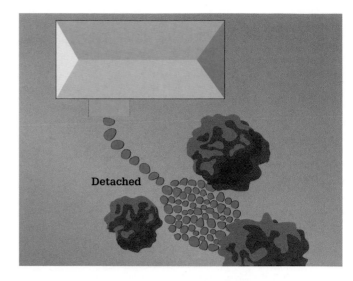

Detached

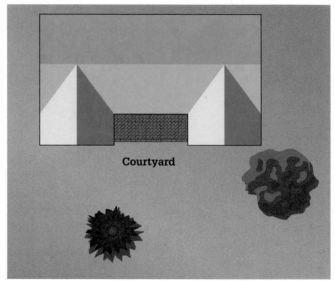

Courtyard

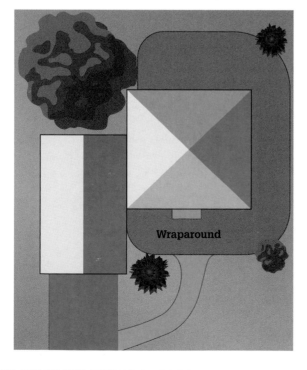

Wraparound

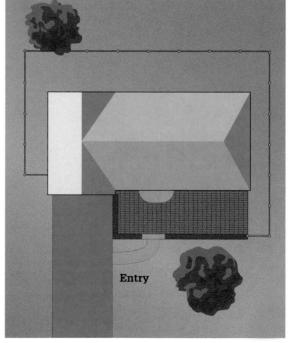

Entry

Zoning Laws, Building Codes & Utilities

Any alterations made to your lot could fall under your municipality's zoning laws. In the case of a new patio, zoning laws might limit locations for the patio and how much ground it can cover. The latter relates to the allowable percentage of development on the lot, so that adding a large patio now could preclude future plans for a home addition. You also must make sure the patio conforms to setback restrictions (required distance from lot lines) and easements (zones that must be accessible for utilities and other public services). If your patio dreams include walls, fire features, or overheads, these structures may be subject to standards set by the local building code, and you might need to obtain building permits for the projects.

Discuss your complete plans with an official at the local municipality's planning office for zoning laws. Basic patios often get the go-ahead with little scrutiny. If you run into snags, ask about alternatives; for example, a concrete patio may not be allowed over an easement, but a less permanent, sandset surface may be approved.

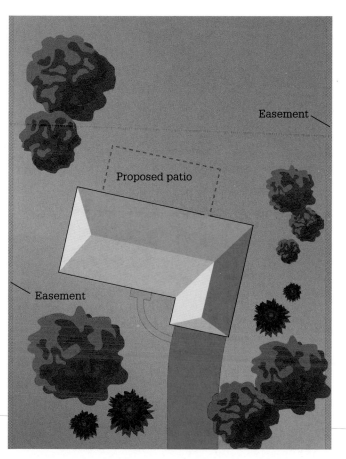
Easement

Proposed patio

Easement

Also contact the local utility companies to have all utility lines marked on your property. This is absolutely necessary before digging in your yard, and it could affect your patio plans. Most states are part of the North American One Call Referral System, which will contact all of the utilities in your area and notify them regarding your construction project. Utility companies that have lines in your yard will automatically send out a representative to mark the lines. Call 888-258-0808.

Access

Like most recreation and relaxation areas, a patio tends to be used more often if it's easily accessible. The same is true of visual access. Full views, or even just glimpses, of the patio from several interior rooms will beckon you outdoors on nice days.

Another important consideration involves the rooms that lead to the patio. Ideally, these access areas have a similar feel and purpose to that of the patio. For example, if outdoor dining is one of your primary activities, locating the patio near the kitchen will prove to be an enormous convenience. Similarly, a patio used frequently for large parties should not be accessed through a bedroom or other private space. This is not only an inconvenience; guests feel uncomfortable walking through private or formal areas of a home.

Atmosphere

Perhaps the most important elements of all are the everyday factors that affect the quality of life on a patio:

Sunlight. Does the site get enough to work with? Too much is better than too little.

Noise. Are noise levels acceptable? You can put up a fence to block your view of the street, but will the traffic be too loud? Conversely, will you always be shushing the kids for fear of disturbing the neighbors?

Privacy. Will you feel overly exposed and on display or perhaps too shut in?

Views. What you see from the patio has a big impact on the atmosphere. If no good views are available, can you add plants and decoration to dress up the space?

Contact your municipality's planning office to discuss the following: site and size of the patio, setback restrictions, allowable lot coverage, exact locations of your lot lines, and easements.

Dealing with Drainage

It's not uncommon for patios to experience drainage issues. One common cause is the hard paved surface, which sheds water instead of absorbing it and deposits it along the lower edge of the patio. There the water collects to create a swampy area of grass. During heavy rains, runoff water can build up enough force to wash out flowerbeds bordering a patio. Another drainage problem occurs when the water has no escape, a common condition with sunken or recessed patios that are surrounded by retaining walls or ascending slopes.

Another cause of poor drainage is the addition or removal of soil or plants, which can alter natural drainage patterns.

Fortunately, all of these drainage problems can be solved with an appropriate drainage system. For patio runoff, a drainage swale or perimeter trench is usually effective. These are gravel-filled trenches containing a perforated drainpipe that collects excess ground water and diverts it to a storm sewer or other collection point. A trench running along the lowest edge of the patio can collect water directly from the patio surface. If the patio is at the top of a natural slope leading to a low point in the yard, a drainage swale located in the low point keeps the rest of the yard relatively dry.

Diverting excess water is only half of the battle—the water also needs a place to go. If allowed by the city, the water can be diverted to the street's gutter or a storm drain, or it can be sent to a dry well on your own property. A dry well is simply an underground pit filled with coarse gravel or rocks. Water from a trench or swale drainpipe feeds into the well, where it is slowly drained into the surrounding soil. See page 108 for instructions to install a drainage swale and page 111 for making a dry well.

Enclosed or recessed patios may require their own drainage systems, typically with some type of floor drain. The patio surface slopes toward the drain, located either in the center or along one side, where runoff water collects in a subsurface catch basin. From there, an underground drainpipe carries the water to a collection point. If you think your patio will need this type of system, consult an engineer or qualified landscape professional early in the planning process to discuss your options.

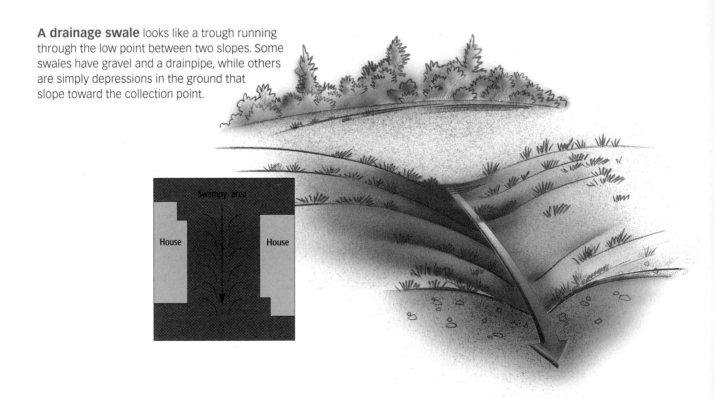

A drainage swale looks like a trough running through the low point between two slopes. Some swales have gravel and a drainpipe, while others are simply depressions in the ground that slope toward the collection point.

Swampy area

House

House

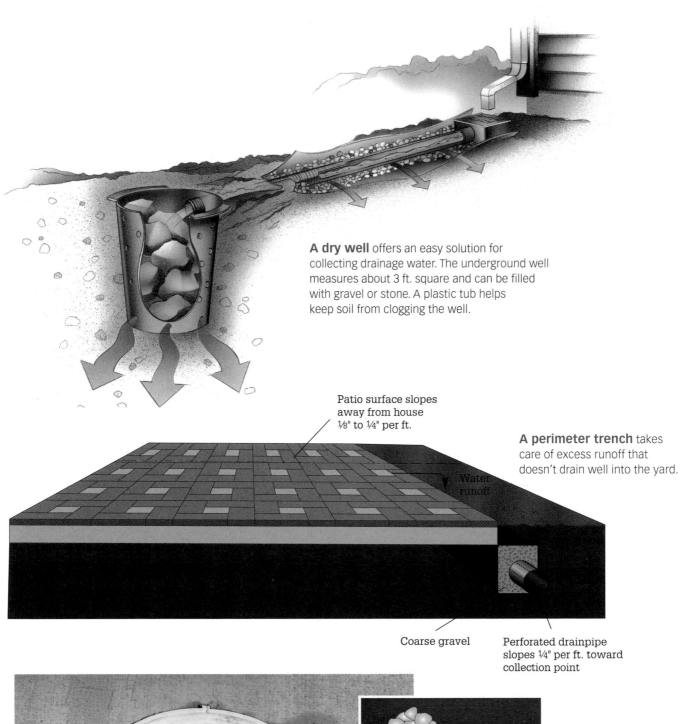

A dry well offers an easy solution for collecting drainage water. The underground well measures about 3 ft. square and can be filled with gravel or stone. A plastic tub helps keep soil from clogging the well.

Patio surface slopes away from house ⅛" to ¼" per ft.

A perimeter trench takes care of excess runoff that doesn't drain well into the yard.

Water runoff

Coarse gravel

Perforated drainpipe slopes ¼" per ft. toward collection point

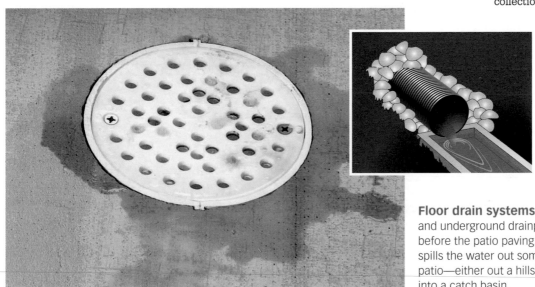

Floor drain systems with a catch basin and underground drainpipe must be installed before the patio paving. The drainpipe then spills the water out someplace away from the patio—either out a hillside slope (inset) or into a catch basin.

Size & Layout

The ideal size and configuration for your patio is determined by the space needed for each primary activity, including plenty of room for easy access and intervening traffic. With the floor space allocated, you can begin playing around with different layouts, design elements, and even patio shapes until the form of the space accommodates all of its functions. All the while, bear in mind the big picture—making sure the proportions and general design of the patio are in keeping with your house and the rest of the landscape.

How Much Space?

It's time to think again about all the uses you have planned for the patio. If you already have the patio furniture, set it up on the proposed site and experiment with different arrangements to get a sense of how much space each furniture grouping will need. If you don't have the furniture yet, see the illustration (this page) for suggestions on spacing. Next, decide which areas you want to dedicate to specific activities and which can be flexible for multiple uses. Cooking and dining areas are best left as static (or "anchored"), while an informal sunbathing spot defined by a couple of lounge chairs can easily be re-arranged. An outdoor kitchen has its own spacing and layout considerations—see page 212.

To plan traffic routes, allow a minimum of 22" of width for main passages between and alongside activity areas (32" minimum for wheelchair access). The main goal is to have enough room for people to move around the patio without disrupting anyone.

Take a Step Back

As your patio plans develop, try to envision the design within its grand context. Does its size seem appropriate for the house and lot? While it's important to make a patio large enough for all its intended uses, there's also a risk in making it too large. With interior rooms, some people like the grandeur and openness of a sprawling great room with cathedral ceiling, while others find the expansive space uncomfortable for personal activities like reading or quiet conversation.

Architects often design in terms of "human scale," creating spaces that are large enough to accommodate the human body in its everyday activities but small enough to provide a comfortable sense of space and enclosure. On a patio you can establish the proper scale with clear barriers, such as fences and overheads or with boundaries that rely more on perception—low walls, plantings, or even just a change in flooring materials.

This modest patio could have been much larger, but the owners preferred a smaller-scale design to suit their needs—they use it primarily for family meals—and to match the bump-out on the house.

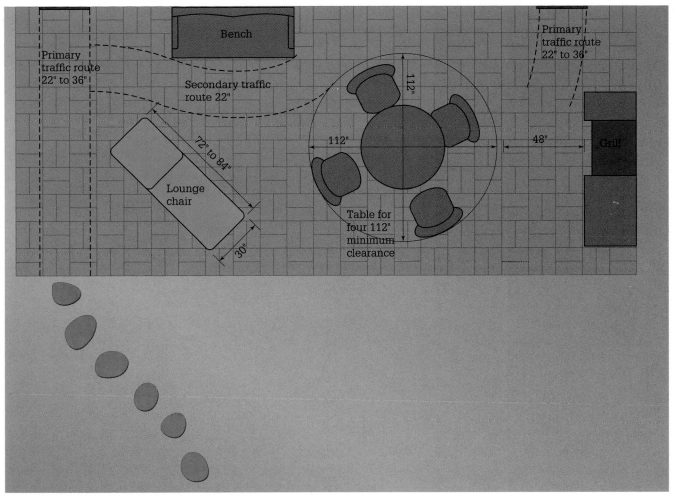

Bench

Primary
traffic route
22" to 36"

Primary
traffic route
22" to 36"

Secondary traffic
route 22"

112"

112"

48"

Grill

72" to 84"

Lounge
chair

30"

Table for
four 112"
minimum
clearance

**(Above) When arranging
your patio,** consider the
placement of furniture and
permanent structures as well
as the space needed for
primary traffic routes. These
routes should have a
minimum width of 22" to
allow for comfortable
passage throughout the patio.

Play
area

Dining &
socializing

Garden
area

**(Left) Make an outdoor
"floor plan"** when designing
your landscape. Think of each
area of your yard as an outdoor
room, and plan your landscape
so it includes spaces for favorite
activities. The front yard, like a
formal living room, often is a
decorative space used to
welcome guests to your hone,
but the backyard usually serves
as private recreational space for
family and friends.

Climate Control

Careful planning can't change the weather, but it can help you make the best of prevailing conditions. By controlling or utilizing sunlight (and shade), wind, and natural air currents, you are in essence creating a microclimate for your patio and can effectively make it the most comfortable place in your outdoor landscape.

Sunlight & Shadows

The unalterable pattern of the sun is one of the few climatic systems you can count on. The tricky part is positioning your patio so it receives the right amount and intensity of sunlight at the time of day—and the season—when you'll use it most. The sun's path changes throughout the year. In summer, it rises high in the sky along the east–west axis, creating shorter shadows and more exposure overall. In winter, the sun's angle is relatively low, resulting in long shadows in the northwest, north, and northeast directions. To avoid shadows altogether, you can locate a patio away from the house and other structures.

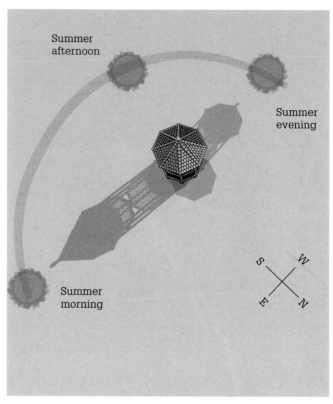

Shadows follow the east-west axis in the summer.

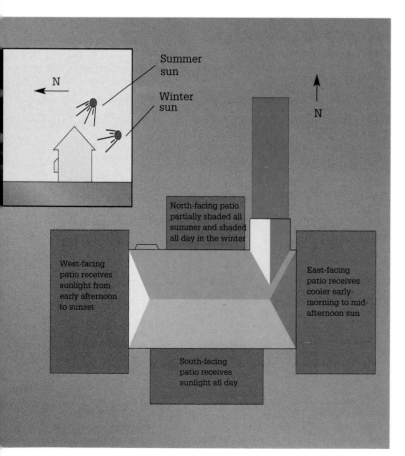

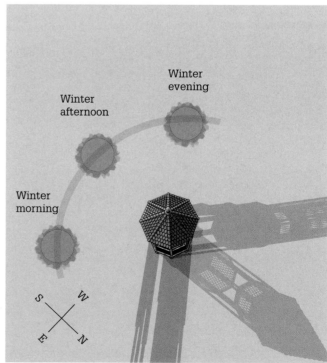

Winter shadows point to the northeast and northwest and are relatively long at midday.

Wind

Strong wind can ruin your patio peace as surely as a rainstorm. Shielding yourself from wind takes careful planning, and sometimes trial-and-error experimentation. Since you can't protect against all wind, first determine the direction of prevailing winds—the most frequent and strongest wind currents affecting your site (prevailing winds may change with the seasons), then decide on the best location for a wind barrier. Contrary to appearances, a solid barrier often is not the most effective windbreak. This is because the air currents swoop over the top of the barrier and then drop down on the backside, returning to full strength at a distance roughly equal to the barrier's height. A more reliable windbreak is created with a lattice or louvered fence that diffuses and weakens the wind as it passes through the barrier.

Patio Materials & Orientation

The surface material you choose can affect the patio's environment. Dark-colored, solid surfaces, like brick or dark stone, absorb a lot of heat during the day and may become uncomfortable to walk on. However, after the sun goes down, stored heat released from the paving can warm the air on the patio. Solid walls also reflect heat and can restrict cooling breezes. Because cold air drops, low-lying patios or those positioned at the base of an incline tend to be cooler than higher areas of the landscape.

If you're building an overhead specifically for shading, experiment with alternative materials, such as bamboo screening or fabric, to filter sunlight for a bright, warm glow without the harshness or heat of direct rays.

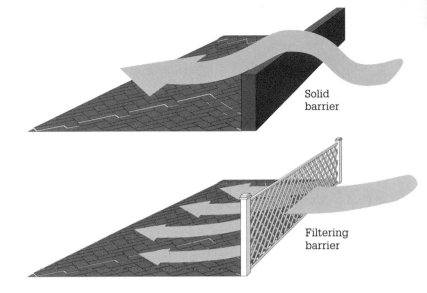

Solid barrier

Filtering barrier

Solid barriers drive wind currents upward, creating a forcible reversal in direction. **Filtering barriers** allow wind to pass through, reducing its force in the process.

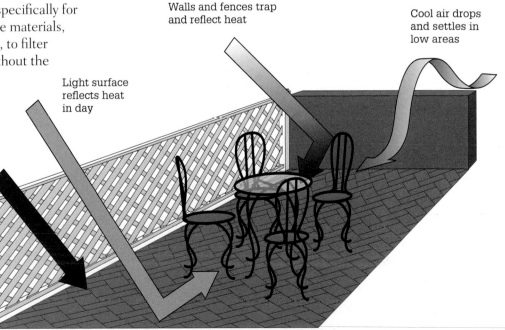

Walls and fences trap and reflect heat

Cool air drops and settles in low areas

Light surface reflects heat in day

Dark surface absorbs heat in day releasing heat at night

Surface materials, barriers, and the patio's elevation within the landscape all have an effect on the space's microclimate.

Exterior Design

Now comes the fun part. A big, empty outdoor room is just waiting for you to make your mark. Colors, textures, and details of all description are at your disposal. And the elements you choose today will not only set the tone and feel of your new living space; together they will become the framework for enhancements and embellishments for years to come. If you're the type who gets anxious at the prospect of filling a blank canvas, don't worry. A little creative thinking and a critical eye will surely lead to a satisfying design.

Start with some of the standard style questions: Formal or Informal? Traditional or Modern? Organic or Sleek? Minimal or Complex? Keeping your general preferences in mind, you can move on to more specific goals of integrating the patio with your house style and thinking in terms of design concepts. Now is a good time to take a second look through Chapter 1 for inspiration.

Blending House & Patio

How much the patio should fit with the house depends on their mutual relationship. A front entry patio or a courtyard patio is closely tied to the home's architecture and will be perceived as an extension of the home. At the opposite extreme, a detached patio can have a style and character all its own.

Marrying the styles of the house and patio doesn't necessarily mean the patio has to mimic the house. Pairing a modern patio to a traditional house, for example, can result in a stronger overall design than one that simply carries through with a single theme (think of I.M. Pei's ultramodern addition to the Louvre museum courtyard).

With a patio located next to the main part of the house, as most are, you gain the option of borrowing some of the patio's space. That is, a patio can make a house look bigger on the outside or feel bigger on the inside. To make the most of this effect, incorporate some of the house details into the patio design. A patio wall that matches or nicely complements the house siding suggests that the patio was part of the original house plan. Paving the patio with a material similar to the flooring in the nearest interior room creates continuity that expands the visual boundaries of the room.

This elegant freestanding pergola looks like it was designed by the home's original architect, with its color and column detailing inspired by the trim on the house windows.

Glass doors allow for the eye to flow seemlessly from inside the house to the patio in this modern home.

To appreciate the importance of balance in this patio composition, picture it without the potted trees and the boulders along the right side.

Design Principles

Design principles describe different ways of looking at a space. Never hard-and-fast rules, design principles are helpful if they get you to ask questions about your plan. They prompt both creativity and criticism, so you can narrow down the choices and make deliberate style decisions. Here are a few principles to consider:

Unity & Variety

Unity is making sure every element of a plan is appropriate for the overall scheme. Topping a formal red-brick patio with traditional wrought iron furniture would be part of a unified plan; decorating a rustic patio with ornate classical urns would not. Variety, while not exactly the opposite of unity, is there to remind you to mix it up a little. A patio, walkway, and set of steps all made with the same concrete pavers are certainly unified, but the design would probably look more interesting with a contrasting border or interspersed accent pavers.

Balance

The purpose of balance is to avoid a lopsided plan in which the eye is always drawn to one element or area. For example, if one side of a patio is dominated by an arbor, you can balance the setting with a grouping of planters on the opposite side. Because balance in design is purely visual, you don't necessarily have to match elements by size or type. An eye-catching sculpture or a colorful wall can balance a prominent water feature.

Proportion

To determine proportion, look at the size and overall impact of the space relative to its surroundings. The patio as a whole should fit with the house and yard, but so should its individual elements. A tall, imposing pergola extending well above the house's roofline only makes the house look smaller. Proportion is also about maintaining scale within the space. Placing a modest furniture set amid a vast sea of pavers only emphasizes the lack of enclosure.

Simplicity

Even professional designers have a hard time reining in their creative urges. Respecting simplicity doesn't mean the design has to be minimal, or even modest. It's more a matter of knowing when to say when. As a rule of thumb, choose your materials and design elements because you really like them and will enjoy being surrounded by them. Just keep in mind that too much decoration or variety results in a complicated design that prevents you from appreciating individual details.

Making a Plan

Everyone takes a different approach to planning a project. Some head to the drawing board, literally, and work out everything on paper before all else. Others jump right into the grunt work and figure out the details as they go. Whichever route you prefer, make sure to take care of the big stuff first: gaining approval from the local planning and zoning department and marking utility lines before you start digging (see page 65).

Project Drawings

Drawings can be useful for many stages of a building project. Scaled drawings, such as a site plan, are good for showing relationships between elements and overall proportions within a plan. And because you can see everything laid out in front of you, drawings are especially helpful for estimating materials and making complete shopping lists. Various scaled drawings of your project might be required by the city for obtaining permits. If you end up hiring out part of the work, detailed drawings will be a valuable reference tool for seeking bids and later to keep the project on track during construction. At any stage of the planning process, sketches and other informal drawings are useful for conveying or experimenting with ideas.

A site plan is an overhead view of the project site, including all existing elements as well as proposed additions. For early planning decisions, you might add notes about prevailing winds, views from the patio site, lot grading and drainage routes, gutter downspouts, and outdoor faucets and electrical outlets. As you refine your patio plans, you can create more detailed, smaller-scaled plan drawings of the patio site and immediate surroundings.

You may already have the basic framework for a site plan—in the original house blueprints, deed map, or property plans. Check with your city or county planning offices, mortgage company, or title company for maps of your property. Without a base map to start from, you can take your own measurements of the lot and house to create an initial site map. Make several copies of the first drawing, or use tracing paper for subsequent drawings so you'll always have a clean base map to work from.

For building projects like overheads or walls, you'll find it helpful to work from a set of construction drawings such as the Patio Arbor project on page 192. If you're designing your own custom structure, you might not need a full set; a plan view and a few elevation drawings might suffice.

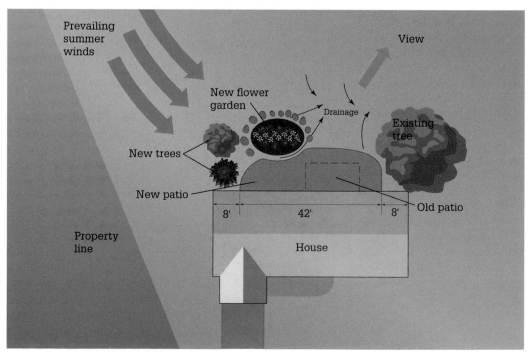

A detailed site map might include notes for sun and wind patterns, lot contours, and landscape features, in addition to property boundaries and the house footprint.

Prevailing summer winds

View

New flower garden

Drainage

New trees

Existing tree

New patio

Old patio

8' 42' 8'

Property line

House

A Patio Mock-up

A great way to test your patio plans is to lay it all out in a life-size mock-up. Start with the footprint of the patio, using a garden hose to represent the perimeter. Next, set up your furniture as you envision it in the new space (use card tables and folding chairs if you don't have the real stuff yet). Use sand, string, or rope to represent the outlines of built-in structures (like kitchen counters, overheads, walls, or fire pits) and significant plantings.

Now try it out. Sit in the chairs, walk the traffic routes, position the lounger and observe how the sun hits it at your preferred time of day. The idea is to get a feel for the space to make sure everything meets your needs. If you keep stepping over the edge of the patio as you rise from the table, perhaps you need to extend the boundary another foot. Have some meals outdoors to judge the comfort level and test traffic flow to and from the indoor kitchen. If you're planning a tall wall or fence, hang a tarp over some stakes and string. Consider the barrier's length, height, and position: Will it serve its purpose for the patio? How will it affect views from inside the house?

The emperor's new patio?
This might look silly, but It works. A full-size mock-up lets you live within your patio plan to give your ideas a test run before starting construction.

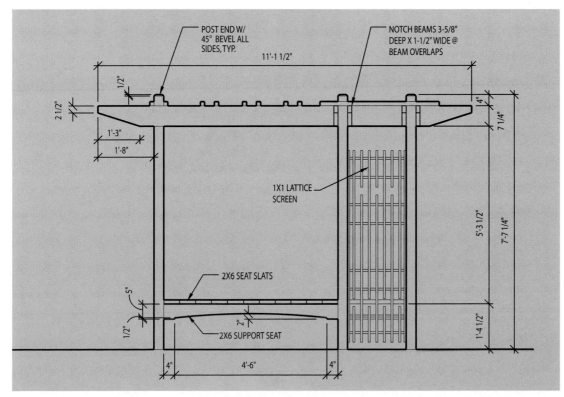

POST END W/ 45° BEVEL ALL SIDES, TYP.

NOTCH BEAMS 3-5/8" DEEP X 1-1/2" WIDE @ BEAM OVERLAPS

11'-1 1/2"

1/2"

2 1/2"

1'-3"

1'-8"

4"

7 1/4"

1X1 LATTICE SCREEN

5'-3 1/2"

7'-7 1/4"

2X6 SEAT SLATS

5"

1/2"

2"

2X6 SUPPORT SEAT

1'-4 1/2"

4"

4'-6"

4"

2-dimensional construction drawings (elevation view shown) help you work out the details of a building project. Use a scale ruler for accurate representation, and include dimensions throughout, plus labels for materials and special features.

Construction: Tools & Materials

This chapter is intended to be a straightforward guide to help you get exactly what you need for your patio project. For a similar reference geared specifically to patio surface materials, see pages 40 to 47.

As you shop for tools and materials and weigh the various options against your budget, keep in mind the value of quality. In most cases, a fairly priced item of high quality offers more value in the long run than its cut-rate counterparts. Better materials not only last longer and need fewer repairs, they also look better, giving you more satisfaction each time you use your patio. When it comes to tools, it's always best to spend a little more for a quality product, even if you plan to use it only once or twice. Avoid the cheap, brand-less tools sold in bins, which are prone to breaking under stress and often wear out before the project is completed.

Building materials, like wall brick and lumber, are commonly available at large home centers (as are tools for all types of projects), making for convenient, one-stop shopping. But if you're looking for something special, shop some retailers a little closer to the source. That is, a brickyard for brick and mortar or a lumberyard for specialty woods.

In This Chapter

- Masonry Tools
- Landscaping & Specialty Tools
- Power Tools
- Mortar
- Brick & Concrete Block
- Lumber & Hardware

Masonry Tools

Most patio projects involve masonry in one form or another: brick paving, mortared stone, concrete block, tile, and poured concrete, just to name a few. Masonry work requires specialty tools that aren't found in standard household tool kits. Fortunately, most are inexpensive hand tools and are commonly available at home centers, hardware stores, or masonry supply dealers, such as brickyards and landscaping centers. Also, many of the tools used to build a masonry patio are the same ones needed for future repairs.

Measuring and marking tools for masonry projects:
- Framing square (A), for marking right angles and checking projects for squareness; same as a carpenter's framing square.

- Wood dowels (B), used as spacers between bricks or concrete blocks to represent mortar joint; standard size is ⅜" in diameter.
- Standard levels (C), or "spirit" levels, available in 2-ft., 4-ft., and 6-ft. lengths; used to check plumb (vertical plane) and level (horizontal plane).
- Story pole (D), a homemade tool made with a long, straight board with measured markings; lets you space bricks and other units without measuring with a tape.
- Mason's string (E), or mason's "line," a strong, thin cord used for laying out a project site or aligning masonry units.
- Line level (F), attaches to a mason's string for checking for level in a variety of situations.
- Tape measure (G), long, flexible tapes (50 ft. or 100 ft.) are especially handy for measuring project sites and landscape elements.
- Chalk line (H), for marking layout lines on any flat surface; same as carpenter's version.

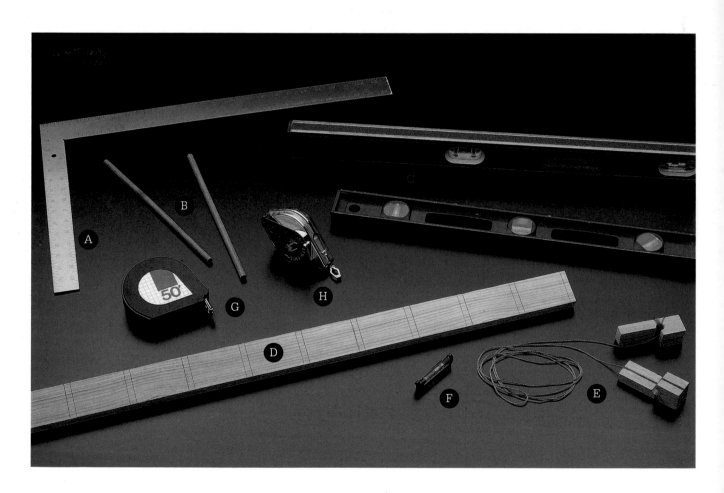

Standard masonry tools for building and repair work:

• Darby (A), for smoothing screeded concrete • Mortar hawk (B), for holding mortar • Pointing trowel (C), for tuck-pointing large mortar joints (such as with mortared stone) • Wide pointing tool (D), for placing mortar or tuck-pointing on brick or block structures • Jointer (E), for finishing mortar joints • Brick tongs (F), for carrying bricks • Narrow tuck-pointer (G), for tuck-pointing or placing mortar in brick or block • Mason's trowel (H), for applying and working with mortar • Masonry chisels (I), for splitting brick, block, and stone • Bull float (J), for floating large poured concrete slabs • Mason's hammers (K), for chipping or breaking up brick and stone • Maul (L), for driving stakes and other heavy hammering actions • Square-end trowel (M), for concrete finishing • Side edger (N), for rounding over the outside edges of concrete slabs and steps • Step edger (O), for finishing the inside corners of concrete steps • Joint chisel (P), for removing dried mortar • Control jointer (Q), for creating control joints in wet concrete • Tile nippers (R), for trimming ceramic tile • Sled jointer (S), for smoothing long mortar joints • Steel trowel (T), for finishing concrete • Magnesium float (U), for floating concrete; alternative to wood float • Screed board (V), homemade tool for screeding concrete.

Landscaping & Specialty Tools

Projects that alter your landscaping, like many patios do, often require a lot of physical labor. Removing large areas of sod, digging postholes, tamping soil and gravel beds, and other tough jobs can be made much easier with the help of rented power tools.

Specialty masonry tools, including power concrete mixers, brick splitters, and tile saws, are also available for rent. And for any backyard project, a sturdy wheelbarrow and a few good shovels are indispensable; if you don't already have these, now's the time to buy them.

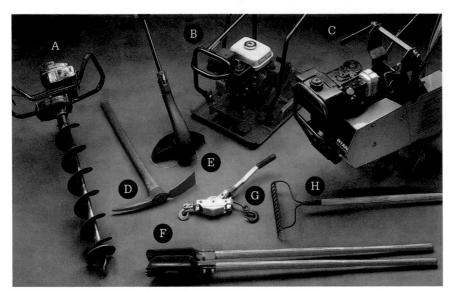

Tools for site preparation:
- Power auger (A), for digging postholes for fences and other building projects; available for rent.
- Power tamper (B), or plate compactor, for compacting gravel; available for rent.
- Power sod cutter (C), for large-scale sod removal; available for rent.
- Pick (D), for digging in hard or rocky soil.
- Weed trimmer (E), for quick removal of weeds and tall grass.
- Posthole digger (F), or clamshell digger, a hand tool for digging postholes.
- Come-along (G), an all-purpose winching tool, handy for moving large rocks, tree parts, etc.
- Garden rake (H), standard rigid-tine rake, essential for grading soil and gravel.

Other tools for patio projects:
- Wheelbarrow (A), with a volume capacity of at least 6 cu. ft.
- Power concrete mixer (B), recommended for projects requiring more than ½ cu. yard of wet concrete; available for rent.
- Masonry hoe (C) and mortar box (D), for mixing mortar and small batches of concrete.
- Square-edged spade (E), good for grading soil and gravel, cutting straight lines in sod, and settling wet concrete.
- Hand tamper (F), for tamping and compacting gravel and soil.
- Sod cutter (G), a hand tool for stripping sod for reuse.

Power Tools

Whether you're building forms, constructing an arbor, or setting masonry anchors, power tools make your work considerably easier and usually more accurate. The power tool market has seen a huge expansion in recent years. Most sizable hardware stores and home centers now carry a full range of mid- to professional-grade tools from several manufacturers. The tools shown here are among the most common and versatile types for cutting, drilling, and shaping wood, metal, and plastic. Each tool is likely to be used again and again for all types of household projects.

Commonly used power tools:

- Power miter saw (A) makes clean, consistent cuts at any angle from 0° to 45°. Note: 90° is indicated as 0° on most saws.
- Circular saw (B) is the king of project saws and can be fitted with a masonry blade for cutting brick, tile, and concrete; a cordless saw (small trim version shown) is especially convenient for outdoor projects.
- Reciprocating saw (C), a multipurpose saw that makes straight or curved cuts in almost any material, including heavy timbers; also great for demolition projects.
- Cordless drill (D), an indispensable tool for basic drilling and screwdriving tasks; corded models are equally useful, if somewhat less convenient.
- Jigsaw (E) makes detailed curved cuts in various materials, including thin sheets and fragile products.
- ½" hammer drill (F), a heavy-duty drill with hammering motion for effective drilling into brick, stone, concrete, and mortar; most also have a standard drill setting (no hammer).

Mortar

Masonry mortar is used in patio projects for setting pavers or stone over concrete slabs, for filling in between the paving, for building brick or block walls, and for masonry repairs. Masonry mortar is a mixture of Portland cement, sand and water (and may contain hydrated lime).

The right type of mortar for any given project depends on the environment (indoors, outdoors, above grade, below grade, climate), the structure (low garden wall, retaining wall), and the type of masonry unit (brick, block, stone). The main types of mortar and their general characteristics are given here.

Recommendations for mortar types are also given for specific projects later in the book. However, the best way to ensure you're using the right type of mortar for the job is to ask your masonry supplier. They can point you to specific products suited for your climate and the masonry material you're using.

Mortar is most commonly available as a dry, premixed form. All you do is mix in water according to the manufacturer's directions. For some repair projects, adding a fortifier may be recommended. Mortar mix can also be tinted with additives to match or complement masonry materials (see photo, bottom of page).

Type N
Medium-strength mortar for above-grade outdoor use in freestanding walls (non-loadbearing walls not used as retaining walls), soft-stone masonry, and tuck-pointing.

Type S
High-strength mortar for exterior use at or below grade. Generally used for paver patio surfaces, walkways, driveways, and brick or block retaining walls.

Type M
Very high-strength mortar used for some paving applications, load-bearing exterior walls, and retaining walls.

Refractory Mortar
A specialty mortar made to withstand high temperatures; used for building with firebrick in fire pits, fireplaces, and barbecues. Chemical-set mixtures will cure even in wet conditions.

Mortar tint samples are available at masonry dealers. Take samples home to find the right color for your new patio materials or for blending with existing structures.

Brick & Concrete Block

Brick used for building walls is made of the same material as paving brick but comes in somewhat different forms. The two main types of standard brick for walls are common brick and face brick. Common brick, also called building brick, has a rough, often flawed surface and may be slightly irregular in dimension, making it suitable for informal walls with an unfinished appearance. Face brick has a smooth, consistent surface and is a good choice for formal walls and accents. It's more expensive than common brick but also more consistently sized, so it's easier to work with. As with brick pavers, standard brick is available in so many colors and styles that it's best to visit a few brickyards before deciding on the best one for your patio.

Concrete block, also called cinder block, is utilitarian in look and purpose. For patio walls that you plan to cover in stucco or other surface treatment, use concrete block instead of brick; it's cheaper than brick and goes up much faster.

Lumber & Hardware

If your patio plans call for anything in wood, make sure to use lumber that can stand up to the weather. Redwood and cedar are two of the most commonly available species of naturally rot-resistant woods. Teak is a premium rot-resistant hardwood typically used for outdoor furniture. The most economical choice of outdoor lumber is pressure-treated pine (or other softwoods), which is chemically treated to resist rot and decay for many years. All of these woods will weather to a somewhat silvery-gray color within a season or so. Periodically applying an exterior stain will help new wood keep its natural coloring and help prolong the life of the wood. Treated lumber is better off painted or stained with a dark color to hide its less attractive appearance.

When it comes to hardware, the same rule of weather resistance is even more critical. All fasteners, anchors, and framing connectors used outside must be galvanized or made of a rust-resistant metal, such as stainless steel or aluminum.

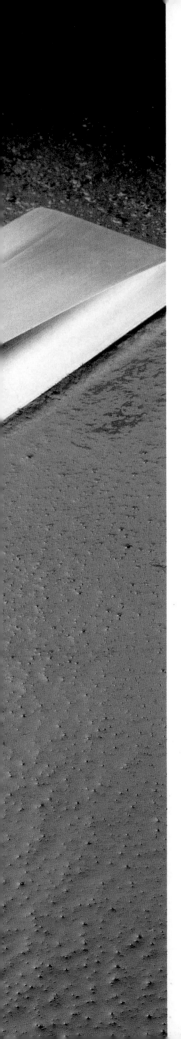

Construction: Techniques

This chapter is full of background information to prepare you for the projects in the next section. You'll also be referred back to here for detailed steps on specific techniques and building processes. Masonry work in particular involves techniques and tricks that are new to most do-it-yourselfers. The time-honored art of bricklaying, for example, takes some practice even to get the basic motions down, but the work is quite satisfying and the results of your efforts will last for many years.

Poured concrete is another material that requires specific knowledge and a feel for working with the medium. The key to success is preparation. Here, you'll learn the entire process, from buying concrete to finishing the slab.

In this chapter and throughout the book, you'll find recommendations for materials, building techniques, and other project details. However, the best source for construction specifications on your own project is your local building department. Every municipality has its own building codes—a set of laws that protect you and everyone who will use the things you build by making sure the structures meet minimum standards.

In This Chapter

- Working with Concrete
- Working with Brick & Concrete Block
- Working with Stone

Working with Concrete

Poured concrete plays a role in many patio designs. It makes a great primary surface material or a clean, durable edging. A small concrete pad laid in front of an entry door can serve as a hard-wearing stoop that can be surrounded by brick or other materials to complete the patio flooring. Concrete is also the best material for building structural footings—the monolithic supports, typically at or below grade, that form the foundation for masonry walls. The basic techniques for creating all of these concrete forms are shown here.

Concrete is made from a simple mixture of sand, larger aggregates (typically gravel), Portland cement, and water. Cement is the bonding agent that holds it all together. Mixing cement with water begins an irreversible chemical process of hardening that can't be stopped. The best insurance policy against running out of time is thorough site preparation. Here is the basic process:

1. Lay out the project, using stakes and strings.
2. Clear the project area and remove sod.
3. Excavate the site to allow for a subbase, footings (as needed), and concrete.
4. Lay a subbase for drainage and stability, and pour footings, as needed.
5. Build and install reinforced wood forms.

Ask your local building department whether your project will require frost footings or metal reinforcement, such as rebar, reinforcing mesh, or fiber additives. For large-scale concrete projects, a landscape engineer or building inspector can advise you on how to prepare the project site.

Overview

Before you start digging, have your yard checked for buried utility lines; then test the grade of the site and surrounding ground. Correct any drainage problems to eliminate or prevent boggy areas and to protect your project from excess water (see page 67). With your yard ready, you can begin staking out the site and preparing the surface.

After the site has been excavated, add a layer of compactible gravel to the ground to provide a level, stable foundation for the concrete and allow for drainage underneath the slab or footing.

Once gravel is in place, you can build the forms. It is then time to gather everything you need for the concrete pour. Good preparation means fewer delays at critical moments, and it leaves you free to focus on placing and finishing the concrete, instead of rebuilding loose forms or locating misplaced tools. The ideal temperature for pouring and finishing concrete is between 50° and 80°F.

Concrete, one of the world's most enduring building materials, is made with water, Portland cement, sand, and aggregates. Varying the ratios of ingredients yields different properties suited to specific situations.

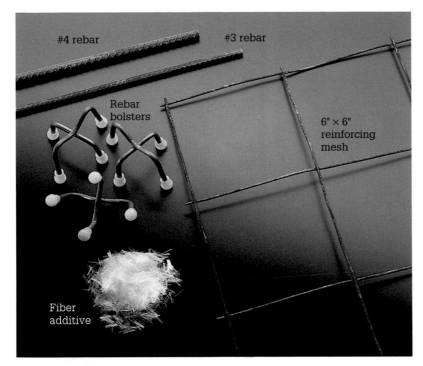

#4 rebar

#3 rebar

Rebar
bolsters

6" × 6"
reinforcing
mesh

Fiber
additive

Reinforcing materials for concrete include metal rebar, in common sizes of #3 (⅜" diameter) and #4 (½" diameter), used in slab, footing, and wall construction; wire mesh, for reinforcing slabs; bolsters, for supporting rebar or mesh from underneath to suspend the material within the concrete; and fiber additive, used to increase the strength of specific concrete mixes.

Shown cutaway

Isolation joint

Concrete slab

Compactible gravel subbase

Isolation joints are used to separate concrete projects from the house foundation and other structures. The standard material for an isolation joint is ½"-thick asphalt-impregnated fiberboard, which can be glued to the adjoining structure with construction adhesive prior to the concrete pour.

Estimating Concrete ▶

To find the volume of concrete required for your project:
1. Measure the width and length of the project in feet, and then multiply those dimensions to find the square footage.
2. Measure the thickness of the project in inches, and then convert to feet (4" = ⅓ ft.; 6" = ½ ft.).
3. Multiply the square footage by the thickness to find the cubic footage.

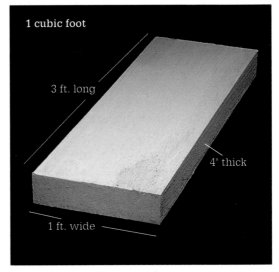

1 cubic foot

3 ft. long

4" thick

1 ft. wide

For example: 1 ft. x 3 ft. x ⅓ ft. = 1 cu. ft. To convert to cubic yards, divide by 27 (27 cu. ft. = 1 cu. yard).

CONCRETE COVERAGE		
Volume	Slab Thickness	Surface Coverage
1 cu. yd.	2"	160 sq. ft.
1 cu. yd.	3"	110 sq. ft.
1 cu. yd.	4"	80 sq. ft.
1 cu. yd.	5"	65 sq. ft.
1 cu. yd.	6"	55 sq. ft.
1 cu. yd.	8"	40 sq. ft.

Coverage rates for poured concrete are determined by the thickness of the slab. The same volume of concrete will yield less surface area if the thickness of the slab is increased. The chart above shows the relationship between slab thickness, surface area, and volume.

Mixing & Ordering Concrete

When it comes to buying and mixing poured concrete, the best options for most do-it-yourself projects are mixing bags of dry mix or having ready-mix delivered by a concrete truck. A less expensive option is to buy the dry ingredients in bulk and mix everything on site. Although bulk is less expensive than bagged mix, it requires you to mix the proper proportions. If you choose this route, ask your masonry supplier for mixing recommendations based on their specific materials.

Mixing Your Own Concrete

Dry concrete mix is typically sold in 60-pound bags at home and landscape centers everywhere. All you add is water. There are several types of premixed concrete, each with specific properties—such as fast-drying or fiber-reinforced concrete. Choose the formulation that best suits your application.

A 60-pound bag of concrete mix yields roughly ½ cubic feet of solid concrete. For a patio surface, the number of bags adds up quickly. If you're planning a large slab that must be poured all at once or any job requiring more than a cubic yard, you're probably better off ordering ready-mix. For small jobs, you can mix a couple of bags at a time in a mortar box or a wheelbarrow. For somewhat larger jobs, consider renting a power concrete mixer.

Any successful concrete pour starts with the mix—achieving the right amount of water per dry ingredients. Using bagged concrete ensures accurate proportioning of the dry ingredients, but adding the right amount of water requires judgment on your part. Follow the instructions on the bag, carefully adding more water as needed.

Properly mixed concrete is damp enough to form in your hand when squeezed, yet dry enough to hold its shape. If too dry, the mixture will be difficult to work, and the aggregate will not easily float down from the surface to produce a smooth, even finish. The mixture will easily slide off a trowel if the mixture is too wet. This consistency will result in a weakened finished surface that may be prone to cracks and other defects.

Once you're satisfied with the mixture, place the concrete immediately. There's no need to panic, but be aware that any lost minutes will ultimately come out of your allowed time for finishing the concrete and making it look good.

Ordering Ready-mix Concrete

Professional delivery of ready-mix concrete is recommended for jobs that call for 1 cubic yard or more. Many ready-mix companies have a 1-yard minimum for delivery orders. If you don't need a full cubic yard, find a spot on your lot for dumping the extra—concrete trucks must unload completely at the end of each delivery, so you'll get the full yard whether you want it or not.

Ordering ready-mix costs more than mixing yourself, but it's much faster for large projects. Ready-mix companies are listed in the phone book under "Concrete." Make sure you're ready when the truck arrives, because mixed concrete won't wait.

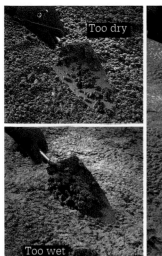

Too dry

Too wet

Correct

A good mixture is crucial to the success of any concrete project.

To mix concrete by hand, pour dry mix from bags into a mortar box or wheelbarrow. Form a hollow in the mix and pour in 1 gallon of clean (drinkable) water for each 60-lb. bag of mix. Work the mixture with a mason's hoe or garden hoe, carefully adding water to achieve the desired consistency. Do not overwork the mix.

To mix concrete with a power mixer, fill a bucket with 1 gallon of clean (drinkable) water for each 60-lb. bag of dry mix in the batch (three bags is workable for most mixers). Pour in ½ of the water, and then add all of the dry ingredients. Mix for 1 minute. Add water as needed to reach the desired consistency, then mix for 3 minutes. Empty the mix into a wheelbarrow, and rinse the drum immediately.

Preparing for Concrete Delivery ▸

- Fully prepare the building site. Make sure your forms are complete and adequately secured. Forms must support the weight of the concrete.
- Prepare a clear delivery path to the project site, so you're ready to pour when the truck arrives. Lay planks over the forms and gravel base to form a smooth path for wheelbarrows.
- Enlist as many strong helpers as possible. A big pour is fast, furious, and exhausting.
- Discuss your project with the experts at the ready-mix company. They will help you determine how much and what type of concrete you need.
- Call the supplier the day before the scheduled pour to confirm the quantity and delivery time.
- Read the receipt you get from the driver. It gives the time the concrete was mixed. Before you accept the concrete, make sure no more than 90 minutes have elapsed between the mixing and delivery times.

Be ready for the concrete delivery, with wheelbarrows, plenty of help, and a clear path for moving the concrete to the pour site, as well as an open area for the truck to park.

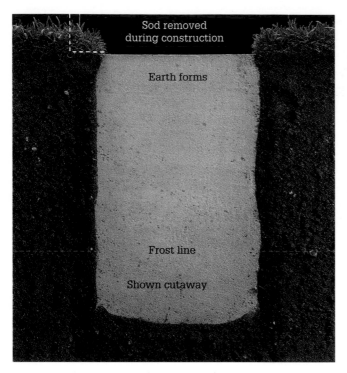

For below-grade-level footings without exposed sides, use the earth as a form. Strip sod from the project area, then rest the edges of a board on the earth to screed. (Gravel base not shown.)

For grade-level or raised footings, where a smooth, finished appearance is important, build level wood forms. Screed the concrete flush with the tops of the form boards. (Gravel base not shown.)

Building Footings

Footings provide a stable, level base for brick, block, stone, and poured concrete structures. They distribute the weight of the structure evenly, prevent sinking, and keep structures from moving during seasonal freeze-thaw cycles.

The required depth of a footing is usually determined by the frost line, which varies by region. The frost line is the point nearest ground level where the soil does not freeze. In colder climates, it is likely to be 48" or deeper. Frost footings (footings designed to keep structures from moving during freezing temperatures) should extend 12" below the frost line for the area. Your local building inspector can tell you the frost line depth for your area.

Footings for walls should be twice as wide as the structure. They should also extend at least 12" past the ends of the project area.

To find out if your planned structure requires footing and/or footing reinforcement, describe your structure to your local building inspector. In some cases, 8"-thick slab footings can be used, as long as the subbase provides plenty of drainage.

For footings that will support poured concrete structures, add metal rebar tie-rods, as required by the local building code.

How to Pour a Footing

Step A: Dig Rough Trenches for the Footings

1. Lay out the location of the project using rope or hose, then use stakes and mason's string to outline footings that are twice as wide as the proposed project.

2. Measure the diagonals to make sure the stake outline is square, and then use a framing square to make sure the corners are square. Adjust as needed.

3. Strip away sod 6" outside the project area on all sides, and then excavate the trench for the footing to a depth of 12" below the frost line. The bottom of the trench should be roughly level.

4. Lay a 6" layer of compactible gravel subbase into the trench. Tamp the subbase thoroughly.

Step B: Build Forms & Add Reinforcement

1. Build and install 2 × 4 forms to outline the footings, aligning the forms with the mason's string (see page 93). Drive stakes along the outside of the forms to anchor them in position, and then adjust the forms to level.

2. If your project abuts another structure, such as a house foundation, slip a piece of ½"-thick asphalt-impregnated fiberboard into the trench between the footing and the structure. This creates an isolation joint. The board allows the structure to

Tools & Materials
Rope or hose ▪ Mason's string ▪ Tape measure ▪ Shovel ▪ Framing square ▪ Level ▪ Compactible gravel ▪ Hand tamp ▪ 2 × 4 lumber ▪ Circular saw ▪ Handsaw (optional) ▪ Wood-trimming knife ▪ Hammer ▪ 3" deck screws ▪ Stakes ▪ Fiberboard ▪ Construction adhesive ▪ #3 rebar ▪ 16-gauge wire ▪ Concrete ▪ Mixing container ▪ Wheelbarrow ▪ Hoe ▪ Long, straight 2 × 4 ▪ Tie-rods, if necessary ▪ Float ▪ Plastic sheeting ▪ Vegetable oil or commercial release agent ▪ Bolt cutters.

move independently, minimizing the risk of damage. Use a few dabs of construction adhesive to hold the board in place.

3. Make two #3 rebar grids to reinforce each footing. For each grid, use bolt cutters to cut two pieces of #3 rebar 8" shorter than the length of the footing and two pieces 4" shorter than the depth of the footing. For longer footings, make several grids to cover the greater spans.

4. Bind the pieces of rebar together with 16-gauge wire, forming a rectangle. Set the rebar grids upright in the trench, leaving 4" of space between the grids and the walls of the trench.

5. Coat the inside edges of the forms with vegetable oil or a commercial release agent.

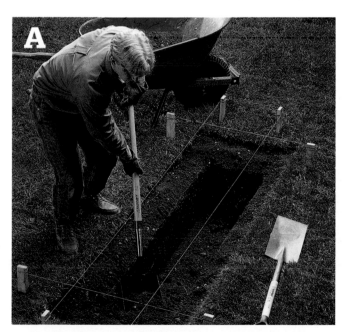

Strip away sod 6" outside the project area on all sides, then excavate the trench for the footing to a depth of 12" below the frost line.

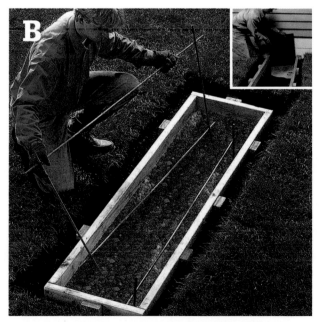

After you build and install a 2 × 4 form frame for the footing, reinforce each footing with #3 rebar grids. If your project is right up next to another structure, create an isolation joint by using a piece of fiberboard (inset).

Step C: Pour the Footings

1. Make sure you have a clear path from your concrete source to your project area. Build a ramp, if necessary, from 2 × 6 lumber. Mix the concrete according to manufacturer's instructions. Work the concrete with a shovel to remove air pockets. Do not overwork the mix.

2. Pour the concrete in evenly spaced loads, starting at the end farthest from the concrete source. Pour the concrete so it reaches the tops of the forms. Do not pour too close to the forms.

3. Screed the surface of the concrete by dragging a short 2 × 4 along the top of the forms. Add concrete to any low areas that form. Screed the surface again and add tie-rods, if needed. Float the concrete until it is smooth and level.

4. When the concrete is hard to the touch, cover the footings with plastic and let the concrete cure 2 to 3 days. Remove the forms and backfill around the edges of the footings. Add compactible gravel to bring the surrounding areas level with the surface of the footings.

5. Let the footings cure for 1 week to maximize strength.

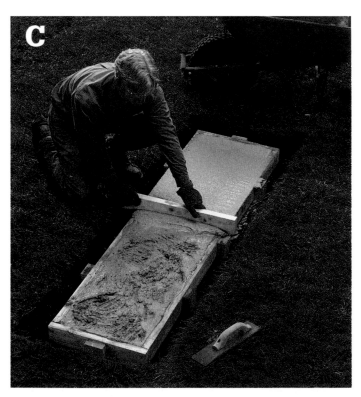

Mix and pour concrete so it reaches the tops of the forms. Use a 2 × 4 to screed the surface. Add tie-rods, if needed. Float the concrete until it is smooth and level.

Building Wood Forms

Forms are the rigid wood frames that contain poured concrete and give the final structure its shape, much like a mold for plaster. Forms for patio and yard projects are typically made from 2 × 4 lumber and sit directly on or just above the gravel subbase or are placed at the top of a deeper excavation so that the below-grade portion of the concrete is contained by the surrounding earth.

The mason's strings that outline your project are a good reference guide for positioning form boards. Patio slabs should slope away from the house or other structure at ⅛" per foot. To create this slope, multiply the distance of your project by ⅛". For example, for a 10"-ft.-long slab, the surface elevation will drop a total of 1¼" (10 × ⅛" = 1¼"). Slope your layout strings accordingly, then measure from the strings to set the form.

Ask the local building department about required specifications for your project. A typical large patio slab should be 4" thick, with wire mesh for internal reinforcement. Other projects, such as footings for walls, may require rebar for reinforcement. When installing metal reinforcement, leave at least 1" of clearance between the metal and the form boards. Use bolsters or small chunks of concrete to raise wire mesh off the subbase, but make sure it's at least 2" below the top of the form. Overlap joints in rebar by at least 12", and then bind the ends together with heavy-gauge wire. Overlap pieces of wire mesh by 12".

Creating Curves ▶

Create curves with ⅛" hardboard attached at the inside corners of the form frame. Drive support stakes behind the curved form.

How to Build Wood Forms

Step A: Set the Slope

1. Outline and excavate the project area.

2. Establish a slope of ⅛" per foot, adding and removing soil as needed, and working away from the house until the soil is evenly sloped.

Step B: Prepare the Forms

1. Cut 2 × 4s to create a frame with inside dimensions equal to the total size of the project.

2. Starting with the longest form board, position the boards so the inside edges are directly below the mason's strings that outline the project.

3. Cut several pieces of 2 × 4, at least 12" long, to use as stakes. Trim one end of each stake to a sharp point.

4. Drive the stakes at 3-ft. intervals at the outside edges of the form boards, positioned to support any joints in the form boards.

Step C: Assemble the Forms

1. Drive 3" deck screws through the stakes and into the form board on one side, so the form board is about 1" above ground.

2. Set a level so it spans the staked side of the form and the opposite form board, and use the level as a guide as you stake the second form board so it is level with the first.

3. Once the forms are staked and leveled, drive 3" deck screws at the corners.

4. Coat the insides of the forms with a vegetable oil or a commercial release agent to prevent the concrete from bonding with them.

5. Tack nails to the outsides of the forms to mark locations for control joints at intervals roughly 1½ times the slab width (but no more than 30 times its thickness).

6. Install metal reinforcement, if necessary.

Tools&**Materials** Circular saw or handsaw
▪ Hammer ▪ Level ▪ Wood-trimming knife ▪ 2 x 4s ▪ 3" deck screws ▪ Vegetable oil or commercial release agent.

Lay out the project area with stakes and mason's string, then determine a ⅛"-per-ft. slope and adjust the strings accordingly.

Position boards with inside edges directly below the mason string's outline. Position 2 × 4 stakes to support joints (inset).

Set a level so it spans the staked side of the form and the opposite form board, level the second form board with the first and attach to the stakes with 3" deck screws.

Placing Concrete

Placing concrete involves pouring it into forms, then leveling and smoothing it with special masonry tools. Attention to detail when placing your concrete will result in a professional finished appearance for your project.

When pouring concrete, never overload your wheelbarrow, and always load from the front—not the side—to avoid tipping. Experiment with sand or dry mix to find a comfortable, controllable load (or "pod").

This also helps you get a feel for how many wheelbarrow loads it will take to complete your project.

To avoid disturbing your building site, lay planks over the forms to make a ramp for the wheelbarrow. Make sure you have a flat, stable surface between the concrete source and the forms, and use supports for your plank ramp. Always remember to start pouring concrete at the farthest point from the concrete source, and work your way back.

How to Place Concrete

Step A: Place Concrete in the Forms

1. Make sure you have a clear path from the source to the site. Use 2 × 6 lumber to build a ramp, if necessary. Lay planks over your forms, and use supports for your plank ramp. Load your wheelbarrow with fresh concrete—remember to load from the front, not the side, to avoid tipping.

2. Pour the concrete in evenly spaced pods, starting at the end farthest from the concrete source and working backward. Do not pour too close to the forms: pour so the top of the pod is a few inches above the top of the forms. If using a ramp, stay clear of the end.

3. Continue to place concrete pods next to preceding pods, working away from the first pod. Do not pour too much concrete at one time, or it may harden before you can start tooling.

4. Distribute the concrete evenly in the project area, using a masonry hoe. Work the concrete until it is fairly flat and the surface is slightly above the top of the forms. Remove any excess concrete with a shovel.

5. Immediately work the blade of the spade between the inside edges of the form and the concrete to remove trapped air bubbles that can weaken the concrete.

6. Rap the forms with a hammer or the blade of the shovel to help settle the concrete and draw the finer aggregates in the concrete against the forms.

Pour concrete in evenly spaced loads (called a "pod"), starting at the end farthest from the concrete source. Use a masonry hoe to distribute concrete evenly (inset).

Use a screed board to remove excess concrete before bleed water appears. Use a sawing motion from left to right, keeping the screed flat.

Cut control joints at marked locations with a mason's trowel, using a straight 2 x 4 as a guide.

Step B: Screed the Surface

1. Use a screed board—a straight piece of 2 × 4 long enough to rest on opposite forms—to remove the excess concrete before bleed water appears.

2. Move the screed board in a sawing motion from left to right, keeping the screed flat as you work. If screeding leaves any valleys in the surface, add fresh concrete to the low areas and screed to level.

Step C: Cut the Control Joints

Cut control joints at marked locations with a mason's trowel, using a straight 2 × 4 as a guide. Control joints help prevent jagged, disfiguring cracks that can occur as natural heaving and settling occur.

Step D: Float the Surface & Groove the Joints

1. Wait until bleed water disappears, then float in an arcing motion, with the leading edge of the tool up. Stop floating as soon as the surface is smooth.

2. Once any excess bleed water has dried, draw a groover across the precut control joints, using a straight 2 × 4 as a guide. You may have to make several passes to create a smooth control joint.

Step E: Shape the Edges

1. Shape the edges of the concrete with an edging tool placed between the forms and the concrete. You may have to make several passes to create a smooth, finished appearance.

2. Use a wood float to smooth out any marks left by the groover or edger.

3. Cover the concrete with plastic and let it cure for 1 week.

Understanding Bleed Water ▸

Timing is key to an attractive concrete finish. When concrete is poured, the heavy materials gradually sink, leaving a thin layer of water—known as "bleed water"—on the surface. To achieve an attractive finish, it's important to let bleed water dry before proceeding with other steps. Follow these rules to avoid problems:

Settle and screed the concrete and add control joints immediately after pouring and before bleed water appears. Otherwise, crazing, spalling, and other flaws are likely.

Let bleed water dry before floating or edging. Concrete should be hard enough that foot pressure leaves no more than a ¼"-deep impression.

Do not overfloat the concrete; it may cause bleed water to reappear. Stop floating (Step D) if the surface starts to get shiny, and resume when it is gone.

NOTE: Bleed water doesn't appear with air-entrained concrete, which is used in regions where temperatures often fall below freezing.

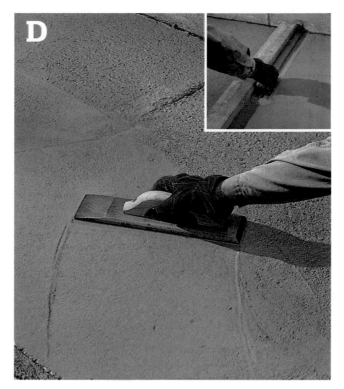

When bleed water disappears, float in an arcing motion, with the leading edge of the tool up. Stop floating as soon as the surface is smooth. Then draw a groover across precut control joints, using a straight 2 x 4 as a guide (inset).

Shape concrete with an edging tool between the forms and the concrete, then use a wood float to smooth out marks left by the groover or edger.

Working with Brick & Concrete Block

With its uncommon versatility, brick finds its way into all sorts of patio projects. Sandset brick paving is the most popular application. This often requires cutting many individual bricks, but the basic construction is like assembling a puzzle. Mortared brick applications call for a little more planning, as well as learning how to mix and apply mortar. Concrete block has much more limited use than brick as a patio material but is nevertheless a good, economical option for building low walls and planters that can be covered with a surface finish, as in the Mortarless Block Wall project.

Planning a Mortared Brick Project

Mortared brick structures require more planning than non-mortared because you must account for the combined thickness of the mortar joints and lay out the project so that all joints are consistent in size. The first step is finding the actual dimensions of the brick you'll use. Often the actual dimensions differ from the nominal (or "stated") dimensions, due to an allowance for the mortar joint.

Some brick pavers have lugs on their sides to create a consistent gap of about ⅛" between bricks for filling with sand in sandset applications. If you're mortaring brick pavers for a patio surface, you'll probably space the bricks at ½" for the mortar joint. This means that the lugs won't come into play. However, make sure you know whether the lugs are included in the brick's nominal dimensions. For wall brick, the nominal dimensions typically include a ⅜" addition to the width and height, to account for a ⅜"-thick mortar joint. When you have the brick on site, use dowels or plywood spacers to represent the mortar joints, and dry-lay the bricks to determine the final layout.

If you're planning a brick (or block) wall, ask the local building department about structural requirements for various wall heights. In many areas, a freestanding wall that's 3 ft. tall or lower doesn't need a frost footing. Walls 2 ft. or lower often can be built on a thickened (8" is standard) part of a larger slab.

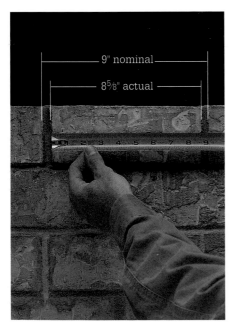

Wall brick typically is sized for a ⅜" mortar joint. As shown here, a 4 × 9" (nominal) brick actually measures 8⅝".

Using wood spacers for mortar joints when dry-laying bricks is a foolproof way to design your brick structure.

Standard mortar joint thickness is ½" for brick paving. Plan your layout accordingly.

How to Mark and Cut Bricks

Step A: Mark Straight Cutting Lines

When you can't avoid cutting bricks, the first thing you have to do is mark the cuts. If you're making many identical cuts, use a T-square and pencil to mark groups of bricks at the same time. Align the ends and hold the bricks in place as you mark.

Step B: Score Straight Cuts

1. To avoid cracking them, set bricks on a bed of sand as you work. If the cutting line falls over the core (solid portion), score the brick on two sides; if it falls over the web area (where there's a hole), score all four sides.

2. For small jobs, use a mason's chisel and hammer both to score and to cut the bricks. To score a brick, use a hammer to tap on the mason's chisel, leaving cut marks $\frac{1}{8}$" deep. For large jobs, you can ensure uniformity and speed up the process by scoring the bricks with a circular saw and masonry-cutting blade. Set the saw's blade and depth between $\frac{1}{8}$" and $\frac{1}{4}$". Carefully align the ends of the bricks, and clamp them securely at each end, using pipe clamps or bar clamps.

Step C: Make Straight Cuts

Use a mason's chisel and a hammer to split the bricks. Hold the chisel at a slight angle and tap it firmly with the hammer.

Step D: Mark Angled Cuts

Set the bricks in position, allowing $\frac{3}{8}$" for mortar joints, where necessary. Mark the cutting lines, using a straightedge to make sure the cutting lines are straight and accurate.

Step E: Score Angled Cuts

Making angled cuts is a gradual process—to avoid breaking the good part of the brick you have to make a series of cuts that move toward the final cutting line. First, score a straight line in the waste area of the brick, about $\frac{1}{8}$" away from the starting point of the marked cutting line.

Step F: Complete Angled Cuts

To make the remaining cuts, keep the chisel stationary at the point of the first cut. Pivot it slightly; score and split again. Keep the pivot point of the chisel at the edge of the brick. Repeat the process until all the waste area is removed.

Use a T-square and pencil to mark several bricks for cutting. Make sure the ends of the bricks are aligned.

Use a circular saw with a masonry-cutting blade to score a group of bricks. Clamp the bricks, making sure the ends are aligned.

To split a brick, align a mason's chisel on a scored line. Tap the chisel with a hammer until the brick splits.

To mark angled cuts, set the bricks in position and mark the angle of the cut, using a pencil and a straightedge.

Mark a line in the waste area of the brick, about ⅛" away from the starting point of the cutting line.

Make a series of cuts, gradually removing angled sections until all of the waste area is removed.

Using a Brick Splitter ▸

If your project requires many cuts, it's a good idea to rent a brick splitter, a tool that makes accurate, consistent cuts in bricks and pavers. Always read and follow manufacturer's instructions on a rental tool, and refer questions to the rental center.

In general, a brick splitter is easy to use. Just mark a cutting line, and then set the brick on the table of the splitter. Align the cutting line on the brick with the cutting blade on the splitter.

Once the brick is in position on the splitter table, pull down sharply on the handle. The cutting blade will cleave the brick along the cutting line.

Note: Always wear eye protection when cutting masonry products, including bricks and pavers.

How to Cut Concrete Blocks ▸

Mark cutting lines on both faces of the block, then score ⅛" to ¼"-deep cuts along the lines, using a circular saw equipped with a masonry blade.

Use a mason's chisel and maul to split one face of the block along the cutting line. Turn the block over and split the other face.

Option: Cut half blocks from combination corner blocks. Corner blocks have preformed cores in the center of the web. Score lightly above the core, then rap with a mason's chisel to break off half blocks.

How to Mix & Throw Mortar

The first critical element to handling mortar effectively is the mixture. If the mortar is too thick, it will fall off the trowel in a heap, not in the smooth line that is your goal. Add too much water and the mortar becomes messy and weak. Follow the mortar manufacturer's mixing directions, but keep in mind that the amount of water specified is an approximation.

If you've never mixed mortar before, experiment with small amounts until you find a mixture that clings to the trowel just long enough for you to deliver a controlled, even line that holds its shape after settling. Record the best mixture proportions for future batches. Always mix mortar in workable batches, so you'll have time to use it all before it becomes too hard to work. Hot, dry weather shortens the working time; you can add water (called "retempering") to thin, hardening mortar, but you must use retempered mortar within two hours.

Step A: Mix the Mortar

Empty the mortar mix into a mortar box or wheelbarrow, and create a well in the center. Pour about ¾ of the recommended amount of water into the depression and mix it in with a masonry hoe. Continue adding small amounts of water until achieving the desired consistency. Do not overwork the mortar or mix too much at one time; it's much easier to work when it's fresh.

Step B: Load the Trowel

Set a piece of plywood on blocks at a comfortable height, and place a shovelful of mortar on the plywood. Using a mason's trowel, slice off a strip of mortar from the pile. Slip the trowel, point-first, under the strip to pick it up. Snap the trowel gently downward to dislodge excess mortar clinging to the edges. A good load of mortar is enough to set three bricks. Don't get too far ahead of yourself—if you throw too much mortar at one time, it will set up before you're ready.

Step C: Throw the Mortar

Position the trowel at your starting point. In one motion, begin turning your wrist over and quickly move the trowel across the surface to spread the mortar consistently along the bricks. The goal is to lay a rounded line about 2½" wide and about 2 ft. long.

Step D: Furrow the Mortar

Drag the point of the trowel through the center of the mortar line, using a slight back-and-forth motion. This action, called "furrowing," helps distribute the mortar evenly.

Mix the mortar with some of the water, then add more water as needed.

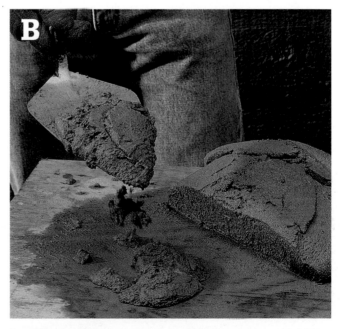

Load the trowel, then snap it down to remove excess mortar.

Throw the mortar by tipping the trowel, then quickly drawing it backward along the line of bricks.

Furrow the mortar line with a back-and-forth motion of the trowel point.

Butter Your Bricks ▸

"Buttering" is a term used to describe the process of applying mortar to a brick before adding it to the structure being built. To butter a brick, apply a heavy layer of mortar to one end, and then cut off the excess with a trowel.

Make Practice Runs ▸

Make practice runs on a 2 × 4 to help you perfect your mortar-throwing and bricklaying techniques. You can clean and reuse the bricks to make many practice runs if you find it helpful, but do not reuse the bricks in your actual projects—old mortar can impede bonding.

Working with Stone

Stone is an especially satisfying material to work with because of its natural shape and contours. Arranging the randomly sized pieces into an attractive patio floor is an opportunity to make your personal mark, and you'll always enjoy knowing that the pattern you made is truly original. Laying stone is also hard work. At times, those same character traits you love will test your patience. The tips and techniques shown here can help your project go smoothly.

Stone weighs 165 pounds per cubic foot, on average. Even flagstone, which may be only a few inches thick, can be quite heavy and difficult to move in large pieces. It's a good idea to wear a lifting belt when working with any stone. And always use the proper lifting technique, bending at your knees and not at your waist. Even smaller stones will strain your back after a while if you don't lift properly.

When you're ready to start laying your patio, organize the bulk shipment of stones, grouping the pieces by size and shape. You might want to reserve thicker stones for a border or other treatment, then lay out the good paving stones for the main section of the patio. This will allow you to view all of the stones at a glance and pick the size or shape needed for the next piece of the puzzle. It also makes it easier to alternate sizes of laid stones, so you don't reach the edge of the patio and have nothing but small pieces to draw from. If you won't finish the project in a day or so, move any leftover stones to prevent killing the grass.

Cutting Stone

You can cut most natural stone by placing it directly on a bed of flat, soft ground—such as grass or sand—to help absorb some of the shock of hammer blows and prevent unwanted breakage. Another option is to build a simple cutting platform, called a "banker," which supports stones in a bed of sand. Made of 2×2 lumber sandwiched over ¾" plywood, a banker can be used on the ground or set atop a stable base of concrete block to allow you to cut at a comfortable height.

Always wear safety goggles and gloves when cutting stone to protect yourself from flying shards and particles. The best tools for most cutting are basic stone chisels, for scoring cutting lines, and mauls for working the chisel. A standard brickset chisel and carpenter's hammer are too light for cutting most stone. Standard hammers also have brittle, hardened heads that can chip when used with most masonry chisels. For safety, maintain your chisels by grinding the striking ends if they become "mushroomed" (forming a curled edge where the steel has been pushed out by repeated hammer blows). Pieces of this edge can break off during hammering and become dangerous projectiles.

(Above) A banker creates a stable yet cushioned surface for cutting stone. To build one, screw a frame of 2 × 2s to both sides of a ¾" plywood center, and then fill the top surface with sand.

(Left) Organizing stones by size and shape makes it easy to find the best pieces during installation.

Mark a cutting line on both sides of the stone, using a crayon or chalk.

How to Cut Flagstone

Step A: Mark the Stone
Trying to split a large flagstone in half can lead to many unpredicted breaks. For best results, chip off small sections at a time. Mark the stone on both sides with chalk or a crayon, indicating where you want it to split. If there is a fissure nearby, mark your line there, since that is probably where the stone will break naturally.

Step B: Score the Stone
Score along the cutting line on the backside of the stone (the side that won't be exposed) by moving a chisel along the line and striking it with moderate blows, using a maul. Option: Scoring stones with a circular saw (see sidebar, (this page).

Step C: Break the Stone
Turn the stone over so the topside is facing up. Place a pipe or 2 × 4 directly under the chalk line, then strike the waste end (the portion you want removed) forcefully with the maul to break the stone.

Chisel along the cutting line on the backside of the stone.

Place a pipe under the cutting line, then strike the waste end to break the stone.

Option: Breaking a Large Flagstone

If a paving stone is too big for your needs, set the stone on the patio subsurface and strike a heavy blow to the center with a sledgehammer. It should break into several useable pieces.

Option: Use a sledgehammer to break a large stone into smaller, randomly shaped pieces.

Using a Circular Saw ▸

If you have a lot of cutting to do, reduce hammering fatigue by using a circular saw with a silicone-carbide or diamond-cutting masonry blade to score the stones ⅛" deep with each pass, then use a maul and chisel to split them completely. When cutting with a circular saw, keep the stones wet to reduce dust.

Dressing Stones ▸

"Dressing" is a general term for trimming or smoothing a stone for a more finished appearance. To remove unwanted bumps or jagged edges from a stone, use a pointing chisel and a maul. Position the chisel at a 30° to 45° angle at the base of the piece to be removed. Lightly tap all around the break line, and then gradually tap with greater force to chip off the piece. Carefully position the chisel before each blow with the maul.

Construction: Preparing the Site

Preparing the area for a new or expanded patio often involves more than excavating the immediate project site. If your house is new and your landscape undeveloped, now is the time to make sure the ground around the house is graded properly to shed water away from the house and patio. Or, if alterations have been made to an existing landscape, checking the grade of the new or newly exposed soil is a critical final stage for preventing drainage problems in the future.

Now is also the time to deal with existing (and potential) drainage problems that could affect the new patio and surrounding yard areas. See page 67 for an overview of common drainage problems and their solutions. Implementing two of those solutions is covered here: creating a drainage swale to collect and channel water from natural low spots in your yard and building a dry well to provide your own underground water collection point. The basic procedures shown can easily be adapted to fit your situation.

Another preparation issue for some projects is the design challenge of a sloping lot. If a hillside is encroaching on your planned patio space, you can reshape the area with a retaining wall or terracing.

When you're ready to start on the patio, head straight to the layout and surface preparation projects. First, you'll set up layout strings to mark the site. Then you'll complete the excavation. From there, creating a smooth, firm base of gravel will get you ready for installing most patio surfaces, and you're on your way to having a new outdoor room.

In This Chapter

- Grading Soil
- Building a Drainage Swale
- Building a Dry Well
- Retaining Walls & Terracing
- Laying Out & Preparing the Patio Site

Grading Soil

Because water flows downhill, the soil around your house and patio must be sloped to direct rainwater and snowmelt where you want it to go. The first 6 ft. leading from the house is the most critical area. Improper grading here is one of the most common causes of water getting into a basement or crawl space.

The standard minimum slope for drainage is ¾" per foot. A steeper slope is fine, but anything flatter than ¾" per foot can lead to standing water or excessive soil saturation. When it comes to the patio site itself, you'll take care of the slope during the excavation.

Regrading may require hauling in extra soil to build up low areas. When practical, you can remove soil in high areas and simply move it to the low spots. If you plan to grow grass or add plantings in the graded area, keep in mind that the top layer of soil must be fertile topsoil.

How to Measure & Establish a Grade

Step A: Measure the Slope

1. Drive a pair of stakes into the soil, one at the base of the foundation, and another at least 8 ft. out into the yard along a straight line from the first stake.

2. Attach a string fitted with a line level to the stakes and adjust the string until it's level. Measure and flag the string with tape at 1-ft. intervals.

3. Measure down from the string at the tape flags, recording your measurements as you work. Use these measurements as guidelines for adding or removing soil to create a correct grade.

Step B: Add & Distribute Soil

1. Starting at the base of the house, add soil to low areas until the desired height is reached.

2. Using a garden rake, evenly distribute the soil over a small area. Measure down from the 1-ft. markings as you work to make sure that you are creating a ¾" per 1-ft. pitch.

3. Add and remove soil as needed, working away from the house until soil is evenly sloped. After you've completed an area, repeat steps A and B to grade the next section of your yard.

Step C: Lightly Tamp the Soil

Use a hand tamp to lightly compact the soil. Don't overtamp the soil or it could become too dense to grow a healthy lawn or plants.

8' Level line

Measure at 1' intervals

Tools & Materials

Hammer or maul ▪ Tape measure ▪ Mason's string ▪ Line level ▪ Spade ▪ Garden rake ▪ Hand tamper ▪ Grading rake (optional) ▪ Stakes ▪ Tape ▪ Topsoil (as needed).

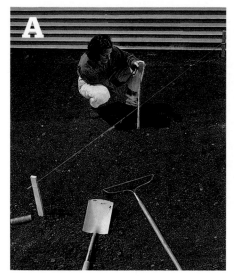

To check the slope, level the string with a line level, and then measure down at 1-ft. intervals.

Beginning at the foundation, use a garden rake to distribute soil, checking and adjusting the slope as you work.

Use a hand tamp to lightly compact the soil in the graded area.

Step D: Remove Debris

1. After all the soil is tamped, use a grading rake to remove any rocks or clumps. Starting at the foundation, pull the rake in a straight line down the slope.

2. Dispose of any rocks or construction debris.

3. Repeat the process, working on one section at a time until the entire area around the house is graded.

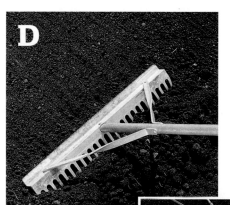

Pull a grading rake in a straight line down the slope to remove rocks, clumps, and debris.

Variation: Creating Level Areas

You may want to create some perfectly level areas for playing lawn games such as croquet, badminton, volleyball, or lawn bowling.

1. Outline the perimeter of the area with evenly placed stakes.

2. Extend a string fitted with a line level between a pair of stakes and adjust the string until it's level. At 2-ft. intervals, measure down from the marked areas of the string to the ground.

3. Add and remove topsoil as necessary, distributing it with a garden rake until the surface under the string is level.

4. Repeat the process until the entire area is leveled.

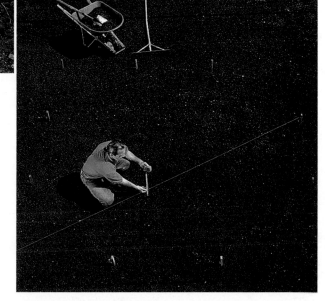

Variation: For a very level ground, use strings on stakes to measure from the string to ground every 2 ft. Add topsoil as necessary.

Building a Drainage Swale

If your yard has areas where rainwater collects and creates boggy spots or has slopes that send runoff water into unwanted places, you need to improve or redirect its drainage. You can fill small, low-lying areas by top-dressing them with black soil, but in large areas the best solution is to create a swale.

A swale is a shallow ditch that carries water away from the yard to a designated collection area, usually a gutter, sewer catch bin, stream, or lake. Some communities have restrictions regarding redirecting runoff water, so contact your city or county inspector's office to discuss your plans before you begin. This is especially important if you're planning a swale that empties into a natural water source, such as a stream, pond, or lake.

If you're building a swale between your house and a neighboring yard, talk to your neighbor about the project before you begin. If drainage is a problem in their yard as well, they may be willing to share the expense and the work of the project.

Building a swale is relatively simple, but it involves the labor of digging a trench. We'll show you how to construct the swale using a shovel, but there are rental tools that you might want to use instead. For larger yards or those with very dense soil, renting a trencher is an option worth considering. This machine, which can be adjusted to dig to an approximate depth, makes quick work of loosening the soil. If you decide to use a trencher, you'll still need to use a shovel to create the V shape and to smooth the sides of the trench, as pictured below.

Another machine you may want to rent is a sod cutter, which cuts the sod into even strips that can be replaced when the swale is complete. If you plan to reuse the sod, store it in a shady area and keep it slightly moist until you replant it.

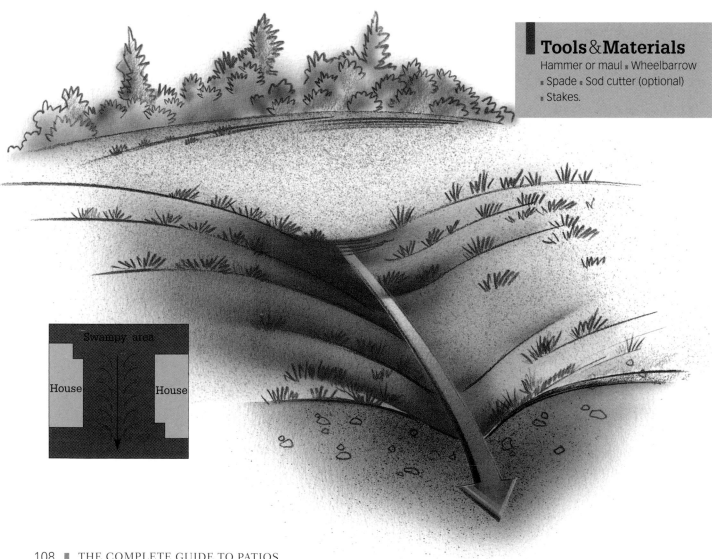

Tools & Materials
Hammer or maul ▪ Wheelbarrow ▪ Spade ▪ Sod cutter (optional) ▪ Stakes.

Swampy area

House   House

How to Make a Drainage Swale

Step A: Mark the Route

After identifying the problem area, use stakes to mark a swale route that directs water toward an appropriate runoff area. To promote drainage, the outlet of the swale must be lower than any point in the problem area or along the planned route.

Step B: Remove the Sod

Carefully remove the sod from the outlined area. Set it aside and keep it moist, so that it can be replaced when the swale is complete.

Step C: Dig the Trench

1. Following the marked route, dig a 6"-deep, V-shaped trench with wide, rounded sides.

2. Shape the trench so it slopes gradually downward toward the outlet, making sure that the bottom and sides of the trench are smooth. Set the topsoil aside for other projects.

Step D: Replace the Sod

1. Lay the sod back into the trench. Compress it thoroughly, so the roots make contact with the soil and there are no air pockets beneath it.

2. Water the sod and keep it moist for several weeks.

Mark a route for the swale with stakes, making sure that the outlet for the water is at the lowest point.

Carefully remove the sod with a spade and set it aside, keeping it moist until you're ready to replace it.

Dig a 6"-deep trench that slopes to the center, creating a V shape. Use the shovel to smooth the sides as you work.

Replace the sod, compressing it against the soil. Water the sod and keep it moist for several weeks.

Swale with Drain Tile ▶

If you have very dense soil with high clay content or severe drainage problems, you'll need to lay perforated drainpipe in the trench for the swale. Follow these steps to make a swale with drain tile:

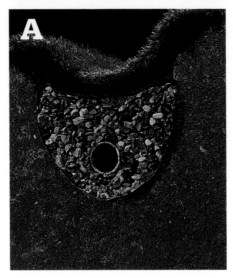

Dig a 1-ft. deep trench, angled downward to the outlet point. Line the trench with landscape fabric. Spread a 2" layer of coarse gravel along the bottom of the swale, then lay perforated drainpipe over the gravel, with the perforations facing down. Cover the pipe with a 5" layer of gravel, and then wrap landscape fabric over the top of the gravel.

Cover the swale with soil and the original or fresh sod. Set a splash block at the outlet under the exposed end of the drainpipe to distribute the runoff water and prevent erosion.

Types of Gravel ▶

Gravel comes in two forms: rough and smooth. When buying gravel for shaping projects, select rough gravel.

Rough gravel clings to the sides of the trench, creating an even drainage layer.

Smooth gravel is typically used as a decorative ground cover. When used for shaping projects, it tends to slide toward the middle of the trench.

Rough gravel

Smooth gravel

Building a Dry Well

ownspouts and other house drainage systems are common obstacles for new patio projects. The problem is simple: the water needs a place to go. Sometimes downspouts can be extended or repositioned to clear the patio area, and natural drainage routes in your yard can be altered with a swale. But often the best solution is to capture the water and divert it to a dry well in your yard.

A dry well system typically consists of a buried drain tile (drainpipe) running from a catch basin at the water source to a collection container some distance away. A basic system is easy and inexpensive to install. In the project shown here, a perforated plastic drain tile connects to a dry well fashioned from a plastic trash can, which has been drilled with holes that are then filled with stone rubble. Water can percolate into the soil as it makes its way along the drainpipe, while the well serves as a large collection area that drains excess water slowly into the surrounding earth.

How to Install a Dry Well

Step A: Dig the Trench

1. Using stakes, mark a path running from the problem area to the location of the dry well. Carefully remove a 12" strip of sod and set it aside, keeping it moist so you can reuse it later. Dig a trench, 10" wide and 14" deep, along the staked path.

2. Slope the trench slightly toward the dry well, about 2" for every 8 ft., to ensure that water flows easily along the drain tile. To check the slope, place a stake at each end of the trench, and then tie a string between the stakes. Use a line level to level the string, then measure down from it at 2-ft. intervals. Add or remove soil as needed to adjust the slope of the trench.

3. Remove the sod in a circle, 4" wider than the dry well container, and then dig a hole at least 4" deeper than the container's height.

> ## Tools & Materials Hammer or maul
> ▪ Wheelbarrow ▪ Spade ▪ Mason's string ▪ Line level ▪ Tape measure ▪ Jig saw ▪ Drill and ¾" bit ▪ Stakes ▪ Landscape fabric ▪ Gravel ▪ Plastic trash can ▪ Perforated drain tile ▪ Large stones ▪ Catch basin.

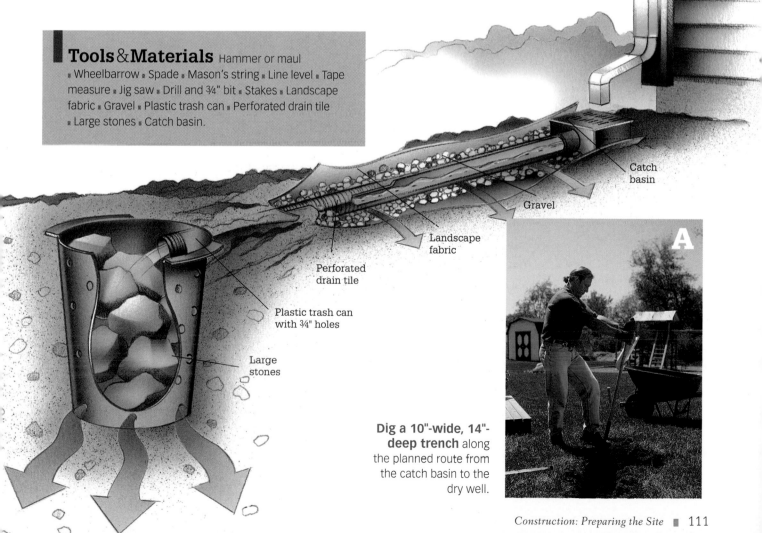

Catch basin

Gravel

Landscape fabric

Perforated drain tile

Plastic trash can with ¾" holes

Large stones

Dig a 10"-wide, 14"-deep trench along the planned route from the catch basin to the dry well.

Line the trench with landscape fabric; then lay a 1" layer of gravel along the bottom of the trench.

Prepare the dry well container, then place it in the excavation, insert the drain tile, and fill it with large rocks. Position the basin to collect the excess water in the problem area.

Attach a catch basin to the drain tile opening, and position the basin to collect the excess water in the problem area.

Step B: Lay the Drain Tile

1. Line the trench and hole with landscape fabric, folding the excess fabric back over each side of the trench and around the edges of the hole.

2. Lay a 1" layer of gravel along the bottom of the trench, and then lay the drain tile in place, with the perforations facing down.

Step C: Create the Dry Well

1. About 3" from the top, trace the outline of the drain tile onto the side of the trash can, then use a jigsaw to cut a hole. Using a power drill and a bit, drill drainage holes through the sides and bottom of the trash can, one hole every 4" to 6".

2. Place the trash can in the hole, positioning it so the large hole faces the trench. Insert the drain tile perforated side down, with at least 2" of tile extending inside the trash can.

3. Fill the trash can with large stones. Arrange the top layer of stones so they are flat in the container.

4. Fold the landscape fabric over the rocks, and then fill the hole with soil.

Step D: Connect the Catch Basin

At the other end of the trench, opposite the dry well, connect the catch basin to the drain tile. Position the catch basin so excess water will flow directly into it.

Cover the drain tile with 1" of gravel, then backfill the trench with soil and fold the landscape fabric over it.

Step E: Refill the Trench

1. Fill the trench with gravel until the drain tile is covered by 1" of gravel. Fold the edges of the landscape cloth down over the gravel-covered drain tile.

2. Fill the trench with the soil you removed earlier.

3. Replace the sod, lightly tamp it with the back of a shovel, and then water it thoroughly.

Retaining Walls & Terracing

A sloping yard often means limited space for a patio. And while a steeply sloping patio might seem like fun to the kids, it would be decidedly inconvenient for dinner parties. The answer, then, is to build retaining walls. Retaining walls cut into a slope (and in some cases, replace the slope), bridging the upper and lower levels while adding more useable area to both.

Terracing is a series of low retaining walls built to tame a long or steep slope. Terracing divides a difficult slope into manageable sections—with individual walls at 3 ft. high or so—and is a much easier project than building a single, towering retaining wall. It's also safer and more reliable and, best of all, creates multiple levels for planting.

Options for Building Retaining Walls

Low retaining walls can be built with a variety of materials, including wood landscape timbers and railroad ties; masonry products, such as brick, concrete block, and poured concrete; and natural stone of many different types. The most popular material for do-it-yourself projects is interlocking concrete blocks made specifically for retaining walls. While many styles have a somewhat commercial look, this block is popular because it requires no mortar—most types are simply stacked in ordered rows—and it automatically sets the "batter" for the wall, the backward lean that most retaining walls have for added strength.

Due to the structural factors involved, the recommended height limit for do-it-yourself retaining walls is 3 ft. Anything higher is best left to a professional. As walls get taller, the physical stresses involved and resulting potential problems rise dramatically. Retaining walls of any size may fall under your municipality's building code. Contact the city to obtain a permit for the project.

This curved, interlocking-block retaining wall is a creative solution for a difficult sloping lot.

Natural cut stone makes an especially attractive retaining wall with a timeless appearance.

Retaining Wall Construction

The primary function of any retaining wall is to hold back the earth behind it. The wall must constantly contend with the weight of the soil, but more importantly, it must deal with the water that flows down and exerts pressure on the back of the wall. Most walls are backfilled with coarse gravel to promote drainage, while a drainage system transports water from behind the wall. Common drainage systems include a perforated drainpipe that diverts water to one end of the wall and weep holes or pipes that allow water to pass through the bottom of the wall. All retaining walls must have some means of drainage to reduce pressure and prevent deterioration of the wall material due to standing water.

For stability, basic retaining walls are built with a "batter" (the backward angle) and may be tied into the hillside at intervals with "deadmen" (lateral supports that are built into the wall at one end and buried in the soil for anchorage at the other end). Walls are generally built on top of a base of compacted gravel. Tall retaining walls, particularly masonry walls, involve much more engineering than simple, low walls. Most are built on a wide concrete footing, with metal reinforcement throughout the footing and wall.

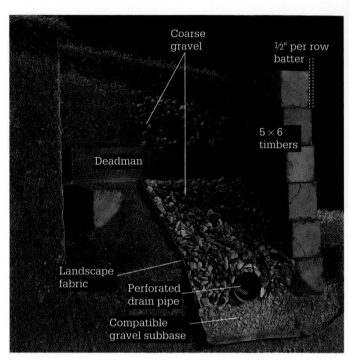

Typical retaining wall construction includes a gravel subbase, coarse gravel surrounded by landscape fabric, deadmen for lateral support, and a batter of ½" or more per row of building material.

Reshaping Your Site ▸

Retaining walls and terracing are effective ways to reshape a landscape. How you configure the walls depends largely upon where you need more useable space—above or below the wall. Shown here are two methods of reshaping the same natural slope. In photo A, the retaining wall is placed at the bottom of the original slope. Extra soil is brought in to fill behind the wall, thus creating more level land on top. In photo B, the wall divides the original slope. Soil cut from the base of the hill is reused as fill behind the top of the wall. The result is a newly controlled area for building a patio below the wall, as well as a modest gain of level ground above. Moving the wall further into the original slope would provide more usable space below the wall but would require removing and disposing of the excess soil. Ideally, any soil removed during reshaping can be used as fill in the same wall project or put to another use elsewhere on your property.

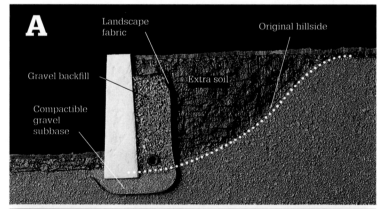

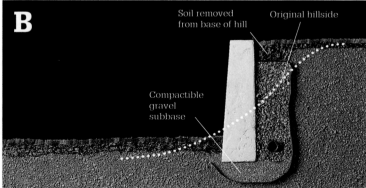

Laying Out & Preparing the Site

Laying out a new patio is a simple process of setting up stakes and mason's lines, measuring for accuracy, then adjusting the lines for the desired slope of the finished patio surface. With your layout complete, you can begin excavating the ground and preparing the site with a gravel subbase and other materials, as needed. All of these steps are given here. How far you go depends on your patio material:

For setting brick, concrete pavers, or flagstone in sand, complete the process through page 119, adding your own edging material before installing the sand base.

For a new concrete slab, stop after completing the gravel base (Step E, on page 117).

For loose material, complete the site preparation through Step F, on page 117, to install landscape fabric, but do not add sand unless your surface material calls for it.

The compacted gravel subbase is a critical element for most patio constructions. It provides a stable, even foundation for the upper surface layers and ensures proper drainage underneath. Water passes easily through the gravel layer without disrupting the patio surface. In cold climates, this helps minimize frost heave because the gravel doesn't retain water, like soil does, so there's less water to freeze and expand. For most patio surfaces, a 4" layer of compactible gravel is appropriate. However, if you're planning a concrete slab, check the local building code for specific requirements.

Tools & Materials
Hammer or maul ▪ Mason's strings ▪ Tape measure ▪ Line level ▪ Standard (carpenter's) level ▪ Spade ▪ Power or hand tamper ▪ Stakes ▪ Straight 2 × 4 (about 6 ft. long) ▪ Gravel ▪ Landscape fabric (not needed for concrete slabs).
Extra Supplies for Sandset Base
▪ Garden rake ▪ Hand tamper ▪ 1"-diameter pipes (for brick or concrete pavers); 2"-diameter pipes (for flagstone) ▪ Sand.

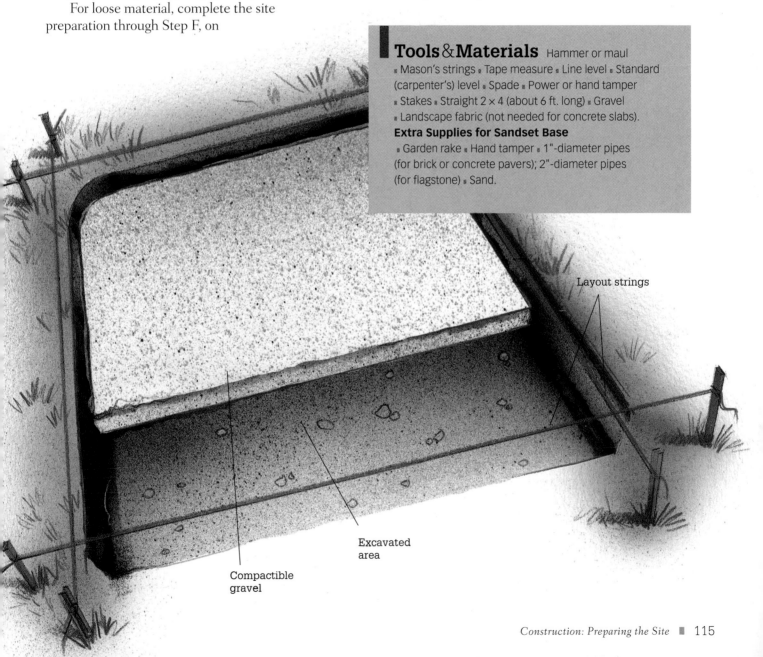

Layout strings

Excavated area

Compactible gravel

How Deep & How Much?

To determine the depth of the patio excavation, just add up the thicknesses of the layers:
X" surface material (measure what you have)
      + 4" of gravel
      + 1" to 2" of sand, if required
      = Total excavation depth

For example: A sandset patio with 3"-thick brick pavers requires an excavation that's 8": 3" + 4" + 1" = 8".

This is for a patio surface at grade level. If you want the brick pavers to rise 1" above the surrounding yard, excavate to only 7".

To estimate quantities for gravel and sand, multiply the square footage of the site by the depth of the layers (in feet) to calculate the amount in cubic feet. Then convert the amount to cubic yards.

For example: A 10 × 20 ft. patio covers 200 sq. ft.

Gravel: 200 × 0.33 (4" layer = 0.33 ft.) = 66 cu. ft.
            66 ÷ 27 = 2.4 cu. yards

Sand: 200 × .083 (1" layer = $1/12$ ft.) = 16.6 cu. ft.
          16.6 ÷ 27 = .61 cu. yards

For a sandset patio, you'll also need sand for filling in between the pavers or stones. When buying sand, look for unwashed coarse sand, which is suitable for patios and is less expensive than finer, washed material. Typically, sandset brick and concrete pavers require a 1"-thick layer of sand for bedding. Sandset flagstone calls for a 2"-thick layer.

How to Lay Out the Site & Add a Gravel Subbase

Step A: Plot the Site Outline

1. Determine the dimensions of the finished patio. Be sure to account for edging materials, if applicable.

2. Using stakes and mason's strings, plot a rectangle (or square) that matches the patio's finished dimensions. If the patio will have curved edges or corners, position the strings at the outermost points of the edges. Drive the stakes at least 12" beyond the edges of the finished patio site. Tie the strings to the stakes so they are straight and taut and set several inches above the ground.

3. Measure diagonally between opposite corners where the layout strings meet (as shown in photo, measure between points A and C, then between points B and D). If the measurements are equal, the layout is square. If not, adjust the stakes and strings until the measurements are equal. Tip: To plot a right angle (90°) from a single layout line, see the sidebar: Plotting Right Angles & Curves (page 118).

Step B: Level the Strings

1. Using a line level as a guide, adjust one of the strings until it is level. Mark the string's height onto the stakes at both ends.

2. Use a standard level to transfer the height marks of the leveled string over to the neighboring stakes. Retie the second and third strings to follow the height marks. Then, use a line level to level the second and third strings and mark their heights at the opposite ends.

3. Repeat the transfer process to level the fourth string and mark its stakes. Confirm that all strings are level, using the line level.

Step C: Establish the Slope

1. For proper drainage, a patio should slope away from the house at $1/8$" per foot. To establish this slope, first multiply the length of the patio (from the high end to the low end) by $1/8$ (0.125). For example, if the patio is 15 ft. from the house to the far edge, it should drop $17/8$" (15 × 0.125 = 1.875, or $17/8$).

2. At the four low-end stakes, measure down from the level line marking and mark the drop distance. Retie the ends of the strings at the new marks. This completes the patio layout.

Step D: Excavate the Site

1. Remove sod from the entire site, using the layout strings as a guide. Depending on the edging you're using, you may have to excavate beyond the strings to allow room for the edging. Also, if the patio has any curves, you can use a garden hose to lay out the curves or use the compass technique and spray paint to plot a uniform corner radius (see sidebar: Plotting Right Angles & Curves, on page 118).

2. Excavate the site according to your depth calculations. Measure down from the layout lines to check the depth, and use a 2 × 4 and a level to check for high and low spots throughout the area. Maintain a uniform depth from the strings to ensure an even downward slope.

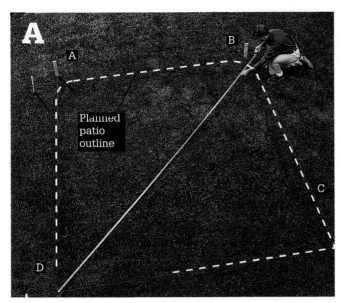

Install mason's lines to represent the patio borders, and then measure between corners to check for squareness.

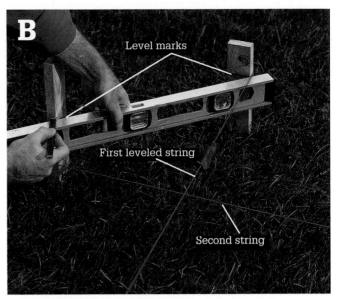

Transfer the height marks of the leveled string to begin leveling the remaining strings.

Option: An alternative method for checking depth over the interior of the excavation is to set up a temporary cross string that's even with the perimeter layout strings. Position the cross-string stakes outside of the perimeter lines. Move the cross string as needed to check the depth across the site's interior.

Step E: Add the Gravel Subbase

1. Pour compactible gravel over the site, raking it into a smooth layer that's at least 4" thick. Use a 2 × 4 to check for high and low spots, adding gravel and regrading as needed.

2. Pack the gravel subbase, using a power tamper or hand tamper, until the surface is firm and flat. Check the slope by measuring down from the side strings, as during the excavation. The space between the strings and the subbase should be equal at all points. Use a 2 × 4 and level or a cross-string setup to measure the subbase throughout the interior of the site.

Step F: Install Landscape Fabric

Landscape fabric is a tough fiber mesh material commonly used as a weed barrier and to separate layered materials. It's better than plastic for most applications because it allows water to flow through, unlike plastic. Fabric is also much more resistant to tearing.

If you're preparing your site for a concrete slab, you don't need landscape fabric.

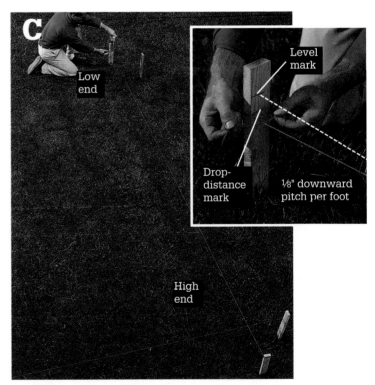

Reposition the strings at the low end of the patio to create a ⅛" per foot downward slope.

Roll out strips of fabric to cover the entire subbase, overlapping the edges of strips by at least 6". If desired, you can secure the strips along seams with U-shaped wire stakes driven into the subbase every 12" or so.

Excavate the site, and use a 2 × 4 or measure down from a cross string to check for evenness.

Compact the gravel subbase for a smooth, firm surface.

Install a weed barrier of landscape fabric, overlapping the rows by at least 6".

Plotting Right Angles & Curves ▸

With a complete square or rectangle, you can always measure the diagonals to check for squareness (see Step A, on page 118). But sometimes it helps to start a layout with an accurate 90° angle. The best way to create one using layout strings is with the "3-4-5" method (actually a simple application of the Pythagorean theorem: $a^2 + b^2 = c^2$). Here's how it works:

1. Set up a layout string in a straight line, then mark the string 3 ft. from one end.

2. With a helper, pull out two tape measures; hold one at the starting point and the other at the 3-ft. mark.

3. Have the helper cross the tapes at the 4-ft. and 5-ft. marks, as shown in the photo. Drive a stake at the tape intersection, and then run a string from the starting point to the stake. The two strings will form a perfect 90° angle.

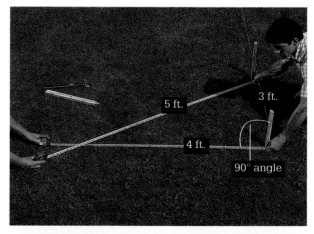

Plotting a curve starts with a 90° angle (see procedure, above). The basic idea is to create a square with four stakes set at equal distances, then pivot from the stake opposite the 90° angle to create the curve. Here's how to do it:

1. Set up two perpendicular strings starting from the same point. Drive one stake along each string at an equal distance from the starting point. These stakes mark the beginning and end of the curve.

2. Drive a fourth stake to complete the square, and measure the diagonals to make sure they are equal.

3. Tie a string to the fourth stake. Hold the string and a can of spray paint in one hand so the paint nozzle is even with the outer stakes. Keeping the string taut, swing the can in an arc while painting the curve onto the ground.

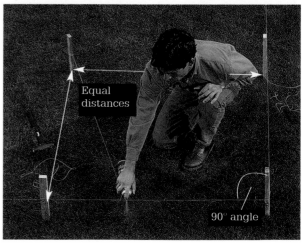

How to Prepare for Sandset Paving

Step A: Install Edging & Screed Pipes

1. Complete the site layout, excavation, and gravel bed procedure to create a subbase for the sand layer. Be sure to add landscape fabric to inhibit weed growth. Install edging material as desired.

2. For a standard 1"-thick sand bed (for pavers), lay down two or more 1"-diameter (outer diameter) pipes to use as depth guides for loading and screeding the sand layer. Plastic PVC pipe works well, because it is smooth and lightweight, but any 1" pipe will do. As an alternative, you can use 1"-thick wood strips cut from 2× lumber.

Note: For flagstone patios, use 2"-diameter pipe or 2"-thick wood strips.

3. Select a very straight 2 × 4, about 6 ft. long, to use as a screed board. Position the pipes so the board can easily span across them.

Step B: Add the Sand

1. Lay a 1"-thick (or 2"-thick, for flagstone applications) layer of sand over the landscape fabric and smooth it out with a garden rake. The sand should just cover the tops of the screed pipes.

2. Water the sand thoroughly, then pack it lightly with a hand tamper.

Step C: Screed the Surface

1. Screed the sand to an even layer by resting your screed board on the pipes and drawing it backward along the tops of the pipes. Use a slight sawing motion as you pull back the board. Add extra sand as needed to fill in low spots (and your footprints), then water, tamp, and screed the sand again until it is smooth and firmly packed.

2. Remove the screed pipe(s) along one side of the patio site. Leave the other pipes in place. As you fill in the area with pavers, you can remove the remaining pipes more easily without disturbing the sand base.

3. Fill the groove left by the removed pipe(s) with sand, and pat the area smooth with the hand tamper. Now you're ready for paving.

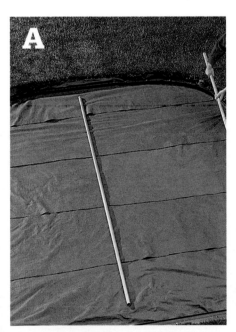

Lay the screed pipes over the landscape fabric, spacing them to fit the screed board.

Fill in sand level with the screed pipes, then water and lightly tamp the sand.

Pull the screed board along the pipes to screed the sand smooth.

Projects: Patio Surfaces

The flooring surface will become the foundation and the heart of your new outdoor room. If you're still deciding on a material, there are plenty to choose from in this chapter. Have a look through the steps of the projects to see what's involved and to get a better idea of the cost and time required. All the traditional favorites are included, as are some new products, like snap-together wood tiles, along with several other ways to completely renew an old concrete slab patio. For an in-depth discussion of the materials themselves, see Chapter 2.

When you're ready to break out the tools, the next big decision is how to get the materials to the patio site and where to store them while you complete the job. This requires a balance of convenience and practicality. With the exception of poured concrete and some mortared projects, most patio surfaces can be completed at a leisurely pace. Keeping this in mind, be realistic about how long your project will take; if you're looking at a few weekends, you won't want a pile of gravel killing your lawn in the meantime. Conversely, you can waste a lot of time and energy hauling brick from the garage or end of the driveway to your backyard.

As for hauling the materials home, do the math to determine whether it's better to pick up the supplies or have them delivered.

In This Chapter

- Sandset Brick
- Concrete Pavers
- Mortared Brick
- Sandset Flagstone
- Mortared Flagstone
- Seeded Concrete & Wood
- Basic Concrete Slab
- Tile on Concrete
- Loose Material
- Framed Wood
- Wood Tile
- Installing Edging

Sandset Brick

Traditional brick pavers set in sand makes for one of the easiest yet most rewarding patio projects. The installation process is straight-forward and, because there's no mortar involved, flexible from a timing standpoint. To pave with any of the classic patterns, such as running bond or her-ringbone, you'll start at one corner of your patio bor-der or edging. For an accurate layout, make sure the sides of the edging form a 90° angle at the starting corner. If you're not using edging or any kind of for-mal border, set up mason's lines to guide the brick placement (see page 115).

In the project shown here, the patio is bordered with "invisible" plastic edging (see page 164 for installation), and the bricks are laid in a standard run-ning bond pattern, in which each course, or row, is offset from neighboring courses by half-bricks. The main field of pavers is bordered by a single row of bricks laid perpendicular to the edging. The bricks

are spaced ⅛" apart. This is set automatically by lugs on the sides of the pavers. If your pavers don't have lugs, use spacers cut from ⅛"-thick hardboard or ply-wood to ensure consistent gapping.

Following the main procedure are four alterna-tive patterns that you can apply using the same basic steps shown in the main project. Another option is using a dry-mortar technique for the look of tooled mortar joints without the trouble of a mortared installation.

Tools & Materials
Supplies for site layout and preparation (page 80) ▪ Rubber mallet ▪ Brick cutting tools ▪ Level ▪ Hand tamper ▪ Pencil & straightedge ▪ 2 x 4 or 6' level ▪ Push broom ▪ Power tamper ▪ Jointing tool (optional) ▪ Brick pavers ▪ Sand.

Dry-lay rows of pavers to find the dimensions of the patio surface.

Place the first two border pavers, setting them in the sand with a rubber mallet.

Lay border pavers in 2 ft. sections, then fill in with field pavers.

How to Build a Sandset Brick Patio

Step A: Dry-lay the Pavers for Sizing

This step is optional. It's an easy way to determine your exact patio dimensions while minimizing the number of cut bricks required. This technique works well for running bond and other square-laid patterns. For angled patterns, like herringbone, dry-laying the bricks is too difficult. Instead, wait to install two sides of the patio edging until you reach the end of the installation.

1. Lay out two perpendicular rows of pavers on a flat surface, such as a driveway. These rows represent the total width and length of the finished patio. Measure the rows to determine the exact dimensions of the patio surface.

Step B: Prepare the Surface & Lay the First Border Pavers

1. Lay out and prepare the patio site. Make sure to install landscape fabric as a weed barrier. Install edging material as desired (page 162). Complete the sand bed, and remove one or more of the screed pipes in the area where you will begin paving.

2. Set the first border brick at the starting corner of the patio edging. Make sure the paver rests firmly against both perpendicular sides of the edging.

3. Lay the second border paver, setting a ⅛" gap between the two bricks (unless pavers have spacers). Set the pavers by tapping them into the sand with a rubber mallet. Use these pavers as a guide for setting the depth of the remaining bricks.

Step C: Begin the Field Pavers

1. Working outward from the corner, install border pavers in 2 ft.-long sections. If the bricks have spacer lugs, make sure the lugs are touching. If there are no lugs, use ⅛" spacers between the bricks. Set each paver by tapping it with the mallet.

2. Begin setting the field (interior) pavers, placing them tightly against the border bricks. For a running bond pattern, start the first row with a half-brick (see page 97 for help with cutting bricks). You can save time by cutting multiple bricks at a time. Start the second row with a full brick. Alternate successive rows of field bricks with half-bricks and full bricks for the entire installation.

Check each section of pavers with a level or straightedge to ensure a flat surface.

Remove screed pipes as you near them, replacing sand and retamping the surface.

Pave around curves, setting even gaps; fill in with cut pavers as needed.

Step D: Check the Surface

1. Complete each section of paving so that the border pavers stay ahead of the field bricks.

2. After each section is set, use a level or straightedge to make sure the pavers are level with one another to create a smooth, flat surface. If a brick is lower than the rest, lift it out and add sand as needed, then reset the brick. Remove sand to lower bricks that are too high. Be careful not to displace bricks or loosen the pattern when resetting bricks.

Tip: If desired, you can set up a mason's string to keep pavers in line as you install the rows.

Step E: Remove the Screed Pipes

1. As the paving approaches the remaining screed pipes, remove the pipes and fill in the gaps with sand.

2. Tamp the sand bed smooth with a hand tamper, being careful not to disturb the set pavers. Step carefully on the laid brick, or you can lay down a sheet of plywood to keep the pavers in place when underfoot.

Step F: Complete the Paving

1. Continue installing 2 ft. sections of border pavers and field pavers. As you approach the opposite side of the patio, reposition the edging, if necessary, so full pavers will fit snugly without needing to be cut.

2. At rounded corners and curves, install border pavers in a fan pattern with even gaps between the pavers. Gentle curves may accommodate full, uncut border bricks, but for sharper bends you may need to mark and cut border pavers into wedge shapes to make them fit.

3. Lay the remaining field bricks. Where partial pavers are needed, hold a full brick over the gap, and mark the cut with a pencil and straightedge, then make the cut.

4. After all of the pavers are installed, permanently anchor the edging along all sides, then backfill with soil or other material as needed.

Step G: Check Your Work

1. Select a very straight 2 × 4 that's about 6 ft.-long to use as a straightedge, or use a 6 ft.-long level. Set the straightedge on the pavers at different angles to check for high or low spots. Adjust high pavers by tapping them into the sand. Remove low pavers and add a thin layer of sand underneath. Check the entire patio surface.

2. After adjusting all uneven pavers, use a mason's string to check the rows for straightness. Adjust crooked pavers as needed.

mallet, tap pavers to set them at the appropriate height.

Step H: Fill the Joints with Sand

1. Spread sand over the patio surface. Using a push broom, sweep the sand across the pavers to fill the joints. Don't worry about filling the joints completely at this stage.

2. Tamp the surface with a power tamper to compress the patio surface and help settle the sand deep into the joints.

Step I: Complete the Joint Packing

1. Sweep up the loose sand from the patio, and then soak the surface thoroughly. This helps settle the sand further into the joints.

2. Let the patio dry completely. Repeat Step H and this step one or more times until the joints are completely filled and evenly packed. The more rounds of filling, tamping, and watering, the tighter the joints will become.

Option: Dry-mortaring the Joints

For a finished masonry look, install the pavers with ⅜" gaps, using plywood spacers for consistent spacing. Fill the joints with a dry mixture of 4 parts sand and 1 part dry mortar. After spreading the dry mixture and tamping the patio, sprinkle the surface with water. Finish the wet mortar joints with a jointing tool. After the mortar hardens, scrub the pavers with a coarse rag and water to clean up the surfaces.

Inspect the entire installation for uneven or misaligned pavers. Using a rubber mallet, tap pavers to set them at the appropriate height.

Sweep sand into the joints between bricks, and then tamp the patio with a power tamper.

Soak the patio, then let it dry to complete each round of packing the joints.

90° Herringbone Pattern

The 90° herringbone requires a lot of cut half-bricks along the border of the patio, but the main pattern is easy once you get started. For this pattern, you must use bricks that are twice as long as they are wide.

Begin the pattern with 2 bricks set in the corner of your edging (make sure the edging forms an accurate 90° angle). Add half-bricks next to the ends of the first 2 bricks. Start the next row with 2 more bricks set into the V created by the first row. Complete the basic pattern with 2 bricks set perpendicular to the rest. Repeat the pattern with the next row.

45° Herringbone Pattern

The 45° herringbone is set at a 45° angle to the main edges of the patio. Like the 90° herringbone, this pattern must start from an accurate 90° corner, and the bricks must be exactly twice as long as they are wide. Filling in along the borders requires many angled cuts, for which it's worth it to rent a wet saw.

Set the first brick so it touches both sides of the edging and is angled at precisely 45°. Use a 45° angle square to ensure an accurate angle. Set 3 more bricks in an alternating pattern as shown here. Make sure the outside bricks touch the edging. Lay the remaining rows in the same zigzag pattern. Measure from the starting corner periodically to make sure the ends of the rows are equidistant from the corner.

Basketweave Pattern

You can lay a basketweave pattern starting from the side edging of the patio or from a centerline. The centerline technique shown here is a good way to ensure an accurate layout. If your patio is square or rectangular, you can avoid cutting bricks altogether using this pattern. Just work from a centerline, and install edging along the sides and ends of the patio after the bricks are laid. Use only bricks that are twice as long as they are wide.

Snap a chalk line down the center of your sand bed, making sure it is perpendicular (90°) to your base piece of edging. Working from the centerline out for each row, lay bricks in a pyramid shape, setting 12 bricks total in the first row, 8 in the second row, and 4 in the third row. To complete the paving, add to each row incrementally to maintain the pyramid. This ensures that every row stems from the centerline, keeping the whole layout in order.

Pinwheel Pattern

The pinwheel pattern has a very simple, straightforward layout. The trick is in finding the right pavers or accent pieces to fill the middle of each brick motif. Choose something that is exactly the same thickness as the primary brick and slightly smaller than the pinwheel cavity. Don't use a thinner unit for the center and then try to compensate with extra sand underneath. It will eventually settle down and create an uneven surface.

Like the basketweave, this pattern looks best when there are no cut bricks along the edges. To accomplish this, install only two adjacent sides of the edging (the patio must be square or rectangular) before laying the brick. Add the remaining two sides after the paving is down. For accuracy, make sure the two base sides of edging form an exact 90° angle.

Concrete Pavers

Concrete pavers are made for easy installation. They are manufactured with uniform dimensions, and many are cast with spacing lugs that automatically set a gap between pavers. Most paver patios are set in sand, following the same basic steps for laying a brick paver surface. In fact, if you're using rectangular pavers that are made to look like brick, follow the steps on page 122 to complete your patio project. Brick-style concrete pavers can also be mortared over a concrete slab. Again, follow the same steps used for brick (see page 130). Interlocking pavers and other shaped designs generally have too many sides or are too complicated for mortared applications.

Where pavers differ most from brick is in their specialty designs. In this project, a circular patio is laid using varying shapes of pavers—not a single unit is cut. Circular pavers are often sold as a kit. The manufacturer specifies the amount of each paver required for different patio sizes and often includes a diagram for installing the pavers. Whether you're planning a circular patio or other specialty design, ask suppliers about half units and other edging pavers that make for easy and attractive installation. If your project does call for a lot of cuts, rent a masonry saw (also called a tub saw) to make the cuts.

A note about tamping: If your pavers have a raised texture, ask your supplier or manufacturer about using a power tamper to compact the patio surface. They may recommend using a protective layer, such as thin plywood, carpet, or landscape fabric, under the tamper to prevent scuffing the pavers.

Tools & Materials
Supplies for site layout and preparation (page 80) ▪ Tape measure ▪ Level or straight board ▪ Push broom ▪ Power tamper ▪ Stake ▪ Long board (2 × 2 or other) ▪ Spray paint ▪ Tape ▪ Circular concrete paver kit ▪ Edging materials ▪ Sand.

How to Build a Sandset Concrete Paver Patio

Step A: Lay Out & Prepare the Patio Site

Follow the basic steps given on page 115 to set up lay-out strings, excavate the patio site, and add a 1"-thick gravel base and sand bed. You can use squared layout strings to set the slope for the patio, but follow this step to mark the ground for excavation. Also, do not install edging material until all of the pavers are laid.

1. Determine the final diameter of the patio, according to the paver manufacturer's specifications.

2. Drive a stake in the ground at the center of the patio site. Fasten one end of a long board to the center of the stake, using a 16d nail. Measuring out from the nail, mark the board at a distance equal to ½ the patio's diameter, plus 6".

3. Tape a can of spray paint to the board so the nozzle is even with the mark on the board. Pivot the board in a complete circle, painting the grass along the way to mark the excavation area.

4. Complete the excavation and site preparation.

Step B: Set the Pavers

1. Place the round center pavers (or paver) in the center of the sand bed. Measure to the edges of the site to make sure the paver(s) is centered.

2. Lay the first ring of pavers around the center piece(s), following the manufacturer's installation diagram or instructions. Set pavers by tapping them with a rubber mallet.

3. Set the second ring of pavers, offsetting the joints of the first ring for an even layout. Alternate wedge-shaped and square (or rectangular) pavers according to the kit design.

4. Continue setting rings of pavers, following the prescribed pattern. As you work, check for high and low pavers with a level or straight board. Add sand below low pavers, and remove sand below high pavers and reset, using a rubber mallet. Also stand back to make sure the pattern is correct and the over-all shape is round.

Step C: Install Edging & Sand the Joints

1. Install edging tight against the outermost ring of pavers. "Invisible" plastic edging works well because it bends easily around the patio (see page 164).

2. Spread sand over the patio and sweep across the pavers with a push broom to fill the joints. Sweep off excess sand when the joints are filled.

3. Tamp the entire patio surface with a power tamper (see note on page 128 about protecting textured pavers from the tamper). If necessary, refill the joints with sand and tamp again until the joints are full to the top and the pavers are firmly locked in place.

Pivot a board from a central stake to paint the outline of the excavation area.

Set the pavers one ring at a time, offsetting the joints between rings.

Fill the paver joints with sand, and then pack the surface with a power tamper.

Mortared Brick

Mortared brick has a formal, finished appearance and is a great option for resurfacing an old concrete slab patio. The brick must be laid over a sound concrete base, so start your project with an examination of the slab. Surface cracks and blemishes are okay, but major cracking or shifting of slab sections indicates the slab is probably not stable enough, leading to cracks on the new brick surface. See page 140 for installing a new concrete slab, if desired. For minor repairs to the concrete surface prior to laying brick, see page 226.

To help your project go smoothly, dry-lay a section of bricks on the slab to determine the ideal layout. Be sure to account for the mortar joints when testing layouts, using plywood spacers to set the gaps. Your brick may be sized for a ⅜" or ½" mortar joint; both are suitable for a patio surface. This is also the time to plan the installation of the edging material. Mortared brick works well with solid edgings, such as brick, wood timbers, or concrete. In most cases, it's best to install the edging first, and then fill in between with the pavers.

How to Build a Mortared Brick Patio

Step A: Place the Mortar Bed

1. Thoroughly clean the concrete slab. Install edging as desired. If the edging is mortared brick, let the mortar cure before starting on the field pavers.

2. Mix a batch of mortar. Note: Use the mortar type recommended by your brick supplier, based on the type of brick and the local climate. Most situations call for Type S or Type M mortar.

3. Make a screed board, using a very straight 2 × 4. Notch the ends of the board to fit over the edging, making the notch depth equal to the thickness of the brick pavers.

4. Apply a ½"-thick layer of mortar over a workable area along one edge of the patio. Screed the mortar smooth with the screed board, then rake the mortar with a notched masonry trowel. The notches create a strong bond with the mortar.

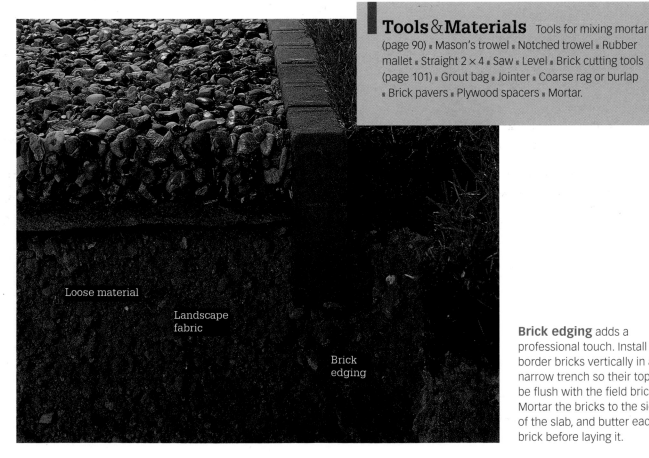

Loose material

Landscape fabric

Brick edging

Tools & Materials Tools for mixing mortar (page 90) ▪ Mason's trowel ▪ Notched trowel ▪ Rubber mallet ▪ Straight 2 × 4 ▪ Saw ▪ Level ▪ Brick cutting tools (page 101) ▪ Grout bag ▪ Jointer ▪ Coarse rag or burlap ▪ Brick pavers ▪ Plywood spacers ▪ Mortar.

Brick edging adds a professional touch. Install border bricks vertically in a narrow trench so their tops will be flush with the field brick. Mortar the bricks to the sides of the slab, and butter each brick before laying it.

Step B: Lay the Pavers

1. Lay the bricks one at a time, using plywood spacers to set the mortar gaps as needed. Set each brick by tapping lightly with a rubber mallet. For a running bond pattern as shown here, start every other row with a half-brick (see page 98 for help with cutting brick).

2. To keep each course in line, stretch a mason's string between two bricks. Reposition the string for each course, and set the bricks even with the string.

3. After each section of pavers is laid, check with a level to make sure the tops of the pavers are even. Tap high bricks down with the mallet, and add mortar beneath low bricks and reset.

4. When all the pavers are set, let the mortar cure.

Step C: Mortar & Finish the Joints

1. Load a grout bag with fresh mortar, then carefully fill the paver joints with the mortar. Do not over-fill the joints, and try to avoid getting any stray mortar on the paver surfaces.

2. After mortaring a workable section—4 sq. ft. or so—tool the joints with a jointing tool. Complete the long continuous joints first, then the short joints between the ends of the bricks. For best appearance, shape the joints to form a slight recess between pavers. Raking the joints too deep creates recesses that catch dirt and are difficult to clean.

3. After tooling each section of joints, let the mortar set a little, then carefully scrape up excess mortar from the edges and faces of pavers, using a small mason's trowel. Be careful not to disturb the finished joints.

4. Let the mortar dry for a few hours, then remove any residual mortar by scrubbing the pavers with a coarse rag (or burlap) and water.

5. Cover the patio with plastic and let the mortar cure for at least 2 days. Remove the plastic, but avoid walking on the patio for 1 week.

Screed the mortar bed to a consistent thickness, using a 2 × 4 screed board set on the edging. Rake the surface of the mortar with a notched trowel.

Set the pavers into the mortar bed, using a rubber mallet.

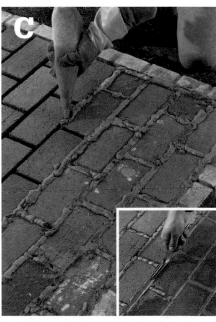

Use a grout bag to fill the paver joints with mortar. Inset: Smooth and shape the mortar with a jointer.

Sandset Flagstone

Creating a patio surface with naturally shaped flagstone is like assembling a giant puzzle that's finished only when you say it is. A sandset patio, as opposed to mortared, has an especially casual look and feel, but even the installation follows an easier pace—since there's no drying mortar to race against, you can take your time fitting the stones and resetting them as needed to achieve the most pleasing layout.

The sandset application also offers several options for filling the joints between stones. You can fill them with sand for a clean, low-maintenance finish, or use small stones or polished pebbles for an interesting contrast of materials. Another popular method is to fill the gaps with soil, then plant ground covers, such as thyme, moss, or grass. Consult a garden supplier for help with choosing the best plants for this application and to determine the ideal size of joints for planting.

Tools & Materials
Supplies for site layout and preparation (page 80) ▪ Rubber mallet ▪ Stone cutting and dressing tools ▪ Level or straight 2 × 4 ▪ Broom ▪ Garden trowel (for soil-joint option) ▪ Flagstone ▪ Sand ▪ Soil (for soil-joint option).

How to Build a Sandset Flagstone Patio

Step A: Prepare the Site & Begin Laying the Stones

1. Follow the steps on page 115 to lay out and excavate the patio site, add a compacted gravel base, and prepare a 2"-thick sand bed. Install patio edging as desired: You can install it now and fit the stones to the patio border, or you can lay the patio stones first and let the edging follow the contours of the stones. For an especially natural look, you can simply use the surrounding earth as a border.

2. Complete a dry run of the stone layout by arranging the stones next to the patio site. Mirror the patio shape as closely as possible, and even mark stones for cutting if desired. Gap the stones ½" to 2" apart, keeping in mind that consistent gapping usually looks better than very random spacing.

3. Drawing from your dry-run arrangement, begin laying the stones one at a time into the sand bed. Set each stone into the sand by striking it with a rubber mallet. Gap the stones no less than ½" apart, and cut stones as needed to fit your layout. Each stone should be evenly supported underneath and not rock back and forth.

Step B: Check the Stones for Level

1. After setting stones over an area of several square feet, set a level or straight 2 × 4 across the stones to check for an even surface. Add sand beneath stones that are lower than its neighbors, and remove sand beneath high stones. Make sure each stone is stable and evenly supported underneath.

2. Continue laying stones and checking for level with each new section. Step back periodically to take a broad view of the installation, making sure the overall layout is attractive.

3. When all of the stones are laid, install edging if you haven't done so already.

Step C: Fill the Joints

1. Spread sand over the patio and sweep across the stones with a push broom to fill the joints. Pack the sand with your fingers or a piece of wood.

2. Spray the entire area lightly with water to help compact the sand. Let the surface dry, then add more sand and spray again as needed until the joints are full and the stones are securely locked in place.

Arrange naturally shaped flagstones next to the patio site to complete most of the puzzle work before the installation. For best appearance, distribute small and large stones evenly to avoid a lopsided layout.

Place the stones in the sand bed and set them firmly with a rubber mallet.

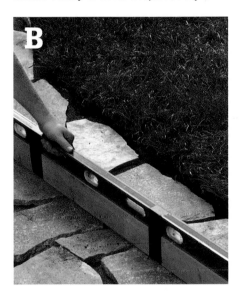

Set a straightedge across sections of the stone to make sure the general surface is even.

Fill the joints with sand, packing with your hand. Spray the patio with water to settle the sand into the joints (inset).

Option: For planting between stones, fill the joints with a soil mixture suited to the type of plants you'll use.

Option: Filling the Joints with Soil for Planting

1. Prepare a soil mixture: Regular soil can become too compacted for effective planting, so it's recommended to fill the joints with a mixture of sand and potting soil. This allows for some compaction while providing for drainage. The best mixture depends on the plants you're using—ask your plant supplier for recommendations.

2. Fill the joints with the soil mixture, using a garden trowel or a tin can. Sweep the stones carefully to move any stray soil into the joints.

3. Soak the joints with a fine mist of water to help compact the soil. Let the soil dry. Repeat filling and soaking the joints to achieve the desired level for planting. These are a few plants that work well:

Alyssum	Saxifrage
Rock cress	Sedum
Thrift	Thymus
Miniature dianthus	Scotch moss
Candytoft	Irish moss
Lobelia	Wolly thyme
Forget-me-not	Mock strawberry

Mortared Flagstone

With its permanent, solid finish, mortared flagstone tends toward a more formal patio setting than sandset stone. It also has a cleaner feel, because there's no sand to get kicked up out of the joints. Yet the mortared application offers the same organic appeal and dramatic lines of any natural flagstone surface. If you'd like to go a step further toward a formal look, you can use cut flagstone, installing it with the same basic steps shown here, but working with a grid layout instead of a random arrangement.

The proper base for mortaring flagstone is a structurally sound concrete slab. If you're covering an old concrete patio, inspect the slab for signs of struc-

tural problems. Wide cracks and uneven surfaces indicate shifting soil or an insufficient subbase. This movement most likely will continue, leading to cracks in your new stone surface. You should remove the old slab and pour a new one or consider sand-setting the stone over the slab.

One of the advantages of mortared stone is that edging along the patio border is optional. Edging is not needed to contain the patio surface, as it is with a sandset application. This gives you the option of leaving the edges of the patio rough to enhance the natural appearance, or even to hang the outer stones over the edges of the slab, to help conceal the concrete below (see Option, below).

Tools & Materials
Paint roller with extension pole ▪ Stone cutting and dressing tools (page 99) ▪ Tape measure ▪ Tools for mixing mortar (page 99) ▪ Mason's trowel ▪ Concrete float ▪ Rubber mallet ▪ 4 ft. level ▪ Straight 2 x 4 ▪ Grout bag ▪ Stiff-bristled brush ▪ Sponge or coarse rag ▪ Jointing tool ▪ Whisk broom ▪ Latex concrete bonding agent ▪ Flagstone ▪ Mortar ▪ Acrylic fortifier ▪ Stone sealer (optional).

How to Build a Mortared Flagstone Patio

Step A: Clean & Prepare the Slab
1. Thoroughly clean the concrete slab. As mentioned, the slab must be in good structural condition, but minor surface flaws are acceptable. If you need to repair cracked edges or fill holes in concrete that will be exposed, see page 226.

2. After all repairs have cured completely and the cleaned surface is dry, apply a latex bonding agent over the entire area that will be mortared. This helps the mortar adhere to the old concrete. Follow the manufacturer's instructions carefully.

Step B: Dry-lay the Stones
1. After the bonding agent has set up per the manufacturer's directions, dry-lay the stones on the patio to find a pleasing arrangement. Work outward from the center, and space the stones ½"-1" apart. Distribute smaller and larger stones evenly throughout the patio to avoid a lopsided layout.

2. Mark stones for cutting, as needed. Make the cuts when you're confident in the layout.

3. Complete the dry run, cutting stones along the patio edge to accommodate edging treatments, or leave the stones uncut to retain their natural shape; see Option, below.

Option: Overhanging the Outer Stones
For a more rustic or natural appearance, allow stones to overhang the edges of the slab below. Thick stones

(4" or so) may be able to overhang as much as 6", provided that the slab supports ⅔ of the stone. For thinner stones, or stones of inherently weak species, don't overhang more than 2" or 3".

Step C: Begin the Mortaring

1. Starting near the center of the patio, set aside some of the stones, maintaining their relative positions in the dry-run layout.

2. Mix a stiff batch of mortar (see page 99). Note: Use the mortar type recommended by your stone supplier, based on the type of stone and the local climate.

3. Spread a 2"-thick layer of mortar over a workable small area of the slab, using a mason's trowel or concrete float.

Step D: Set the First Stone

1. Firmly press the first large stone into the mortar in its original position in the dry-run layout.

2. Tap the stone with a rubber mallet or the handle of a trowel to set it into the mortar.

Thoroughly clean the concrete slab, then apply a concrete bonding agent.

Arrange stones on the patio for an accurate dry-run layout.

Option: If desired, let outer stones extend beyond the edges of the slab.

Move some of the stones aside, then apply mortar for setting the first few stones.

Bed the first stone into the mortar, then check it for level.

Add mortar and stones to complete the surface, checking for level as you go.

Fill the joints with mortar, using a grout bag for a neat application.

Smooth the mortar joints flush with the stone surfaces (inset), and then let the mortar cure completely. After a week, seal the stone, if desired.

3. Use a 4-ft. level and straight 2 × 4 to check the stone for level. Make any necessary adjustments by tapping with the mallet until the stone is level.

Step E: Lay the Remaining Stones

1. Using the first stone as a reference for the overall height of the patio surface, continue laying stones into the mortar, working outward from the center of the slab and adding mortar as needed. Maintain ½"-1" mortar joints, and do not let stones touch in the final layout.

2. Check for level as you work, using the level and 2 × 4. First check each stone for level as you bed it, then make sure the stone is roughly level with all neighboring stones. If a stone is too high, tap with the mallet to lower it; if too low, remove the stone and add mortar underneath, then re-bed the stone. Remove any spilled mortar from the stone surfaces before it dries, using a wet brush or broom.

3. After all the stones are laid, let the mortar set up for at least a full day before walking on the patio.

Step F: Grout the Mortar Joints

1. Mix a small batch of mortar, adding acrylic fortifier to the mix to make the mortar more elastic.

2. Load a grout bag with mortar. Use the bag to fill the joints between the stones, being careful not to spill mortar onto the stone faces. Do not overfill the joints. For large joints, pack the bottoms of the joints with gravel to conserve mortar and increase the strength of the joints.

3. Wipe up any spills, using a brush and sponge.

Step G: Tool the Mortar & Seal the Stone

1. Once the mortar is stiff enough to hold your thumbprint (without mortar sticking to your thumb), smooth the joints with a whisk broom, jointer, or other finishing tool. Rake the joints just enough so the mortar is flush with the stone faces. This prevents water from pooling on the surface and makes the patio easier to clean.

2. Cover the patio with plastic sheeting and let the mortar cure for 3 to 4 days, then remove the plastic and clean the stones with water and a stiff-bristled brush.

3. After a week, apply a stone sealer, if desired, following the manufacturer's directions.

Seeded Concrete & Wood

A poured concrete patio divided by wood forms is an attractive alternative to a monolithic concrete slab. In addition to its decorative appearance, this type of surface is easier to create, since the permanent forms divide the concrete pour into 4 equal sections (or more, as desired). Each section can be poured and finished before moving on to the next, or you can complete all the quadrants in a day. If you choose the latter, you must watch the poured quadrants carefully and finish them at the proper time, so you'll need a couple of helpers. As an optional addition, this project includes steps for seeding the concrete with small stones, or seeding aggregate, introducing color and texture to the concrete surface.

The form lumber used in the project as shown is brown pressure-treated 2 × 4s, chosen because it's more attractive than most green treated wood. If green is all you can find, you can color the wood with a compatible stain. In any case, use high-quality lumber rated for ground contact, and avoid the type with visible incise marks on the surface, a result of certain forms of treatment. For bolder grid lines, you can use 4 × 4 lumber instead of 2 × 4, joining the form pieces with galvanized spikes.

When planning your patio project, consult your local building department to learn about the following requirements:

- Depth of gravel subbase
- Thickness of concrete slabs
- Metal or other slab reinforcement
- Vapor barrier beneath concrete
- Slope of patio

Adapt the project as shown to meet the local requirements. See pages 86 to 95 for background information on working with concrete.

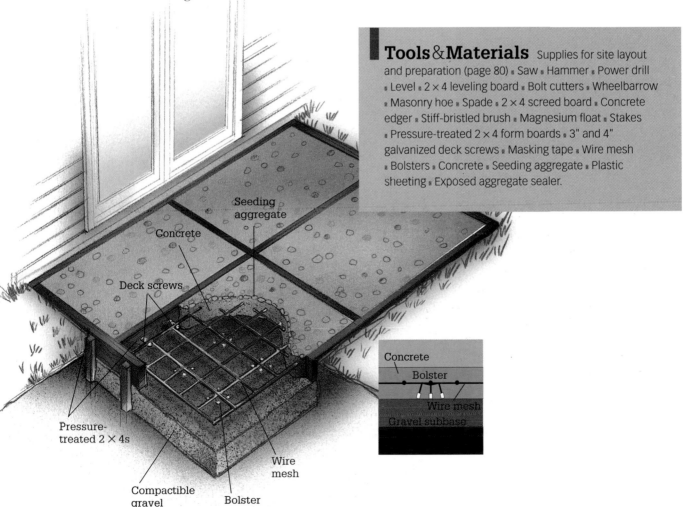

Tools & Materials Supplies for site layout and preparation (page 80) ▪ Saw ▪ Hammer ▪ Power drill ▪ Level ▪ 2 × 4 leveling board ▪ Bolt cutters ▪ Wheelbarrow ▪ Masonry hoe ▪ Spade ▪ 2 × 4 screed board ▪ Concrete edger ▪ Stiff-bristled brush ▪ Magnesium float ▪ Stakes ▪ Pressure-treated 2 × 4 form boards ▪ 3" and 4" galvanized deck screws ▪ Masking tape ▪ Wire mesh ▪ Bolsters ▪ Concrete ▪ Seeding aggregate ▪ Plastic sheeting ▪ Exposed aggregate sealer.

Seeding aggregate

Concrete

Deck screws

Pressure-treated 2 × 4s

Compactible gravel

Bolster

Wire mesh

Concrete

Bolster

Wire mesh

Gravel subbase

How to Build a Seeded Concrete & Wood Patio

Step A: Prepare the Surface & Build the Form Border

1. Define the patio layout, excavate the site, and prepare the gravel subbase. Leave the layout stakes and strings in place as a reference for installing the forms.

2. Cut 4 pressure-treated 2 × 4s to create the permanent outside border of the patio. Lay the boards on the patio subbase and fasten them together at the ends with 3" galvanized deck screws.

3. Secure the form with temporary stakes every 2 ft., setting the top of the form 4" above the subbase (for a 4"-thick slab). The stakes should be below the top edges of the form. Use a long, straight board and a level to make sure the form is level from side to side and that the form slopes down from the high side (house side) at ⅛" per foot.

Step B: Install the Dividers

1. Cut one 2 × 4 form divider to fit between 2 opposing outer form boards. Mark the centers of the outer form boards, and install the divider on the marks, using 3" screws. Make sure the top edge of the divider is flush with the tops of the outer boards.

2. Cut 2 short dividers to fit between the installed divider and the side form boards. Install the short dividers centered along the long divider.

3. Drive 4" galvanized deck screws partway into the inside faces of all of the form boards, spaced every 12". These will act as tie rods to secure the lumber to the concrete slabs.

4. Cover the top edges of the wood with masking tape to protect it during the concrete pour.

Step C: Pour the Concrete for the First Quadrant

1. Cut reinforcing wire mesh to fit inside each quadrant, leaving 1" of clearance between the mesh and forms on all sides. Use bolsters to raise the mesh off the base, making sure the mesh remains at least 2" below the tops of the forms.

2. Mix concrete in a wheelbarrow or power concrete mixer.

3. Place the concrete into the first quadrant. Use a masonry hoe or shovel to spread the concrete evenly. Slide a spade along the insides of the form, and then rap the outsides of the form with a hammer to settle the concrete.

4. Screed the concrete with a straight 2 × 4 that spans across the quadrant. Let any bleed water disappear before continuing.

Stake the form at 2-ft. intervals, checking the form for level and slope.

Install dividers between the outer form boards, then add screws for tying the form to the slabs.

Place concrete into the first quadrant, then screed it level with the top of the form.

Cover the concrete with aggregate. Then float the surface with a magnesium float (inset).

Scrub the surface with a stiff brush and water to expose the aggregate.

Step D: Embed the Aggregate & Begin Finishing

1. Cover the concrete in the quadrant with a full layer of seeding aggregate.

2. Pat down the aggregate with the screed board, then float the surface with a magnesium float until a thin layer of concrete covers the stones. Be careful not to overfloat the surface. If bleed water appears, stop floating and let it dry before completing the step.

3. Tool the edges of the quadrant with a concrete edger, then use a float to smooth any marks left behind.

Note: If you plan to pour more quadrants immediately, cover the first quadrant with plastic sheeting so it does not set up too quickly. Pour the remaining quadrants, repeating Steps C and D. Check each poured quadrant periodically; uncover each quadrant once any bleed water has evaporated, and complete the finishing for that quadrant immediately (Step E).

Step E: Complete the Finish & Apply Sealer

1. After the bleed water has evaporated from the concrete surface, mist the surface with water, and then scrub it with a stiff-bristled brush to expose the aggregate.

2. Remove the tape from the forms. Replace the plastic and let the concrete cure for 1 week. If you're pouring and finishing one quadrant at a time, you can now move on to the next quadrant.

3. After all of the quadrants have cured, rinse and scrub the surfaces again to remove any remaining residue. If desired, use diluted muriatic acid to wash off stubborn concrete residue (follow the manufacturer's instructions for mixing ratios and safety precautions).

4. After the patio has cured for 3 weeks, seal the surface with exposed-aggregate sealer, following the manufacturer's directions.

Basic Concrete Slab

A basic poured concrete slab makes a great patio surface by itself or can serve as a solid base for a finish of tile or mortared brick or stone. Much of the information you'll need to plan and execute a concrete pour begins on page 88. The project shown here outlines the major steps and sequence of the entire job.

Once you have a good understanding of what your own patio project involves, the next step is to consult the local building department to learn about their construction requirements for concrete slabs. Standard patio slabs are 4" thick and usually require internal reinforcement, such as wire mesh. For smaller slabs, the local building code might allow fiber reinforcement instead. If you're planning a brick or block wall on top of the slab,

ask about footing requirements and the proper method for integrating the footing with the slab. Some codes may allow a thickened portion of the slab to serve as the footing. Also check for these code requirements and adapt your project as needed:

- Depth of gravel subbase
- Thickness of concrete slab
- Vapor barrier beneath concrete
- Slope of patio

If your new slab will become your finished patio, you might consider coloring the concrete for a decorative effect (see page 144). A popular method of coloring for do-it-yourselfers is using an acid stain, which can be simply applied with a brush, as shown on page 143.

How to Build a Concrete Slab Patio

Step A: Prepare the Site & Build the Form

1. Follow the basic steps on pages 116 to 118 to lay out the patio with stakes and mason's lines. Excavate the site about 10" wider than the slab to provide plenty of room for staking the forms. Prepare a 4"-thick subbase of compacted gravel (page 117). Leave the layout stakes and strings in place as a reference for installing the form.

2. Build the concrete form from 2 × 4 lumber. Stake the form in place so its top edges are 4" above the gravel base (for a 4"-thick slab). Drive a stake every 2 ft. outside the form, and fasten it to the form so the top of the stake is slightly below the top of the form board. Measure from the layout strings to make sure the form is level from side to side and slopes down from the high side (house side) at ⅛" per foot.

Tools & Materials Supplies for site layout and preparation (page 115) ▪ Supplies for wood forms ▪ Shovel ▪ Power concrete mixer ▪ Wheelbarrow ▪ Asphalt-impregnated fiberboard ▪ Bricks ▪ Vegetable oil or commercial release agent ▪ 6-mil plastic sheeting (for vapor barrier) ▪ Fiber-reinforced concrete ▪ 2 × 4 screed board ▪ Mason's trowel ▪ Darby ▪ Concrete edger ▪ Magnesium float ▪ Groover ▪ Plastic sheeting (for curing concrete).

Stake the form every 2 ft., screwing through the stake to secure the form.

Option: Bend and stake a kerfed 1 × 4 to make forms with curved edges or corners.

An optional divider separates the slab into workable sections.

Option: Creating Curved Forms

Use 1 × 4s to create forms for turns or rounded corners. Make parallel ½"-deep saw cuts, or kerfs, in one side of the form board, then bend the board to create the desired curve. Stake behind the form at close intervals so the curve will retain its shape against the weight of the concrete, then backfill behind the form with soil. For small curves, you can use hardboard instead of a 1 × 4 to create the shape (see page 94).

Step B: Install Isolation Membranes

1. At any joint where the new slab will contact an existing structure, such as the house or existing concrete work, add a strip of 4"-wide × ½"-thick asphalt-impregnated fiberboard. Temporarily hold the strips in place with bricks.

Option: For a large slab or for a patio that will abut a concrete walkway or a slab for vehicle parking, install a 2 × 4 form divider and isolation board to create an expansion joint. The divider closes the end of the main form to create a smaller, more workable section of slab.

2. For slabs larger than 8 ft., mark the locations of control joints (page 95) onto the forms. Plan to make control joints for each 8-ft. section of the slab. Note: If you will be tiling the slab, position control joints so they will coincide with grout joints in the tile layout.

Step C: Place the Concrete

1. Coat the form boards with vegetable oil or a commercial release agent so the concrete won't bond to their surfaces as it cures.

2. If recommended or required by the local building code, cover the gravel subbase with a vapor barrier of 6-mil plastic sheeting.

3. Mix fiber-reinforced concrete for the entire section of the slab, using a power mixer, or order concrete from a ready-mix company (see page 89). If you use ready-mix, have helpers on hand so you can place the concrete as soon as it arrives.

4. Pour pods of concrete into the form, digging into the concrete with a shovel to eliminate air pockets. Remove the bricks supporting the isolation membranes once the concrete can support them. Spread the concrete evenly throughout the section by scooping and placing shovelfuls, rather than dragging it along.

Step D: Screed the Concrete

1. Screed the concrete from side to side, using a straight 2 × 4 resting on top of the form boards. Raise the leading edge of the screed board slightly as you move it across the concrete.

2. As you work, add concrete to fill in any low spots, and rescreed as needed.

Place the concrete in pods, then distribute it evenly throughout the section.

Screed the concrete smooth, riding the screed board along the tops of the form sides.

Let the bleed water disappear, then float the concrete with a darby.

Shape the edges of the slab with an edger (inset). Broom the surface, if desired, for a nonslip texture.

Step E: Cut Control Joints & Float the Surface

1. Cut control joints (if you need them) at the marked locations, using board as a guide to ensure a straight line.

2. Allow the bleed water to evaporate from the concrete surface (see page 95), and then float the concrete with a darby. Let the surface cure for 2 to 4 hours or until it is solid enough to support your weight.

Step F: Complete the Finishing

1. Use an edger along the insides of the form to create smooth, rounded edges. Smooth out any marks left behind, using a magnesium or wood float.

2. Finish any control joints with a groover. For a 4" slab, the groove should be 1" deep.

Option: Apply a broomed finish for a nonslip surface or for adding "tooth" to the surface for a better bond with mortared finishes. While the concrete is still wet but firm to the touch, drag a fine-bristled nylon or horsehair broom across the surface in parallel strokes. Dip the broom in water and shake to clean the bristles between each stroke.

3. Cover the concrete with plastic sheeting, and mist the concrete daily for 2 weeks. If you'll be adding a mortared finish, do not apply any type of curing agent, which seals the concrete and prevents a bond with mortar.

4. When the concrete has fully cured, remove the forms and backfill along the edges of the slab. Color or seal the concrete as desired.

How to Acid Stain Concrete

Acid staining is a permanent color treatment for cured concrete that yields a translucent, attractively mottled finish that's well suited to patios. Unlike paint, which is a surface coating, acid stain is a chemical solution that soaks into the concrete pores and reacts with minerals in the concrete to create the desired color. The color doesn't peel or wear, but it won't hide blemishes or discoloration in the original concrete surface. Some colors of stain may fade in direct sunlight, so be sure to choose a color guaranteed by the manufacturer not to fade.

To apply an acid stain, follow the manufacturer's directions carefully. Here is a typical process:

1. Thoroughly clean the concrete and let dry. Then, wearing protective clothing and eyewear, load the stain into a plastic bucket or all-plastic pump sprayer. Apply stain with a brush or sprayer. Always brush to a wet edge to prevent dark lap marks. Sprayed-on stain may be left alone for a highly mottled finish or brushed or mopped for less mottling.

2. Allow surface to dry, and then remove residual stain with rags or a broom. Rinse. Stain may be reapplied for a darker shade, or another color may be added for accents.

3. Allow stain to dry, according to the manufacturer's directions, and then apply a water-based concrete sealer, using a brush or roller. For faster results, use a hand-pump sprayer.

Note: Always test stain in an inconspicuous area before applying it to your primary surface.

Use a paintbrush to apply stain, using long, even strokes. Minimize brush strokes.

Once stain has absorbed, remove residual stain with rags.

Apply a sealer, using a hand-pump sprayer.

How to Color Concrete

Coloring concrete is a great way to add depth and beauty to a concrete slab. Together with stamps, colored concrete can successfully mimic many other patio surfaces. To achieve vibrant colors, use white Portland cement in the concrete mix.

Dry pigment colors the surface of poured concrete. Not only is it easy to work with, but it is also used and trusted by professionals. You simply dust the powder over the concrete prior to final floating, and then finish with a magnesium float. To achieve an even color, you may want to dust and then spot dust again. Make sure you follow the manufacturer's instructions, and avoid overworking the concrete with the float. Overworking concrete may cause bleed water to rise and dilute the color, and leads to rapid deterioration of the surface.

1. Once you have poured the concrete, smooth the surface and then add the pigment. See page 140.

2. Following the manufacturer's instructions, dust the powdered pigment over the entire concrete surface, throwing out handfuls of the powdered pigment so that it disperses and leaves an even, fine dusting. As you become more comfortable with the product, you'll be able to work faster and cover larger areas at a time by throwing out handfuls of the dry pigment.

3. Float the concrete surface using a magnesium float.

After a concrete slab has been colored and floated, there may still be color inconsistencies. This actually adds depth to a stamped surface, creating a more realistic emulation of stone or brick. Left unstamped, it is also a desirable finished style.

Dust the powdered pigment over the entire concrete surface, following the manufacturer's instructions. Then float the surface using a magnesium float.

How to Stamp Concrete

Stamped concrete adds texture to otherwise ordinary concrete slabs. Stamping mats are available in a variety of textures and patterns and can be rented at most equipment rental centers and concrete supply stores.

As you plan your concrete pro-ject, mark a reference line at or near the center of the project and align subsequent mats with the first, working outward toward the ends of the project. Plan for long seams to fall across the project rather than along the length of it to avoid misaligned seams. You may have to hand-finish textures at corners, along sides, or near other obstructions using specialty stamps, chisels, or other rollers.

The stamping pads should be pressed into slightly stiff concrete to a depth of about 1". Stamping pads can be reused throughout the process.

Step A: Prepare the Surface

1. Pour a concrete slab and mark a reference line for the first mat at or near the center of the form.

2. Toss the powder release agent across the surface in the amount specified in the manufacturer's instructions.

Step B. Stamp the Surface

1. Align the first stamping mat with the reference line on the form, following your layout plan. Once the mat is placed, do not adjust it.

2. Carefully step onto the mat to embed the stamp into the concrete. Be sure to wear sturdy boots that you don't mind getting dirty.

Alternative: If you're using professional-grade stamps, use a hand tamp to set them. Then peel back the stamp to reveal the stamped concrete surface. If you have a couple of mats you can walk from mat to mat, reusing mats as you progress across the concrete surface to avoid walking on the concrete.

3. Butt the second pad against the first, so the seams are flush and aligned. Embed the mat into the concrete. Pull up the first mat and reuse it to lay the next stamp. Continue this pattern, removing and reusing the mats. When the project area is wider than the stamping pads, complete rows across the width before stamping lengthwise.

Stamped concrete can emulate stones or pavers at a fraction of the cost.

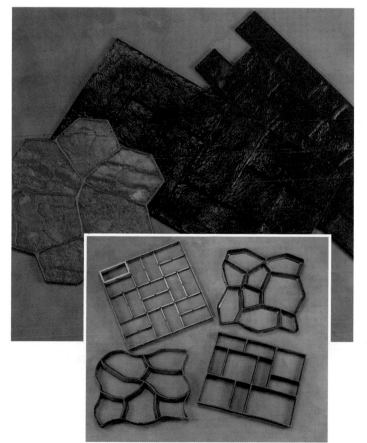

Stamping mats can be pressed onto fresh concrete, as with the professional-grade mats. The DIY molds are less expensive and can be used as either stamp pads or molds. The professional stamps are considerably more expensive but can be rented from concrete rentals or home centers.

After bleed water has disappeared from the surface of your concrete slab, sprinkle the powder release agent across the surface. Follow the manufacturer's instructions.

Align the first stamp with the reference line on the form. Follow your layout plan, butting each stamp up against the previous one and setting it by firmly pressing down (or stepping on it).

Alternative: Set professional-grade mats in place by using a hand tamp (inset). Then peel back the form to reveal the stamp.

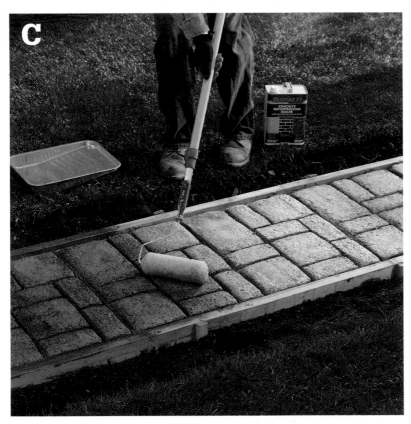

After the leftover release agent from the surface has been removed, apply an acrylic concrete sealer, following the manufacturer's instructions.

Step C: Finish the Surface

1. Allow the concrete to cure for a week, and then apply an acrylic concrete sealer, according to the manufacturer's instructions.

2. Remove the wood forms and backfill around the perimeter or add edging as desired.

How to Simulate Flagstone

Carving joints in concrete can simulate a natural flagstone surface. By adding color to the concrete, you can really throw your neighbors off. And stamps can add even yet another dimension of depth and detail. The finished look is a walkway or patio that resembles a mortared flagstone surface.

Start by studying some flagstone paths in your neighborhood and sketching on paper the look you want to re-create. This way, you can also get an idea of the right color. Keep in mind the color of your house and landscaping, and experiment with tint until you find a complementary hue.

1. Pour concrete according to the basic techniques on page 140. Smooth the surface with a screed board.

2. Follow the directions in this chapter for coloring concrete with dry pigments.

3. Cut shallow lines in the concrete, using a jointing tool or a curved copper pipe. Note: If you stamp the concrete first, you can still add your flagstone lines at this point.

4. Refloat the surface. Remove the wood forms once the concrete has cured. Protect the surface with clear concrete sealer.

Create forms and pour your concrete. Screed the surface smooth.

Cut shallow lines in the concrete, using a jointing tool or curved copper pipe.

Refloat the surface for a smooth, mortared flagstone appearance.

Tile on Concrete

Whether it's ceramic, porcelain, or natural stone, tile turns a concrete slab into a highly decorative patio. Outdoor tile installs almost identically to indoor floor tile. On patios, tile must be installed over a stable concrete slab, either old or new. Inspect an old slab to make sure it is sound and shows no signs of structural flaws, such as major cracking or shifting or an inadequate subbase.

If you're tiling over an old slab that's in good shape structurally but has some surface flaws and may not be smooth enough for tile, you can lay a new subbase made of floor-mix concrete over the old slab. A bond barrier between the old and new layers helps prevent cracks and other problems in the bottom slab from transferring to the new surface. In this project, installing a new subbase is covered in Steps A to E. If your slab is in good shape and you're ready to tile, skip ahead to Step F.

While the installation techniques for outdoor and indoor tile are similar, the materials are not the same for both. Outdoor tile must have adequate thickness and low water absorption to withstand heavy outdoor use and changing weather. As for grout, use an exterior-grade, sanded grout for all outdoor tile. Ask your tile supplier for recommendations on tile, grout, and sealers to make sure your patio will stand up to the local conditions.

Tools & Materials
Basic hand tools (page 149) ▪ Shovel ▪ Aviation snips ▪ Masonry hoe ▪ Mortar box ▪ Hand tamper ▪ Magnesium float ▪ Concrete edger ▪ Utility knife ▪ Trowel or putty knife ▪ Measuring tape ▪ Tile marker ▪ Carpenter's square ▪ Maul ▪ Straightedge ▪ Square-notched trowel ▪ Rubber mallet ▪ Tile cutter or wet saw ▪ Tile nippers ▪ Needlenose pliers ▪ Caulk gun ▪ Sash brush or sponge brush ▪ Paint roller with extension pole ▪ 2 x 4 and 2 x 2 lumber ▪ 2½" and 3" deck screws ▪ ⅜" stucco lath ▪ Heavy gloves ▪ 30# building paper ▪ Dry floor-mix concrete ▪ Dirt ▪ Plastic sheeting ▪ Roofing cement ▪ Tile ▪ Tile spacers ▪ Dry-set mortar ▪ Buckets ▪ Soft cloth for wiping tile ▪ ¼"-dia. caulking backer rod ▪ Grout ▪ Latex-fortified grout float ▪ Grout sponge ▪ Coarse cloth or abrasive pad ▪ Latex tile caulk ▪ Caulk tint ▪ Grout sealer ▪ Tile sealer.

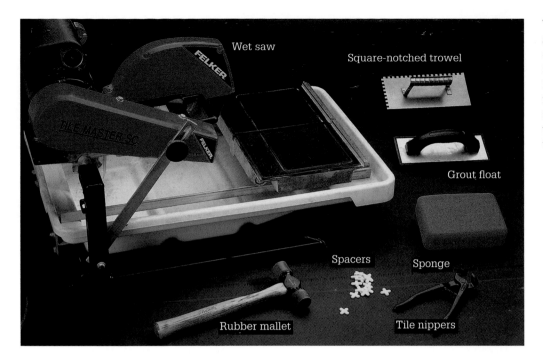

Wet saw

Square-notched trowel

Grout float

Spacers

Sponge

Rubber mallet

Tile nippers

Tools for working with tile are available at most home centers and some tile dealers. If your tile project calls for a lot of cut tiles, rent a wet saw for the job. For minimal straight cuts, use a standard tile cutter, and use tile nippers for curved cuts.

▮ How to Install a Tile Patio

Step A: Install Subbase Form Boards

1. Dig a trench 6" wide and no more than 4" deep around the patio to create room for 2 × 4 forms. Clean dirt and debris from the exposed sides of the patio.

2. Cut and fit 2 × 4 frames around the patio (page 93), joining the ends with 3" deck screws. Cut wood stakes from 2 × 4s and drive them next to the forms at 2-ft. intervals.

3. Set stucco lath on the surface, and then set a 2 × 2 spacer on top of the lath to establish the subbase thickness. Note: Wear heavy gloves when handling metal, such as stucco lath.

4. Adjust the form boards so the tops are level with the 2 × 2. Screw the stakes to the forms with 2½" deck screws.

Step B: Prepare the Site

1. Remove the 2 × 2 spacers and stucco lath, then lay strips of 30# building paper over the patio surface, overlapping seams by 6", to create a bond-breaker for the new surface.

2. Crease the building paper at the edges and corners, making sure the paper extends past the tops of the forms. Make a small cut in each corner of the paper for easier folding.

Build temporary 2 × 2 forms to divide the project into working sections. The forms also provide rests for the screed board used to level and smooth the fresh concrete.

Adjust the form height by setting stucco lath on the surface, then place a 2 × 2 spacer on top of the lath (their combined thickness should equal the thickness of the subbase).

Level off the surface of the concrete by dragging a straight 2 × 4 across the top, with the ends riding on the forms.

Pour and smooth out the next working section. After floating this section, remove the 2 × 2 temporary for between the two sections.

After curing is complete, remove the plastic, disassemble and remove the forms, and trim off the building paper around the sides. Apply roofing cement to two sides of the subbase.

3. Lay strips of stucco lath over the building paper, overlapping seams by 1". Keep the lath 1" away from the forms and the wall. Use aviation snips to cut the lath.

4. Build temporary 2 × 2 forms to divide the project into 3- to 4-ft. sections. Screw the ends of the 2 × 2s to the form boards so the tops are level.

Step C: Place Concrete in the First Section

1. Mix dry floor-mix concrete according to the manufacturer's directions, using either a mortar box or a power mixer. The mixture should be very dry so it can be pressed down into the voids in the stucco with a tamper.

2. Fill one section with concrete, up to the tops of the forms. Tamp the concrete thoroughly with a lightweight tamper to force it into the voids in the lath and into the corners.

3. Drag a straight 2 × 4 across the tops of the forms to screed the concrete surface level. Use a sawing motion as you progress to create a level surface and fill any voids in the concrete. If voids or hollows remain, add more concrete and smooth it off.

4. Use a magnesium float to smooth the surface of the concrete. Apply very light pressure and move the float back and forth in an arching motion. Tip the lead edge up slightly to avoid gouging the surface.

Step D: Fill Remaining Sections

1. Pour and smooth out the next section. Float the section, then remove the 2 × 2 temporary forms between the two sections.

2. Fill the void left behind with fresh concrete. Float the concrete until it is smooth and level and blends into the section on each side.

3. Pour and finish the remaining sections one at a time, using the same techniques.

Step E: Finish the Subbase

1. Let the concrete dry until pressing the surface with your finger does not leave a mark, then cut contours around the edges of the subbase with a concrete edger.

2. Cover the concrete with sheets of plastic, and weigh down the edges. Let the concrete cure for at least 3 days, or according to the manufacturer's directions.

3. After curing is complete, remove the plastic, disassemble and remove the forms, and trim off the building paper around the sides of the patio using a utility knife.

4. Apply roofing cement on two sides of the patio, using a trowel or putty knife to fill and seal the seam between the old and new surfaces. To provide drainage for moisture between the layers, don't seal the lowest side of the patio.

Adjust the tile to create a layout that minimizes tile cutting. Shift the rows until the overhang is equal at each end and any cut portions are less than 2" wide.

Set the first tile in the corner of the quadrant where the lines intersect, adjusting until it is exactly aligned with both reference lines. Position the next tile along one arm of the quadrant, fitting it neatly against the spacer.

Step F: Dry-lay the Tile

1. Dry-lay one row of tile vertically and one horizontally on the subbase so they intersect at the center of the patio. Use tile spacers between tiles to represent joints. Keep the tiles ¼" to ½" away from the house to allow for expansion.

Note: If you're tiling directly over a slab that has control joints, position the tile so that grout joints coincide precisely with the control joints. Later, you'll fill those tile joints with caulk instead of grout to create an expansion joint.

2. Adjust the tile to create a layout that minimizes tile cutting. Shift the rows of tiles and spacers until the overhang is equal at each end and any cut portions are less than 2" wide. Again, make sure a grout joint falls directly above any control joints in the slab.

3. With the layout set, mark the subbase at the joint between the third and fourth row out from the house, then measure and mark it at several more points along the subbase. Snap a chalk line to connect the marks.

4. Use a carpenter's square and a long, straight board to mark end points for a second reference line perpendicular to the first. Mark the points next to the dry-laid tile so the line falls on a joint location. Snap a chalk line that connects the points.

Step G: Place First Legs of Tile

1. Mix a batch of dry-set mortar in a bucket, according to the manufacturer's directions.

2. Spread mortar evenly along both legs of the first quadrant near the house, using a square-notched trowel. Apply enough mortar for 4 tiles along each leg.

3. Use the edge of the trowel to create furrows in the mortar. Apply enough mortar to completely cover the area under the tiles without covering up the reference lines.

4. Set the first tile in the corner of the quadrant where the lines intersect, pressing down lightly and twisting slightly from side to side. Adjust the tile until it is exactly aligned with both reference lines.

5. Rap the tile gently with a rubber mallet to set it into the mortar.

6. Set plastic spacers at the corner of the tile that faces the working quadrant.

7. Position the next tile into the mortar bed along one arm of the quadrant. Make sure the tiles fit neatly against the spacers. Rap the tiles with the mallet to set it into the mortar, then position and set the next tile on the other leg of the quadrant.

8. Fill out the rest of the tiles in the two mortared legs of the quadrant. Wipe off any excess mortar before it dries.

Set tiles into the field area of the first quadrant, saving any cut tiles for last. Cut tile using a wet saw or a tile cutter. For curved cuts, use tile nippers.

Fill in the remaining quadrants, using a straightedge to check joints occasionally. If any of the joint lines are out of alignment, compensate over several rows of tiles. After all tiles are set, remove spacers.

Step H: Fill the First Quadrant

1. Apply a furrowed layer of mortar to the field area of the first quadrant, and then set tiles into it. Save any cut tiles for last. Use a wet saw or a tile cutter for cutting. For curved cuts, use tile nippers.

2. Place several tiles at once, and then set them all with the rubber mallet at one time.

3. As you finish the quadrant, use a needlenose pliers to carefully remove the plastic spacers before the mortar hardens—usually within an hour. Clean all excess mortar from the tiles before it hardens.

Step I: Fill the Remaining Quadrants

1. Apply mortar and fill in tiles in the remaining quadrants, beginning with the next quadrant against the house. Use the same techniques used for the first quadrant.

2. Use a straightedge to check the tile joints occasionally. If any of the joint lines are out of alignment, compensate for the misalignment over several rows of tiles.

3. After all the tiles for the patio are set, make sure all spacers are removed and any excess mortar has been cleaned from the tile surfaces. Cover the project area with plastic for 3 days to allow the mortar to cure properly.

Step J: Remove the Plastic & Install Backer Rod (as needed)

1. After 3 days, remove the plastic from the tile.

2. For installations with expansion joints (see Step F, on page 151): Insert strips of ¼"-diameter (or other size, based on your grout joint thickness) backer rod into any grout joints that are aligned with slab control joints.

Step K: Grout the Joints

1. Mix a batch of tile grout to the recommended consistency. Tip: Add latex-fortified grout additive so excess grout is easier to remove. Use a damp sponge to wipe off grout film.

2. Start in a corner and spread a layer of grout onto a 25-sq.-ft. or less area of the tile surface.

3. Use a rubber grout float to spread the grout and pack it into the tile joints. Scrape diagonally across the joints, holding the float in a near-vertical position. Make sure to scrape off excess grout from the surface of the tile so the tile does not absorb it.

4. Use a damp sponge to wipe the grout film from the surface of the tile. Rinse the sponge out frequently with cool water, and be careful not to press down so hard around joints that you disturb the grout. Wash grout off of the entire surface.

Step L: Finish & Seal the Tile

1. Let the grout dry for 4 hours, and then poke it with a nail to make sure it has hardened. Use a cloth to buff the surface to remove any remaining grout film. Use a coarser cloth, such as burlap, or an abrasive pad to remove stubborn grout film.

2. Remove the caulking backer rod from the tile joints, then fill the joints with caulk tinted to match the grout color.

3. Apply grout sealer to the grout lines using a sash brush or small sponge brush. Avoid spilling over onto the tile surface with the grout sealer. Wipe up any spills immediately.

4. After 1 to 3 weeks, seal the surface with tile sealer. Follow the manufacturer's application and directions, using a paint roller with an extension pole.

After the mortar cures, remove the plastic sheeting. Fill expansion joints with backer rod, if applicable to your project.

Mix a batch of tile grout to the recommended consistency and use a grout float to pack it into the tile joints.

Remove the caulking backer rod, then fill the joints with caulk that is tinted to match the grout color. Apply grout sealer, and then seal the entire surface after 1 to 3 weeks with tile sealer.

Loose Material

Gravel, crushed stone, wood chips, and other loose materials are very easy to install and can become a surprisingly attractive patio surface. The versatile nature of loose material lends itself to everything from creative mixed-media designs to plain surfaces that evoke the simple beauty of Zen rock gardens.

The basic installation of a loose material patio starts with excavating the site, then adding a 2" layer of compacted gravel and edging material. Edging is required to contain the loose surface material. From there, the installation depends on the type of material you're using:

For crushed stone, gravel, and other small aggregates: Add a 1" to 2" layer of surface material and tamp flat

For river rock: Add 2" or more (based on size of rock)

For wood chips: Add a 2" or thicker layer and rake smooth

Ask your supplier for installation recommendations for your specific surface material.

When shopping for a surface material, choose carefully, based on how you plan to use the patio. Visit a few stone yards or landscape supply dealers and discuss your project with knowledgeable staff. If possible, walk around on some sample stock to see how the material feels underfoot. Keep in mind that large stones are more difficult to walk on than smaller aggregate. For the smoothest, hardest surface, use compacted gravel as the finish material, or top your gravel base with granite fines, or "rock dust," and compact the top layer with a power tamper (be sure to slope the surface for drainage).

Tools & Materials

Supplies for site layout and preparation (page 115) ▪ Power tamper or drum roller ▪ Wheelbarrow ▪ Shovel ▪ Rake ▪ Loose material.

Accent pieces do not have to be pavers suitable for walking on. For a more decorative effect, try large, natural rocks strategically set on the loose material. Small or fine loose material is easy to form into shapes with rakes. Here, this raked effect represents the sea in Japanese rock garden architecture.

Complete the site preparation, then install edging along the patio's border.

Option: Lay pavers over the gravel base, according to your custom design. Check them for level.

Add the surface material and rake it smooth. If desired, roll or tamp the new layer for a compacted surface.

How to Create a Loose Material Patio

Step A: Prepare the Site & Install Edging

1. Lay out the patio site following the steps on pages 116 to 117. Excavate to a depth of 4" (or other, depending on your surface material and application).

2. Cover the excavation with landscape fabric, overlapping the strips by at least 6".

3. Add compactible gravel: Use decomposed granite or similar mixed-size material that compacts to a firm, smooth layer. Compact the gravel with a power tamper to create a smooth, evenly compressed 2"-thick subbase.

4. Install patio edging as desired. To help contain the loose patio material, set the edging so it will stand at least ½" higher than the top of the surface material.

Option: Installing Accent Pavers

Set pavers (stone, concrete, wood, or other material) onto the gravel base, as desired. For flagstone and other materials that might not be flat on the bottom, add sand underneath the stone to level it and prevent wobble. When all accent pavers are set, proceed to Step B.

Step B: Add the Loose Material

1. Spread out your surface material over the patio site, raking it into an even layer of the desired thickness.

2. If appropriate for your material, roll the surface layer with a drum roller or tamp with a power tamper to create a smooth, level surface.

3. Spray masonry materials with water to clean the aggregate for a finished appearance.

Creating a Paver Island ▸

An island of flat paving stones (bricks and concrete pads work well, too) floating in a pool of loose material creates an eye-catching patio that combines the visual texture of aggregate and the practical benefits of a flat, stable flooring surface. The basic installation techniques are simple: Set the paver island over the gravel subbase using a sandset application, containing the installation with "invisible" plastic edging. Fill the paver joints about halfway with compressed sand, and then top off with the same loose material used in the surrounding area.

Framed Wood

With a flooring surface that's several inches above the ground, a framed wood patio combines the elevated feel of a traditional deck with the easy access of a patio. This free-standing patio is built on precast concrete footings set on the ground, so it's made to go anywhere. Its simple design is easy to customize for your needs. You can enlarge the patio by adding more footings and using longer lumber or add on to the main patio to create an "L" or other shape. As shown, the patio measures 12 ft. square. The concrete footings used are commonly available at home centers and lumberyards.

Start your project by leveling the site and adding a ground cover as desired. If the patio is located over unstable soil or in a low area of your yard that collects water, consider installing a gravel subbase (see page 117), with or without a decorative topping material. A gravel bed drains well and will help keep the patio footings level. For any project, it's a good idea to install landscape fabric, either under a gravel base or just below your ground cover, to inhibit weed growth.

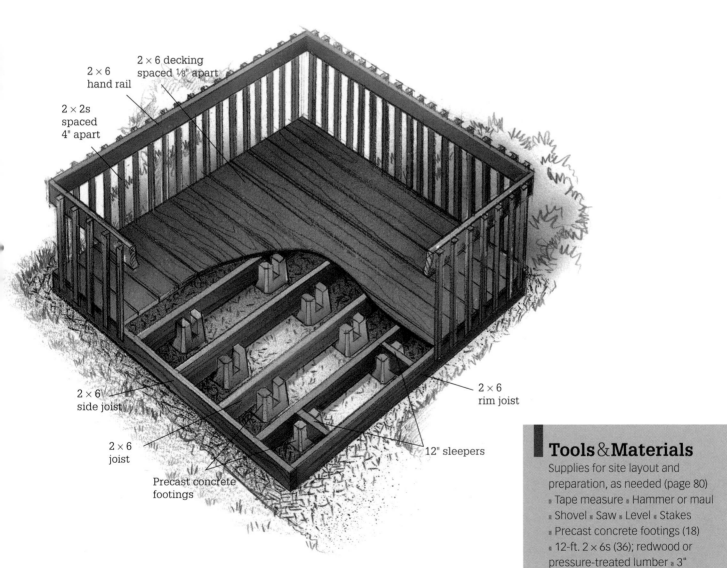

2 × 6
hand rail

2 × 6 decking
spaced ⅛" apart

2 × 2s
spaced
4" apart

2 × 6
side joist

2 × 6
joist

Precast concrete
footings

12" sleepers

2 × 6
rim joist

Tools & Materials

Supplies for site layout and preparation, as needed (page 80) ▪ Tape measure ▪ Hammer or maul ▪ Shovel ▪ Saw ▪ Level ▪ Stakes ▪ Precast concrete footings (18) ▪ 12-ft. 2 × 6s (36); redwood or pressure-treated lumber ▪ 3" galvanized deck screws ▪ Wood sealer/protectant of your choice.

How to Build a Framed Wood Patio

Step A: Install & Level the Footings

1. Measure a 10 × 10-ft. area for the patio foundation, and mark the corners with stakes.

2. Position a footing at each corner, and then measure from corner to corner—from the center of each footing. Adjust until the diagonal measurements are equal, which means that the footings are square.

3. Place a 2 × 6 across the footings for the back row, setting it in the center slots. Check this joist with a level, then add or remove soil beneath footings as necessary to level it.

4. Center a footing between these corner footings. Use a level to recheck the joist, then add or remove soil beneath the center footing, if necessary. Remove the joist.

5. Repeat the process described in Steps 2, 3, and 4 to set and level the footings for the front row.

6. Position the remaining 12 footings at equal intervals, aligned in three rows. Position a 2 × 6 from the front row of footings to the back, and adjust soil as necessary to bring the interior footings into alignment with the front and back rows.

Step B: Install the Joists

1. Measure each of the 10 joist boards; trim any board as needed so that all are exactly 144" long. If desired, seal the ends of the joists with wood sealer/protectant and let them dry completely.

2. Center a 12-ft. joist across each row of footings. Using a level, check the joists once again and carefully adjust the footings, if necessary.

Step C: Add the Side Joists & Rim Joists

1. Line up a 2 × 6 flush against the ends of the joists along the left side of the patio, with the ends extending equally past the front and back joists.

2. Attach the side joist by driving a pair of deck screws into each joist.

3. Repeat this process to install the right-side joist.

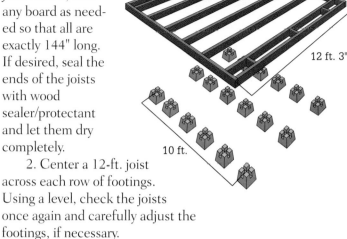

12 ft. × 12 ft. decking

12 ft. 3"

10 ft.

Position the corner footings and the center footing for the back joist. Remove or add soil beneath the footings to level them.

Position the remaining footings and insert the joists. Check to make sure the framework is level, and adjust as needed.

Install the front and back rim joists between the ends of the side joists, securing them with pairs of deck screws.

Position the sleepers in the slots of the footings, then attach them to both joists with pairs of deck screws.

After the framing is completed, measure the diagonals and adjust the frame until it's square.

Install the patio boards by driving a pair of screws into each joist. Use a framing square to leave a ⅛" space between boards.

Step D: Position the Sleepers

1. Measure and cut six 2 × 6 sleepers to fit between the front and back joists and the rim joists. Seal the cut ends with wood sealer/protectant and let them dry completely.

2. Position one sleeper in each row of footings, between the first joist and the rim joist. Attach each sleeper by driving a pair of galvanized deck screws through each of the joists and into the sleeper.

Step E: Square Up the Frame

1. Once the framing is complete, measure the diagonals from corner to corner. Compare the measurements to see if they are equal.

2. Adjust the framing as necessary by pushing it into alignment. Have someone help you hold one side of the framework while you push against the other.

Step F: Lay the Decking

1. Seal the 2 × 6 decking boards with wood sealer/protectant and let them dry. Seal all exposed framing members as well.

2. Lay a 2 × 6 over the surface of the patio, perpendicular to the joists and flush with the rim joist. Secure this board with deck screws.

3. Repeat Step 2 to install the rest of the patio boards. Use a framing square to set a ⅛" space between boards. Rip cut the last board, if needed.

4. At the front of the patio, position a 2 × 6 rim joist flush between the ends of the side joists, forming a butt joint on each end.

5. Attach the rim joist to the side joists by driving a pair of deck screws through the faces of the side joists, into the ends of the rim joist.

6. Repeat #4 and #5 to install the other rim joist.

How to Add a Railing to a Platform Patio

Step A: Prepare the Balusters

1. Place the 2 × 2s flush together, adjust them so the ends are even, and draw a pair of straight lines, 3" apart, across each board, 1½" above the beveled end. Repeat the process and draw a line at 1¼" and 4¼" from the top ends. Using the lines as guides, drill pilot holes through the 2 × 2s.

2. Apply wood sealer/protectant to the ends of the 2 × 2s.

Step B: Attach the Balusters

1. Position a 2 × 2 flush with the bottom of the joist, and then clamp it in place to use as a placement guide.

2. Position the corner 2 × 2s against the side joists, beveled end down, 4" in from the corner.

Check for plumb, then drive deck screws through the pilot holes.

3. Attach the remaining 2 × 2s for each side, spacing them 4" apart.

Step C: Attach the Handrailing

1. Hold a 12-ft. 2 × 6 that forms the top of the railing in place, behind the installed 2 × 2s.

2. Attach the 2 × 2s to the 2 × 6 top rails by driving deck screws through the pilot holes.

3. Connect the top rails at the corners, using pairs of deck screws.

4. Finish the railing by applying a coat of wood sealer, according to the manufacturer's directions.

Tools & Materials 2½" galvanized deck screws
- 2 × 6 × 12" (3) ■ 2 × 2 × 42" (18 per side, one end beveled).

Gang together all of the 2 × 2s, then drill pairs of pilot holes at both ends of each board.

Attach the 2 × 2s to the side joists, leaving a 4" gap between them.

Level the 2 × 6 railing behind the 2 × 2s, then attach it by driving screws through the pilot holes.

Wood Tile

Wood patio tiles (also called deck tiles or decking tiles) are manufactured units made with natural wood slats and are designed primarily for dressing up old concrete slabs. Some types of tiles snap together for installation; others are simply laid down and held snugly together by your own border or edging treatment. There are rigid types suitable for hard surfaces, and flexible versions for laying over tamped loose material. Tiles are made to uniform sizes, commonly 12" or 24" square, making it easy to plan your layout before purchasing the tiles. To order tiles, measure your patio and plan the layout using the manufacturer's given tile dimensions. Factor in border material and edging strips, as needed. Tiles can be cut to almost any size to suit your layout or fit around obstructions.

Interlocking rigid tiles are shown in this project. These tiles are available in a few different styles, which you can mix and match for custom patterns. Because they snap together, the tiles do not require a rigid border to prevent shifting, but manufacturers typically offer decorative edge strips for finishing the edges and corners of the installation.

Like all natural wood, patio tiles will fade to a silvery-gray when exposed to the sun and weather. To retain the wood's natural coloring, seal the tiles with a finish or protectant recommended by the manufacturer, and reapply periodically as needed.

How to Install a Wood Tile Patio Surface

Step A: Begin Laying Tiles

1. Thoroughly clean the surface of the concrete patio. Note: The patio slab must drain well and not collect water for extended periods. Pooled water underneath the tiles will damage them.

2. Starting at one corner of the patio, lay tiles according to your desired pattern. Start with edging strips, if you're using them, or simply set full tiles into the corner. Snap each tile to its neighbors as you place it.

Option: If your layout calls for cut tiles along one edge of the patio, you can create a symmetrical layout by working outward from the center of the patio. Both side edges will have cut tiles of equal width. Snap a chalk line down the center of the patio slab, and lay the first rows of tiles along the chalk line.

3. Continue setting edge strips and full tiles, as needed, to cover the main portion of the patio.

Step B: Make a Template for Cutouts

To fit tiles around obstructions, make a cardboard template that matches the dimensions of an installed tile. Mark and cut the cardboard as needed until the template fits snugly around the obstruction.

Wood patio tiles are made of wood slats held together by an underlying plastic mat or internal tubing. The slats are affixed with screws or staples.

Tools & Materials Tape measure ▪ Jigsaw with down-cutting blade ▪ Sandpaper ▪ Cardboard. **For gravel-base Installation:** ▪ Supplies for site layout and preparation, as needed (page 80) ▪ Pea gravel ▪ Supplies for installing edging.

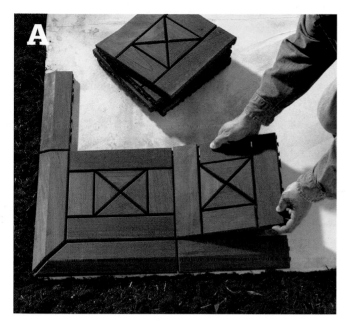

Lay tiles into a corner of the patio, starting with edging strips, if desired.

Step C: Cut Tiles & Complete the Installation

1. Using your cardboard template, trace the cutting lines onto the face (top surface) of a full tile.

2. Cut the tile on the face side, using a down-cutting blade to minimize splintering. If necessary, clamp the tile slats to your work surface to keep them in place during the cut.

3. On the underside of the cut tile, add corrosion-resistant screws to secure any loose slat ends to the support base. Sand any rough edges smooth for best appearance, and install the cut tile.

4. Complete the tile installation. Cut outer tiles as needed, using a jigsaw or handsaw.

Variation: Tiling Over a Gravel Base

To tile over loose material, purchase flexible tiles specific for this type of installation.

1. Lay out the patio site and excavate for a 2"-thick layer of pea gravel and the desired edging material.

2. Cover the excavated area with landscape fabric, overlapping strips of fabric by at least 6". Add a 2" layer of gravel, and prepare as recommended by the tile manufacturer. The gravel base must drain well to prevent standing water, which can damage the tiles.

3. Install edging material as desired. To avoid cutting tiles, you can complete the edging installation after laying all of the tiles.

4. Lay the tiles following the manufacturer's instructions.

Create a cardboard template for marking tile cuts to fit around obstructions.

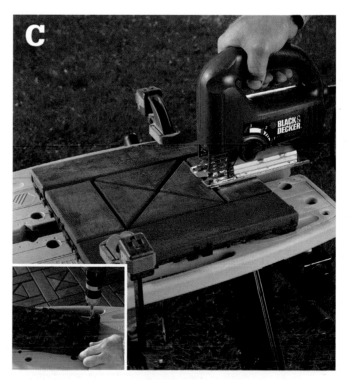

Cut tiles with a jigsaw, then secure the loose ends of slats with screws (inset).

Installing Edging

Edging can play many different roles in patio design. Its most practical purpose is containment, keeping the patio surface material in place so paving doesn't drift off into the yard. As a decorative feature, edging creates a visual border that adds a sense of order or closure to the patio space. This effect can be enhanced by edging with a material that contrasts with the patio surface or can be subdued by using the same material, perhaps in a slightly different pattern. Finally, edging can serve to strengthen the patio as a hard, protective curb that stands up to years of foot traffic.

The best time to install edging depends on your application. For sandset paver and loose material surfaces, edging is typically installed on top of the compacted gravel subbase. Edging along concrete slabs can be applied on top of the slab or along the sides, with the proper order determined by the finish materials.

To minimize the number of cuts required for paving, you can install edging after the patio surface is complete, or install two adjacent sides of edging to form a right angle, providing an accurate guide for starting the paver pattern; install the remaining two sides up against the laid pavers. Another option is to set up temporary edging, which can be easily moved, if necessary, and replace with the real thing when the paving is done.

How to Install "Invisible" Plastic Edging

Choose heavy-duty edging that's strong enough to contain patio materials. If your patio has curves, buy plenty of notched edging for the curves. Also buy 12"-long galvanized spikes—one for every 12" of edging, plus extra for curves.

Tools & Materials

Maul ▪ Tape measure ▪ Snips or saw (for cutting edging) ▪ Heavy-duty plastic edging ▪ 12" galvanized spikes.

1. After your gravel base is tamped, lay landscape fabric, and then set the edging on top of the fabric. Using your layout strings as guides, install the edging with spikes driven every 12" (or as recommended by the manufacturer). Measure down from the strings to make sure the edging is at the correct height. Along curves, spike the edging at every tab, or as recommended.

Option: On two or more sides of the patio, you can spike the edging minimally, in case you have to make adjustments. Anchor the edging completely after the paving is complete.

2. After installing the patio paving, cover the outside of the edging with soil and/or sod.

Secure the edging with spikes driven through the nailing tabs.

Lay sod or backfill behind edging to hide it from view.

How to Install Brick Paver Edging

Brick edging can be laid in several different configurations: on-end with its edge perpendicular to the patio surface (called "soldiers") (A); on-end with its face against the patio ("sailors") (B); or laid flat on its face or long edge, either parallel (C) or perpendicular (D) to the patio. For mortared patio surfaces, brick can be mortared to the edge of the slab for a decorative finish.

Here are the basic installation steps for non-mortared brick edging:

1. Excavate the patio site with a flat shovel to create a smooth, straight edge. The edge of the soil (and sod) will support the outsides of the pavers; the excavation should equal the dimensions of the finished patio. For an edging with bricks set upright, dig a narrow trench along the perimeter of the site, setting the depth so the tops of the edging bricks will be flush with the paving surface (or just above the surface for loose materials).

2. Install the gravel subbase and landscape fabric, as desired.

3. Set the edging bricks into the ground, using your layout strings to keep them in line and to check for the proper height. As you work, backfill behind the bricks with soil and tamp well to secure them in the trench. Tap the tops of the bricks with a rubber mallet and a short 2 × 4 to level them with one another.

Brick Edging Configurations

Brick soldier edging

Brick set on long edges

Brick set on faces, perpendicular or parallel to patio surface

Tools & Materials
Flat shovel ▪ Tape measure ▪ Rubber mallet ▪ 2 × 4 (about 12" long) ▪ Bricks.

A

Excavate the site carefully. Dig a trench for edging bricks installed on end.

B

Install edging along layout lines, setting them flush with a mallet and 2 × 4.

Variation: Using "Invisible" Plastic Edging

This is an easy and effective option for sandset paver patios: Install plastic edging, making sure the top of the edging will be below the top of the brick edging. Install the plastic edging on top of the compacted gravel base. Set brick edging along the inside of the plastic edging, following the basic sandset procedures. Cover the plastic edging with soil or sod after the paving is complete.

Variation: Plastic edging makes it easy to install a flat brick border for sandset patios.

How to Install Stone Edging

Cut stone or dressed stone makes better edging than flagstone, which often has jagged edges that create an uneven border. Semi-dressed stone, with one or more flat sides, is a good option for a more natural look.

1. Excavate the patio site, then dig a perimeter trench to accommodate the stone edging.

2. Add the gravel base and landscape fabric, as desired. Place each stone into the trench and tap it with a rubber mallet to set it into the gravel, then backfill behind the stone with soil to secure it. Use your layout strings to keep the edging in line and to measure for the proper height. Dress stones as needed to make a tight fit.

3. If desired, fill between stones with sand or soil to help lock them together.

Tools & Materials Tape measure ▪ Rubber mallet ▪ Stone cutting tools ▪ Garden spade ▪ Edging stones ▪ Sand.

Set the stones into the trench, using the layout strings for reference.

Fill behind set stones with soil, packing the stones firmly in place.

How To Install Concrete Curb Edging

Check with the local building department for requirements for concrete curbs. They can tell you how to build a curb that will stand up in your climate. A strong curb should be at least 4" thick and 6" or more wide, with internal reinforcement, such as rebar. Note: If the curb will abut a house wall or foundation, install an isolation membrane.

1. Build wood forms on top of a 4"-thick subbase of compacted gravel. Measure from your layout strings to the forms to make sure the forms are level and/or sloped as desired. Add metal reinforcement inside the forms, as recommended or required by the local building code.

2. Fill the forms with fiber-reinforced concrete, then screed the surface flush with the tops of the forms.

3. Float the concrete, then shape the edges with an edger, and finish the curb as desired. Cover the curb with plastic, and let the concrete cure for 1 week before removing the forms.

Tools & Materials Supplies for wood forms
▪ Tools for mixing and finishing concrete ▪ Metal reinforcement ▪ Fiber-reinforced concrete ▪ Plastic sheeting.

Build wood forms and add rebar to strengthen the curb.

Float the top of the curb with a concrete float, and finish the surface as desired.

Cut timbers to length with a reciprocating saw and long blade (or other saw).

Anchor the timbers to the ground with ½" rebar driven with a maul or sledgehammer.

How to Install Timber Edging

Pressure-treated landscape timbers or cedar timbers make attractive, durable edging that's easy to install. Square-edged timbers are best for geometric pavers like brick and cut stone, while loose materials and natural flagstone look good with rounded or squared timbers. Choose one of the standard sizes (4 × 4 or 4 × 6) depending on how bold you want the border to look.

1. Excavate the patio site, then dig a perimeter trench for the timbers so they will install flush with the top of the patio surface (or just above the surface for loose material).

2. Add the compacted gravel base over the site, including a 2" to 4" layer in the perimeter trench.

3. Cut timbers to the desired length, using a reciprocating saw and long, wood-cutting blade or a circular saw or handsaw. Drill ½" holes through each timber; close the ends and every 24" in between. Cut a length of ½"-diameter (#4) rebar at 24" for each hole, using a reciprocating saw and metal-cutting blade.

4. Set the timbers in the trench and make sure they lie flat. Use your layout strings as guides for leveling and setting the height of the timbers. Anchor the timbers with the rebar, driving the bar flush with the wood surface.

Tools&Materials
Maul ▪ Reciprocating saw with wood-cutting and metal-cutting blades ▪ Power drill and ½" bit ▪ Landscape timbers (pressure-treated or rot-resistant species only) ▪ ½" (#4) rebar.

How to Install Lumber Edging

Dimension lumber makes for an inexpensive edging material and a less-massive alternative to landscape timbers. 2 × 4 or 2 × 6 lumber works well for most patios. Use only pressure-treated lumber rated for ground contact or all-heart redwood or cedar boards to prevent rot. For the stakes, use pressure-treated lumber, since they will be buried anyway.

1. Excavate the patio site, then dig a perimeter trench for the boards so they will install flush with the top of the patio surface (or just above the surface for loose material). Dig the trench a few inches wider than the finished patio edge to provide room the edging stakes.

2. Add the compacted gravel base over the site, including a 2" to 4" layer in the perimeter trench.

3. Cut the edging boards to length, using a circular saw or handsaw. Whenever possible, use full-length pieces to avoid butt joints. Seal cut ends with wood preservative. Cut 2 × 4 stakes to length, and then cut one end to a point. The stakes should be about 16" or so; make them longer if they drive into the ground too easily or shorter if they're too hard to drive.

4. Stake the edging boards in the trench close to the ends of each board and every 24" in between. Drive the stakes below the top edge of the board. Fasten the boards to the stakes with pairs of 2½" deck screws. Fasten edging boards together with screws where they meet at corners and butt joints. Use your layout strings as guides for leveling and setting the height of the edging.

5. Backfill behind the edging to support the boards and hide the stakes.

Tools & Materials Circular saw ▪ Power drill ▪ 2× lumber for edging ▪ 2 × 4 lumber for stakes ▪ Wood preservative ▪ 2½" galvanized deck screws.

Set the edging boards in place, and then drive stakes below the tops of the boards.

Secure the edging boards to the stakes at the desired height.

Projects: Finishing Touches

Accessories and amenities—such as fire pits, fountains, and walls or overheads—not only enhance the usefulness of a patio, but they are powerful design tools that can help establish a sense of scale and space. This chapter includes several projects designed to make the most of your new living space. You can customize the final design by choosing the materials and finishing techniques, thus making the projects unique for your patio.

Here's a quick preview of the projects to consider:

In This Chapter

- Raised Garden Bed
- Fire Pit
- Wall Fountain
- Cobblestone Fountain
- Brick Wall
- Mortarless Block Wall
- Patio Arbor
- Trees

Raised Garden Bed

A small garden bed right on, or next to, your patio makes a handy place for growing herbs or the perfect spot for brightening the space with seasonal flowers. It's a spectacular dinner party display that allows guests to pick fresh vegetables or herbs during patio dining.

The garden bed in this project has no bottom, allowing water to drain into the soil (or excavated patio) below. If you're incorporating the bed into your patio surface, install the bed before the surface. If you're locating the bed out in the yard, it will probably be easier to build the bed after completing the patio, so the bed won't be in the way during the paving process.

When properly built and filled with quality top-soil, this flowerbed makes growing healthy plants practically foolproof. Consider the types of plants you want to grow and the amount of sunlight they need. Vegetables and most flowers need 6 to 8 hours of full sun during the day. If your patio area doesn't have that much sun, plant it with woodland and other shade-loving plants. For planting shrubs or vegetables, install landscape fabric (Step C, page 171) along only the sides of the bed, since these plants typically have deeper roots than flowers. And for herbs, use a rich soil filled with peat and fill in around the herbs with wood chips or other mulch.

Tools & Materials Tape measure ▪ Mason's string ▪ Hammer ▪ Shovel ▪ Wheelbarrow ▪ Reciprocating saw with wood-cutting blade ▪ Level ▪ Power drill with 3⁄16" and 1⁄2" bits ▪ Stakes ▪ 8 ft. 4 x 4 cedar timbers (6) ▪ 6" galvanized nails ▪ Wood sealer/protectant ▪ Landscape fabric ▪ Galvanized roofing nails ▪ Topsoil ▪ Mulch.

Use a shovel to remove the grass inside the outline, and then dig a trench for the first row of timbers.

How to Build a Raised Garden Bed

Step A: Prepare the Site

1. Outline a 5-ft. × 3-ft. area with stakes and string to mark the location of the bed. Use a shovel to remove all of the grass or weeds inside the area.

2. Dig a flat 2"-deep, 6"-wide trench around the perimeter of the area, just inside the stakes.

Step B: Build & Level the Base

1. Measure and mark one 54" piece and one 30" piece on each 4 × 4. Hold each timber steady on saw-horses while you cut it, using a reciprocating saw.

2. Coat each timber with a wood sealer/protectant. Let the sealer dry completely.

3. Lay the first row of timbers in the trench. Position a level diagonally across a corner, then add or remove soil to level it. Repeat with remaining corners.

4. Set the second layer of timbers in place, staggering the joints with the joint pattern in the first layer.

5. Drill 3⁄16" pilot holes near the ends of the timbers, and then drive in the galvanized barn nails.

Step C: Complete the Raised Bed

1. Lay the third row of timbers, repeating the pattern of the first row to stagger the joints.

2. Drill pilot holes through the third layer, offsetting them to avoid hitting the underlying nails. Drive the nails through the pilot holes.

3. Drill 1⁄2" drainage holes, spaced every 2 ft., horizontally through the bottom layer of timbers.

4. Line the bed with strips of landscape fabric, overlapping the strips by 6".

5. Drive galvanized roofing nails through the fabric, attaching it to the timbers.

Step D: Fill with Soil & Plants

1. Fill the bed with topsoil to within 4" of the top. Tamp the soil lightly with a shovel.

2. Add plants, loosening their root balls before planting. Apply a 3" layer of mulch, and water the plants.

Level timbers in the trench, then lay the next layer, staggering the joints. Drill holes and drive nails through them.

Place the third layer of landscape timbers over the second, staggering the joints. Secure the timbers in place with nails. Drill 1⁄2" drainage holes through the bottom row of the timbers. Line the bed with landscape fabric.

Fill the bed with topsoil, and then plant your garden. Apply a 3" layer of mulch, and water the garden.

Fire Pit

This fire pit creates a unique space for enjoying fun and safe recreational fires. When determining the location for your pit, choose a spot on your patio with plenty of room for people to sit and enjoy the fire without interfering with traffic flow around the pit. If your pit will be set aside from the patio, find a spot where the ground is relatively flat and even. Some municipal codes require a buffer zone of at least 25 ft. from your home, garage, shed, or any other fixed, combustible structures in your yard. Also make sure to have a garden hose or other extinguishing device accessible at the location.

In this project, two courses of 6" manhole block are used to create a fire pit with a 26" interior diameter, ideal for backyard settings within city limits. Manhole blocks are designed specifically to create rounded tunnels and walls and can be purchased from most concrete block manufacturers.

Three ¾" gaps have been factored into this design to act as air vents, allowing the natural airflow to stoke the fire. This layout makes the circumference of the second course roughly ½" smaller than the first. A slightly thicker layer of surface-bonding cement is added to the top course to make up the difference.

Surface-bonding cement starts out as a white paste and can be tinted to match or complement any color of capstone. The 8 × 16" landscape pavers used here are cut at angles to allow ten pieces to fit around the rim of the fire pit (see illustration on page 173).

There are usually heavy restrictions for fire pits within city limits, regarding pit size, seasonal burning, waste burning, and more. Many municipalities also require that you purchase a recreational burning permit issued by an inspector from the fire department. Check with your local building department or restrictions specific to your area.

When not in use or during winter months, you may want to cover the top of the fire pit to prevent damage that may occur in inclement weather.

Note: It is important to allow your fire pit to cure for at least 30 days before building a fire in it. Heat can cause concrete with a high moisture content to greatly expand and contract, causing the material to severely crack or fragment.

Tools & Materials
Hammer or hand maul ▪ Tape measure ▪ Shovel ▪ Hand tamp ▪ Wheelbarrow or mixing box ▪ Mason's trowel ▪ Spray bottle ▪ Jointing tool ▪ Square-end trowel ▪ Tuck-point trowel ▪ Circular saw with an abrasive masonry blade ▪ Eye & ear protection ▪ Wire brush ▪ 2 x 2 wooden stakes (2) ▪ Mason's string ▪ Spray paint ▪ Compactible gravel ▪ 60 lbs. of concrete (12) ▪ Sheet plastic ▪ 6" manhole blocks ▪ ¼" wood spacers (3) ▪ Chalk ▪ Refractory mortar ▪ Surface-bonding cement ▪ Mortar tinting agent ▪ ½" plywood ▪ 8 x 16" landscape pavers (10).

How to Build a Fire Pit

Step A: Excavate the Site

1. Use a hammer or a hand maul to drive a wooden stake into the centerpoint of the planned fire pit location. Then drive a temporary stake into the ground 10½" from the center stake.

2. Tie a mason's string to the center stake—the string should be just long enough to reach the temporary stake. Hold or tie a can of spray paint to the end of the string. Pull the string taut and spray paint a circle on the ground.

3. Remove the temporary stake and drive it into the ground 22½" from the center stake. Pull the string taut, and spray a second circle on the ground.

4. Strip away the grass between the two circles, and dig a trench 10" deep.

5. Fill the base of the trench with 2" compactible gravel. Tamp the gravel thoroughly.

Step B: Pour the Footing

1. Mix concrete in a wheelbarrow or mixing box and shovel it into the trench until the concrete reaches ground level. Work the concrete with a shovel to remove any air pockets.

2. Screed the surface of the concrete by dragging a short 2 × 4 along the top of the natural form. Add concrete to any low areas and screed the surface again. Finish the concrete by smoothing the surface level with a trowel.

3. When the concrete is hard to the touch, cover it with a sheet of plastic and let it cure for 2 to 3 days. Remove the plastic and let the concrete cure for an additional week.

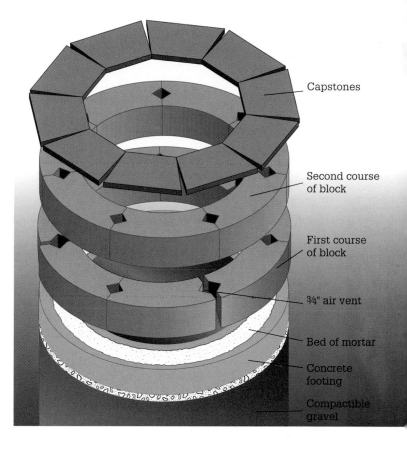

Capstones

Second course of block

First course of block

¾" air vent

Bed of mortar

Concrete footing

Compactible gravel

Outline the location of the footing using spray paint and a piece of string. Then dig a circular trench 10" deep.

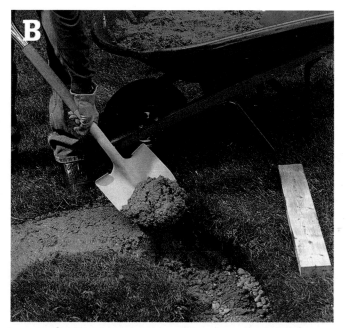

After tamping a 2" layer of compactible gravel in the bottom of the trench, fill with concrete and screed it with a scrap of 2 × 4. Float the surface with a trowel.

Step C: Lay the First Course

1. When the concrete has sufficiently cured, strip away the grass inside the circle and fill it with compactible gravel. Lay out the first course of 6" manhole blocks with three ¾" gaps for air vents, using ¾" wood spacers.

2. Mark the internal and external circumference of the first course on the footing with chalk, and remove the blocks. Take note of any low or high spots on the footing, remembering that low spots can be leveled out with extra mortar at the base.

3. Mix a batch of refractory mortar and lightly mist the footing area with water. Throw a bed of mortar on the misted area, covering only the area inside the reference lines.

4. Set a manhole block into the bed of mortar, centering it on the footing and the chalk reference lines. Press the block into the mortar until the joint is approximately ⅜" thick. Place the second block directly against the first block with no spacing between the blocks and press it in place until the tops of the blocks are flush. Use a scrap of 2 × 4 to help you position the tops of the blocks evenly along the first course.

5. Continue laying the blocks, making sure the spaces for the three air vents are correctly positioned with the ¾" wood scraps. Do not allow the wood spacers to become set in the mortar.

6. Continue laying blocks until the first course is set. Remove any excess mortar with a trowel and finish the joints with a jointing tool. Fill the hollows between the butted blocks (not the air vents) with mortar.

Step D: Lay the Second Course

Dry-lay the second course of blocks over the first, offsetting the layout of the joints between the blocks. Note: Because of the air vents in the first course, the second course is slightly smaller in diameter. When laying the second course, line up the internal edges of the blocks, leaving a slight lip along the outer edge.

Step E: Apply Surface-bonding Cement

1. Mix a small batch of surface-bonding cement according to the manufacturer's instructions. Add a mortar-tinting agent, if desired.

2. Mist the blocks of the fire pit with water. Apply the surface-bonding cement to the exterior of the fire pit walls using a square-end trowel. Make up the difference in diameter between the two courses with a thicker coating of surface-bonding cement inside the edges of the air vents. Do not cover the air vents completely with surface-bonding cement.

3. Use a wet trowel to smooth the surface to create the texture of your choice. Rinse the trowel frequently, keeping it clean and wet.

Mist the footing with water and spread a bed of mortar inside the reference lines. Place the blocks of the first course in position, with three ¾" spacers in the course to create air vents.

Dry-lay the second course of block ⅜" from the outside edge of the first course.

Mist the surface of the walls and apply surface-bonding cement with a square-end trowel. Use more surface-bonding cement on the second course to even out the gap between the courses.

Lay a bed of mortar on top of the second course and set the capstones into place, maintaining a uniform overhang.

Step F: Install the Capstones

1. Make a capstone template from ½" plywood, following the illustration (right). Use the template to mark ten 8 × 16" landscape pavers to the capstone dimensions.

2. Cut the pavers to size using a circular saw with an abrasive masonry blade and a cold chisel. When cutting brick with a masonry blade, make several shallow passes, and always wear ear and eye protection. Refer to pages 97 to 98 for techniques on building with brick.

3. Mist the top of the fire pit with water. Mix a batch of mortar and fill in any block hollows, then throw a bed of mortar along the top of the second course.

4. Butter the leading edge of each capstone, and position it on the mortar bed so the front edges overhang the interior diameter of the manhold block by roughly ⅛". Adjust the capstones as you work so the joints are ⅜"-thick and evenly overhang the exterior edge of the pit. Also make sure the entire layer is even and level. Tool the joints as you work.

5. Use a jointing tool to smooth mortar joints within 30 minutes. Cut away any excess mortar pressed from the joints with a trowel. When the mortar is set, but not too hard, brush away excess mortar from the faces of the capstones with a wire brush.

6. Allow the fire pit to cure for 30 days before its first use.

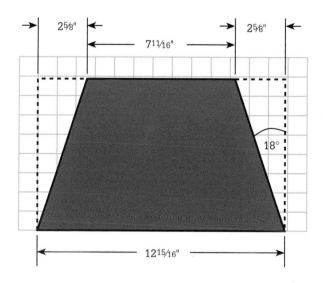

Wall Fountain

Wall fountains have graced patios and private gardens since antiquity. Today, fountains can be purchased as compact, all-in-one units that simply hang on a wall. But this project shows you how to create your own custom water feature, complete with a fountainhead or other statuary, a decorative spill basin, and a hidden reservoir. The tube that circulates the water is also hidden, so the fountain's stream appears to issue magically from an unknown source. By choosing your own decorative pieces and materials, your fountain will become a unique and personal patio accent. Traditional fountain masks and wall-mountable statuary are available at garden centers and specialty dealers in several materials, such as stone, metal, terra-cotta, concrete, fiberglass, and resin.

The secret to this wall fountain is the water tube that runs from the pump to the fountainhead. A free-standing garden wall or low patio wall makes it easy to conceal the tube by running it behind the wall. If you're mounting to a house wall with traditional clapboard or other wood siding, you can thread the tube up through the wall cavity behind the siding using an electrician's fish tape (see Step C, on page 178). A masonry house wall is more difficult. However, a garage wall with any type of exterior finish is usually a convenient location, because you can run the hose into the garage, up the wall, then outside again. When it's impractical to run the water tube inside or behind the wall, you can simply attach it to the face of the wall, and then hide it behind plants or vines. A small trellis covered with vines makes an especially attractive camouflage.

Where you mount the fountainhead depends on your personal design and the fountain equipment. It's a good idea to mock up the installation and run the pump to test the trajectory of the water stream. This will give you an idea of how high to mount the fountainhead and how far from the wall to locate the basin assembly. To minimize splashing, it's recommended that you mount the fountainhead no higher than a distance equal to the diameter of the spill basin. Be sure to choose a water pump with an adjustable flow rate, so you can fine-tune the stream after the fountain is installed. Note: The pump must be plugged into a GFCI outlet.

Tools & Materials
Tape measure ▪ Shovel ▪ Level ▪ Permanent marker ▪ Jigsaw with metal-cutting blade ▪ Metal file ▪ Power drill and bit ▪ Plastic reservoir basin ▪ Submersible pump with adjustable flow ▪ 9-gauge galvanized expanded metal mesh ▪ Flexible plastic or rubber water tubing ▪ Mask or statuary for fountainhead, plus mounting hardware ▪ Spill basin (must be rustproof) ▪ Decorative stones.

How to Build a Wall Fountain

Step A: Install the Reservoir Basin

Note: Select a reservoir basin that is deep enough to completely submerge the pump and is several inches larger in diameter than the spill basin. A sturdy plastic tub with a rigid rim is ideal; the rim can serve as a border for containing the surrounding paving materials.

1. Dig a hole for the basin at the desired distance from the wall. Level and smooth the bottom of the hole so the basin sits perfectly flat and level.

2. Set the basin in the hole and check it for level. Add soil or sand beneath the basin; adjust its height and correct for level.

Step B: Prepare the Mesh Screen

1. Cut a single piece of 9-gauge galvanized expanded metal mesh (available at home centers and steel yards) to fit neatly around the outside of the rim of the reservoir basin. Mark the mesh for cutting with a permanent marker, then make the cut with a jigsaw or bolt cutters.

2. Test-fit the mesh on the basin. At the point closest to the fountain wall, mark the locations for holes in the mesh for running the water tube and pump power cord; if practical, use one hole for both. Cut the hole(s) and file any rough edges smooth to prevent damage to the tube or cord.

Step C: Install the Water Tube

1. Mark a hole for the water tube near the bottom of the fountain wall, making sure the hole is aligned with the center of the reservoir basin.

Note: For brick wall surfaces, the holes must fall in the center of mortar joints; drilling into brick faces is likely to cause cracking.

2. Measure up from the top of the basin and mark a second hole at the point where the tube will enter the back of the fountainhead. Use a level to make sure the two holes are perfectly aligned.

3. Drill the holes, using a bit that's slightly larger than the water tube. Use a hammer drill and masonry bit for drilling into mortar; use a standard drill and bit for wood surfaces.

Note: If you're drilling into a garage wall, you may want to enlarge the lower hole—or make another hole—for running the power cord into the garage.

4. Feed the water tube through the holes, leaving plenty of slack at both ends.

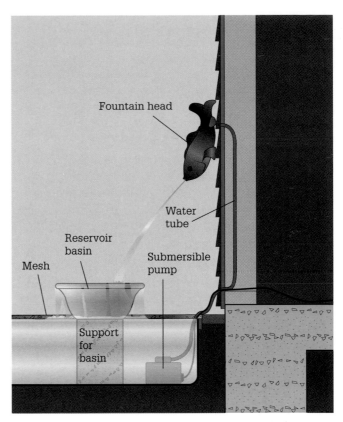

This simple wall fountain requires a reservoir basin, a submersible pump with adjustable flow, mesh, and rubber water tubing to cycle the water. The details can all be customized. In our project, we purchased a ceramic statue and drilled a hole for the water tube. We also chose to use a shallow reservoir basin, and place patio pavers above water level.

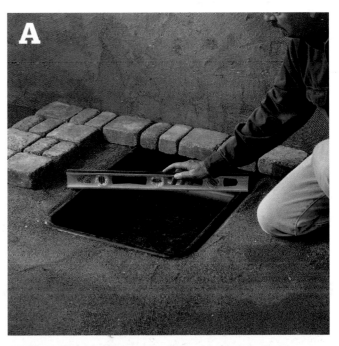

Set the reservoir basin in the hole and check for level.

Variation: To run the tube inside a wall cavity, feed the end of a fish tape (or a straightened coat hanger) down through the upper hole. Use a wire hook or needlenose pliers to retrieve the end from the lower hole. Tape the water tube to the fish tape, and pull the tube up through the wall.

Step D: Mount the Fountainhead

1. Position the fountainhead where it will be installed and mark the wall for mounting hardware, as needed. Install mounting hardware, following the manufacturer's instructions.

2. Trim the water tube to the proper length. Fit the end of the tube into the fountainhead, and then mount the fountainhead as directed.

Step E: Set the Spill Basin & Adjust the Water Flow

1. Measure the distance between the bottom of the reservoir basin and the top of the basin's rim. Cut concrete blocks or stack bricks as needed to create a stable support base for the spill basin. The support base should be level with the top of the reservoir basin.

2. Center the support base in the reservoir basin, then place the water pump into the basin in its final position. Trim the water tube as needed and attach it to the pump outlet as directed by the pump manufacturer.

3. Set the spill basin on top of its support base—without the metal screen—making

sure the spill basin is centered over the reservoir basin.

4. Fill the reservoir basin with water. Plug the pump into a GFCI outlet, and run the pump for a few seconds while you check the water stream; the stream should land near the center of the spill basin. Adjust the pump's flow rate as needed, then turn off the pump.

Step F: Complete the Fountain

1. Remove the spill basin. Set the metal screen in place on top of the reservoir basin, then reposition the spill basin on top of the screen, centered over the reservoir basin, as before.

2. Fill both basins with water so that the reservoir basin maintains a sufficient water level for proper pump operation. Run the pump for a while to make sure the water level is correct.

Note: To protect young children from a drowning hazard, you can fill the spill basin with stones, up to or just below the water level at the top of the basin.

3. Complete the patio paving as needed to conceal the rim of the reservoir basin. Cover the metal screen with a layer of decorative stones to complete the fountain installation.

4. As you use the fountain, check the water level frequently and top off as needed to compensate for water loss due to evaporation and splashing.

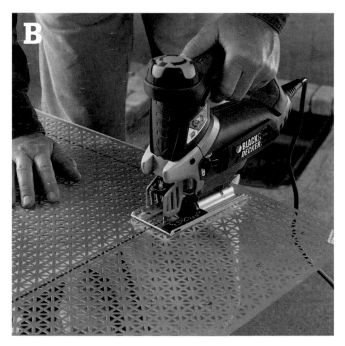

Cut the metal mesh to fit over the top of the reservoir basin, using a jigsaw.

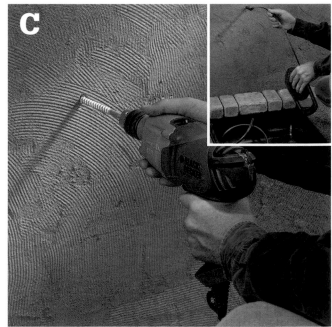

Drill holes for the water supply tube. Use a fish tape to thread tubing inside a framed wall cavity (inset).

(Top left) **Secure the fountainhead** to the wall, following the manufacturer's directions.

(Top right) **Complete the basin assembly** and test the fountain before covering the screen with stones.

(Left) **Adjust the flow rate** until the stream lands near the center of the spill basin.

Cobblestone Fountain

A cobblestone fountain, which is typically set flush with a paved surface, is attractive when the water isn't running and delightful when it is. The simple design of this fountain makes it easy to build into a sandset or loose material patio surface or into the surrounding grass for an appealing focal point that doesn't take up patio space. Tucked into a corner and surrounded by moss or other ground covers, the fountain becomes an oasis for the eyes and the ears.

The water basin of the fountain is a standard 5-gallon bucket. But any watertight plastic vessel at least 12" in diameter and 15" deep will work. To protect children and animals, you must cover the opening of the basin with a sturdy grate. This project calls for 9-gauge expanded metal mesh, which is available at some building centers or at any steel yard.

The cobblestone surface could be cut stone, smooth river rock, or even brick—whatever works with your patio setting. To eliminate weeds and help keep debris out of the basin, cover the excavated area with landscape fabric. Set the pump on bricks to keep it above the floor of the basin and out of residue that will collect there. The pump must be plugged into a GFCI outlet.

Tools & Materials

Shovel ▪ Tape measure ▪ Level ▪ Bolt cutters ▪ Metal file ▪ Hand tamp ▪ Plastic bucket or tub ▪ Sand ▪ Gravel ▪ Bricks (2) ▪ Submersible pump with telescoping delivery pipe ▪ Landscape fabric ▪ 9-gauge ¾" expanded metal mesh, 30 x 36" ▪ 6" paving stones, (approximately 35) ▪ Plants and decorative stones, as desired.

Of course, cobblestone is not the only surface layer suitable for this type of fountain. With strong mesh and tightly woven landscape fabric, there are many pebbles or crushed decorative materials that make lovely fountain coverings. You may need an extra layer of landscape fabric on top of the mesh to prevent pebbles from falling through the mesh.

How to Build a Cobblestone Fountain

Step A: Dig the Hole & Test-fit the Basin

1. Begin digging a hole 2" to 3" wider than the diameter of the bucket or tub you selected for the basin of the fountain. Keep the edges of the hole fairly straight and the bottom fairly level.

2. Measure the height of the basin, add the height of the paving stones you've chosen, and then add 4" to this total. When the hole is approximately as deep as this combined measurement, test-fit the basin and check it with a level. Remove dirt from the hole until the basin is as close as possible to level.

Step B: Dig the Paving Area

1. Cut out the grass or soil in a 30 × 36" rectangle surrounding the hole. To bring the surface of the fountain to ground level, dig this area 2" deeper than the height of the paving stones.

2. Spread sand over the paving area, and then dampen and tamp the sand. Continue adding and tamping the sand until you've created a level 2" layer over the entire area.

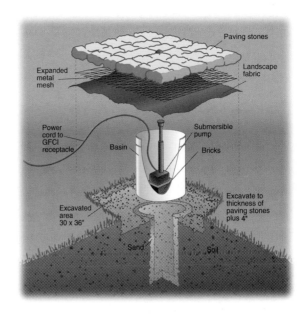

Dig out a 30 × 36" rectangle surrounding the hole, digging 2" deeper than the height of the paving stones.

Dig a hole approximately as deep as the combined height of the basin and the paving stones plus 4".

Step C: Position the Basin

1. Add about 3" of gravel to the hole, and then add a 3" layer of sand. Dampen and tamp the sand; then test-fit the basin again. Adjust until the top of the basin is level with the prepared paving area.

2. Fill the edges of the hole with gravel and/or sand to hold the basin firmly in place.

Step D: Install the Pump & the Gate

1. Clean out any sand or dirt, and then put 2 clean bricks on the bottom of the basin. Center the pump on top of the bricks, then extend the electrical cord up over the edge of the basin and out to the nearest GFCI receptacle.

2. Lay landscape fabric over the paving area. Extend the fabric over the edges of the basin by 5" or 6", and then trim it to shape.

Step E: Fill the Basin & Adjust the Flow Valve

Fill the basin with water. Turn on the pump and adjust the flow valve, following manufacturer's instructions. Adjust and test until the bubbling effect or spray appeals to you. (Keep in mind that the fountain's basic dimensions will be somewhat different when the paving stones are in place.)

Step F: Add the Paving Stones

1. Place the grate over the paving area, making sure the water delivery tube fits cleanly through an opening in the grate. If necessary, use bolt cutters and a metal file to enlarge the opening.

2. Put the paving stones in place, setting them in evenly spaced rows. Be sure to leave an area open around the water delivery pipe so the water has room to bubble up around the stones and then return to the basin.

Step G: Camouflage the Pump's Electrical Cord

Place plants and stones at the edge of the fountain to disguise the electrical cord as it exits the basin and runs toward the nearest GFCI receptacle.

(Above) Add a layer of gravel and then sand, tamping and adding sand until the top of the basin is level with the paving area.

(Right) Place the pump in the bucket, centered on the bricks. Position the electrical cord to run up and out of the hole.

Fill the basin with water and adjust the flow valve on the pump to create a pleasing effect.

Position the grate, and then set the paving stones in place. Be sure to leave space for water to recirculate between the stones.

Arrange plants and stones to disguise the electrical cord as it runs to the nearest GFCI receptacle.

Brick Wall

The ancient technique of bricklaying can be used to create numerous patio accessories—from accent walls to planters to decorative columns or pedestals. This project shows you the steps for building a low brick wall, but you can adapt the basic technique to build other structures.

Because this wall is freestanding, it's built with "double-wythe construction" (with two layers of brick tied together) for added support. Planters and other square or rectangular features are often built with single-wythe walls.

All brick structures must be built upon a solid concrete footing or an acceptable concrete slab. After jotting down some ideas or drawing up plans for your brick project, consult with your local building department to learn about footings and other structural requirements. Keep in mind that walls and other structures are often allowed more design flexibility (that is, fewer restrictions) when they're kept below a certain height, usually 3 ft.

How to Build a Brick Wall

Step A: Establish the Layout

1. Dry-lay the first course of brick by setting down two parallel rows of brick, spaced ¾" to 1" apart.

2. Snap chalk lines to outline the location of the wall on the footing (or slab). Draw pencil lines on the footing to mark the ends of the bricks.

3. Test-fit the spacing with a ⅜"-diameter dowel, then mark the locations of the joint gaps to use for reference after the spacers are removed. Note: ⅜" mortar joints are standard; if your bricks are sized for a different size of mortar joint, use the appropriate spacing.

Tools & Materials Tape measure ▪ Pencil ▪ Chalk line ▪ Mason's trowel ▪ Tools for mixing mortar ▪ Tools for cutting brick ▪ Level ▪ Mason's string and line blocks ▪ Jointing tool ▪ Brush ▪ ⅜" wood dowels ▪ Bricks ▪ Mortar ▪ Corrugated metal wall ties ▪ Top cap blocks.

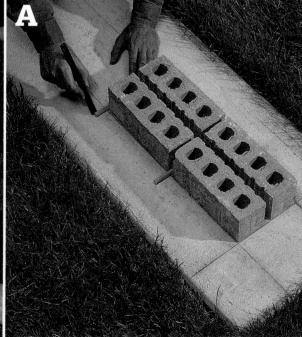

Step B: Lay the First Brick

1. Mix a batch of mortar for the first section of brick. Note: Use a mortar type recommended for your type of brick and your climate. Type N mortar is standard for freestanding, non-load-bearing walls.

2. Dampen the concrete slab with water. Using a mason's trowel, throw a layer of mortar onto the slab for the first two bricks of one wythe, starting at one end of the wall layout.

3. Butter the inside end of the first brick (page 100), then press the brick into the mortar, creating a ⅜" mortar bed. Cut away excess mortar, using the trowel.

Step C: Adjust the First Brick

1. Plumb the face of the end brick, using a level. Tap lightly with the handle of the trowel to adjust the brick if it is not plumb.

2. Level the brick end-to-end, and adjust as needed by tapping with the trowel.

Step D: Begin the Second Wythe

1. Butter the end of a second brick, then set it into the mortar bed, pushing the dry end toward the first brick to create a joint of ⅜".

2. Butter and place a third brick, using the chalk line for reference. Check all of the laid bricks for plumb and level, and adjust as needed.

3. Lay the first three bricks of the second wythe parallel to the first wythe.

4. Level across the wythes, and make sure the end bricks and mortar joints are aligned. Fill the gap between the end bricks with mortar.

(Opposite) Determine the layout of the wall by dry-laying the first course of bricks.

(Top) Set the first brick into the mortar, then remove excess to prevent a buildup behind the wall.

(Middle) Tap the brick lightly with the trowel handle until it is perfectly plumb and level.

(Bottom) Set each new brick into the buttered end of the preceding brick (inset). Check both wythes for level.

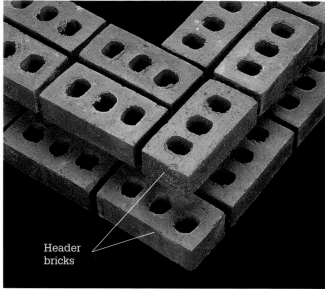

Header
bricks

(Top left) Start with half-bricks on alternate courses to create a running bond pattern.

(Top right) Variation: Use alternating header bricks to cap off the ends of the wythes at wall corners.

(Above) Check the ends of the courses with a straightedge to ensure consistent mortar joints.

Step E: Build Up the Wall End

1. Cut a half-brick, then throw and furrow a mortar bed for the half-brick on top of the first course.

2. Butter the end of the half-brick, then set it into the mortar bed, creating a ⅜" joint. Cut away excess mortar. Make sure the bricks are plumb and level.

3. Add more bricks and half-bricks to both wythes at the end until you lay the first bricks in the fourth course. Align bricks with the chalk lines.

Variation: Building Corners

To build corners, lay a header brick at the end of two parallel wythes. Position the header brick in each subsequent course perpendicular to the header brick in the preceding course.

Step F: Check the Alignment of Courses

Check the spacing of the bricks at the wall end, using a level or straightedge. Properly spaced bricks will form a straight line when you place the straightedge over the stepped end bricks. If the bricks are not in alignment, do not move those bricks already set. Instead, try to compensate for the problem gradually as you fill in the middle (field) bricks by slightly reducing or increasing the width of the mortar joints.

Step G: Tool the Mortar Joints

1. Every 30 minutes, stop laying bricks and smooth out all untooled mortar joints with a jointing tool. Complete the horizontal joints first, then the vertical joints.

2. Cut away any excess mortar pressed from the joints, using a trowel.

3. When the mortar has set, but is not too hard, brush away any excess mortar from the brick faces.

Step H: Build the Other Wall End & Lay the Field Bricks

1. Build the opposite end of the wall following the same procedure used for the first wall end. Use the chalk lines for reference.

2. Stretch a mason's string between the two wall ends to establish a flush, level line between the ends—use line blocks to secure the string, tightening the string until it is taut.

3. Begin to fill in the field bricks of the first course, using the mason's string as a guide.

4. Lay the remaining field bricks. Before laying the last brick, called the closure brick, butter it at both ends. Center the closure brick between the two adjoining bricks, then adjust it as needed with the trowel handle.

5. Fill in the first three courses of each wythe, moving the mason's string up one course after completing each course.

Step I: Tie the Wythes Together

In the fourth course, set corrugated metal wall ties into the mortar bed of one wythe and on top of the brick adjacent to it. Space the ties 2 to 3 ft. apart, and install them every 3 courses.

Option: For added strength, set metal rebar into the cavities between the wythes, and fill in between the wythes with thin mortar.

Step J: Complete the Wall

1. Lay the remaining courses, installing metal ties every third course. Check against the mason's string frequently for alignment, and use the level and trowel to make sure the wall is plumb and level.

2. Lay a furrowed mortar bed on the top course, and place a wall cap to finish the top of the wall and cover the cavity between the wythes. Remove any excess mortar. Make sure the cap blocks are aligned and level.

3. Fill the joints between the cap blocks with mortar.

Line block

Metal wall tie

(Above left) Tool the joints with a jointing tool, then remove spilled mortar from the brick faces.

(Above right) Stretch a mason's string between the wall ends, using line blocks (inset). Butter both ends of the closure brick before setting them.

(Bottom left) Tie the wythes together every three courses, using metal wall ties.

(Bottom right) Cover the top of the wall with cap blocks for a finished appearance.

Mortarless Block Wall

Far from an ordinary concrete block wall, this tile-topped mortarless block wall offers the advantages of concrete block—affordability and durability—as well as a dramatic touch of style. Color is the magic ingredient. Tint added to the surface-bonding cement produces a buttery-yellow that contrasts beautifully with the cobalt blue tile. Of course, you can use any color combination that matches or complements your patio setting.

Mortarless block walls are simple to build. You set the first course in mortar on a concrete footing and stack the subsequent courses in a running bond pattern, without mortar between the blocks. The wall gets its strength from a coating of surface-bonding cement that's applied to the exposed surface. Tests have shown that the bond created in this type of construction is just as strong as traditional block-and-mortar walls.

In this project, the wall is 24" tall and uses 3 courses of standard 8 × 8 × 16" concrete blocks and 8 × 12" ceramic tiles for the top cap, with bullnose tiles to finish the edges. When selecting tile, be sure to get durable exterior ceramic tile, thinset exterior tile mortar, and exterior tile grout.

The footing below the wall must be twice as wide as the wall and extend at least 12" beyond each end. Consult with your local building department to learn about footing size and depth, maximum wall height, and other structural requirements for this type of wall. You may also be allowed to build the wall on top of an approved concrete slab. If you're integrating the wall with a new patio surface, plan the wall according to your surface material. For sandset paving and loose materials, build the wall before laying the patio surface. For a concrete slab, build the wall on top of or next to the slab—check the building code for slab requirements.

Tools & Materials Stakes & mason's string ▪ Hammer ▪ Line level ▪ Tape measure ▪ Shovel ▪ Wheelbarrow or mortar box ▪ Hand maul ▪ Hand tamp ▪ 4-ft. level ▪ Hacksaw ▪ Chalk line ▪ Circular saw with masonry-cutting blade ▪ Masonry chisel ▪ Line blocks ▪ Mason's trowel ▪ Notched trowel ▪ Square-end trowel ▪ Groover ▪ Tile cutter ▪ Caulk gun ▪ Rubber grout float ▪ Sponge ▪ Small paintbrush ▪ Compactible gravel ▪ 2 x 4s for footings ▪ #3 rebar ▪ 16-gauge wire ▪ Vegetable oil or release agent ▪ Cement mix ▪ Sheet plastic ▪ Concrete blocks (end, half, & stretcher) ▪ Type N mortar ▪ Corrugated metal tiles ▪ Wire mesh ▪ Surface-bonding cement ▪ Fortified thinset exterior mortar ▪ 8 x 12" ceramic tile rated for exterior use ▪ Matching bullnose tile ▪ Tile spacers ▪ Sand-mix exterior grout ▪ Silicone caulk ▪ Grout sealer.

How to Build a Mortarless Block Wall

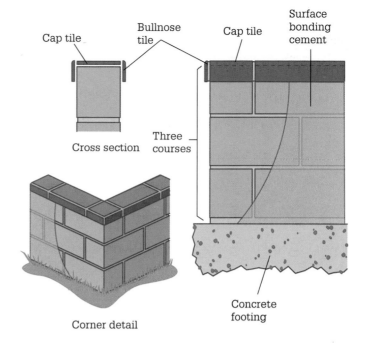

Cap tile | Bullnose tile | Cap tile | Surface bonding cement

Cross section

Three courses

Corner detail

Concrete footing

Step A: Install the Footings & Lay Out the First Course

1. Lay out the location of the wall and then use stakes and mason's string to outline footings that are twice as wide as the proposed wall. Measure the diagonals to make sure the staked outline is square, and then use a framing square to make sure the corners are square. Adjust if necessary.

2. Dig the trenches and set the footings, as described on page 90. When the concrete is hard to the touch, cover the footings with plastic and let the concrete cure for 2 to 3 days. Remove the wood forms and backfill around the edges, and then let the footings cure for a week.

3. Lay out the blocks for the entire first course. If you need to use less than half a block, trim two blocks instead. For example, if you need 3½" blocks, use four and cut two of them to ¾ their length—this produces a stronger, more durable wall.

4. Use a level to make sure the course is plumb and a framing square to make sure the corners are square. Set a mason's string flush with the height of the course, along the outside of the wall.

5. Mark the position of the end and corner blocks on the footing, using a pencil.

Step B: Set the First Course

1. Mix a batch of mortar, and then mist the footing with water, roughly 3 or 4 block lengths from the end of the wall. Lay a ⅜"-thick bed of mortar on the misted area, covering only the area inside the reference lines.

2. Set an end block into the mortar bed at the corner. Place a stretcher block into the mortar bed directly against the end block with no spacing between the blocks. Place the next block with no spacing between the blocks. Place the next stretcher block in exactly the same manner. Use the mason's string as a guide to keep the blocks level and properly aligned.

3. Repeat this process, working on 3 to 4 ft. at a time, until the first course is complete. Periodically check to make sure the wall is plumb and level and that the corners are square.

Lay out the first course of block, cutting blocks as necessary. Mark the ends and corners, then remove the blocks and snap reference lines.

Mist the footing with water, then lay a ⅜"-thick bed of mortar inside the reference lines.

Starting at the first corner, stack a full-sized end block so it overlaps the vertical joint at the corner. Build the corners and then the ends three courses high.

Fill the subsequent courses. On the next to last course lay wire mesh over the block, then install the final course. Fill the block hollows with mortar.

Apply the surface-bonding cement to damp blocks, using a square-end trowel. Smooth the cement and cut grooves as necessary.

Step C: Build Up the Corners & Ends

1. At a corner, begin the second course with a full-sized end block stacked so that it spans the vertical joint where the two runs meet. Make sure the block is level and plumb. If a block requires leveling, cut a piece of corrugated metal tie and slip it underneath. If a block is off by more than ⅛", remove the block, trowel a dab of mortar underneath, and reposition the block.

2. Align a full-sized stretcher block against the end block to form the corner. Use a framing square to make sure the corner is square.

3. Build the corner up three courses high. Keep blocks level and plumb as you go, and check the position with a level laid diagonally across the corners of the blocks.

4. Build up the ends of the wall three courses high; use half-sized end blocks to offset the joints on the ends of the wall.

Step D: Fill the Subsequent Courses

1. Set your mason's string level with the corner and end blocks of the second course.

2. Fill the second course with stretcher blocks, alternating from the end to the corner until the blocks meet in the middle. Maintain a standard running bond with each block overlapping half of the one beneath it. Trim the last block if necessary, using a circular saw and masonry-cutting blade or a hammer and chisel.

3. Use a level to check for plumb, and line blocks and a line level to check for level. Lay wire mesh on top of the blocks.

4. Install the top course, then fill block hollows with mortar and trowel the surface smooth.

Step E: Apply Surface-bonding Cement

1. Starting near the top of the wall, mist a 2 × 5-ft. section on one side of the wall with water. (The water keeps the blocks from absorbing all the moisture from the cement once the coating is applied.)

2. Mix the cement in small batches, according to the manufacturer's instructions, and apply a ¹⁄₁₆"- to ⅛"-thick layer to the damp blocks, using a square-end trowel. Spread the cement evenly by angling the trowel slightly and making broad upward strokes.

3. Use a wet trowel to smooth the surface and to create the texture of your choice. Frequently rinse the trowel to keep it clean and wet.

4. To prevent random cracking, use a groover to cut control joints, which you can fill later with silicone caulk.

Step F: Set the Tiles

1. Lay out the 8 × 12" ceramic tiles along the top of the wall, starting at a corner. If any tiles need to be cut, adjust the layout so that the tiles on the ends of the wall will be the same size.

2. Apply latex-fortified exterior thinset mortar to the top of the wall, using a notched trowel. Spread the mortar with the straight edge, and then create clean ridges with the notched edge. Work on small sections at a time.

3. Place the corner tile, twist it slightly, and press down firmly to embed it in the mortar. Place each tile in this same manner, using tile spacers to keep the tiles separated.

4. Lay out the bullnose tile on each side of the wall. Again, start in a corner and make sure that the tiles at the ends of the wall will be the same size. Cut tile as necessary.

5. Apply mortar to the sides of the wall. Set the bullnose tile in the same way that you set the top tile. Tape the tile in place until the mortar dries.

6. Remove the spacers and let the mortar cure for at least 24 hours.

Step G: Grout the Tile

1. Mix a batch of sanded grout. Note: Adding latex-fortified grout additive makes it easier to remove excess grout.

2. Spread a layer of grout onto a 4- to 5-ft. area of tile. Use a rubber grout float to spread the grout and pack it into the joints between tiles. Use the grout float to scrape off excess grout from the surface of the tile. Scrape diagonally across the joints, holding the float in a near-vertical position.

3. Use a damp sponge to wipe the grout film from the surface of the tile. Rinse the sponge frequently with cool water, and be careful not to press down so hard that you disturb the grout.

4. Continue working along the wall until you've grouted and wiped down all of the tile. Let the grout dry several hours, then use a cloth to buff the surface until any remaining grout film is gone.

5. Apply grout sealer to the grout lines.

Lay out the tile along the wall, and then set it using exterior thinset mortar.

Grout the joints, using a rubber grout float. Wipe the film from the tile and let it dry. Polish the tile with a soft, dry rag.

Patio Arbor

From parties and everyday meals to afternoon naps and sunbathing, this attractive overhead is designed to make the most of all the ways you use your new patio.

The patio arbor combines the sheltering and light-filtering qualities of an arbor roof with the convenience of built-in bench seating. And it fits into the corner, so it won't take up a lot of floor space. You can add as much or as little lattice screen as you like for just the right amount of shade or privacy. An optional roof design lets you extend the roof over an 11 × 11 ft. area—perfect for adding a table that takes advantage of the bench seating.

You can build this project on top of a concrete slab or on the ground for sandset and other surface applications. The location will dictate how you install the posts, and steps are given here for both. Using the ground installation, you can also locate the arbor just off of your patio to extend your outdoor living space into your yard or garden.

Tools & Materials See Materials List, on page 193 for all lumber and hardware required. ▪ Tape measure ▪ Chalk line (concrete slab installation) ▪ Circular saw ▪ Hammer ▪ Clamps ▪ Chisel ▪ Power drill and bits ▪ Ratchet wrench ▪ Jigsaw ▪ Sandpaper ▪ Framing square ▪ Flexible wood strip ▪ Straight 2 x 4s (2) ▪ ¾" plywood.
Additional Supplies for Ground Installation:
▪ Stakes and mason's string for post layout ▪ Shovel ▪ Hand tamper ▪ Reciprocating saw ▪ Trowel or concrete float.

Material List

Description (No. finished pieces)	Quantity/Size	Material
Posts		
Full-height posts* (7)	7 @ field measure	
Add 1 post for optional full roof	4 × 4	
Seat support post (1)	1 @ field measure	4 × 4
Post blocking	2 blocks for each post; field measure	2× pressure-treated lumber; size to match existing deck joists
Roof Frame		
Beams (8)	8 @ 12'	2 × 8
Roof slats (20)	10 @ 8'	2 × 2
Optional Full Roof		
Beams (6)	6 @ 12'	2 × 8
Roof slats (12 long, 12 short)	18 @ 8'	2 × 2
Seats		
Seat supports (6 sides, 6 ends)	5 @ 8'	2 × 6
Seat slats (27)	9 @ 8'	2 × 6
Lattice Screens		
Lattice slats	Field measure	1 × 1 (¾" × ¾" actual dimensions)
Hardware & Fasteners		
16d galvanized common nails or 3½" deck screws		
Post bases (for concrete patios or ground-level decks only)	8, with recommended anchors and fasteners	Simpson AB44 or similar approved base
⅜" × 7" galvanized carriage bolts	16, with washers and nuts	
¼" × 6¼" galvanized carriage bolts	20, with washers and nuts	
2½" deck screws		
3½" deck screws		
3½" galvanized lag screws	22, with washers	
Galvanized metal angle	1	
4d galvanized finish nails		
Waterproof glue		
6d galvanized finish nails		

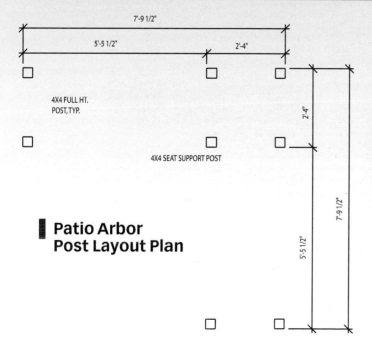

7'-9 1/2"

5'-5 1/2"   2'-4"

4X4 FULL HT.
POST, TYP.

4X4 SEAT SUPPORT POST

2'-4"

7'-9 1/2"

5'-5 1/2"

▎ Patio Arbor
Post Layout Plan

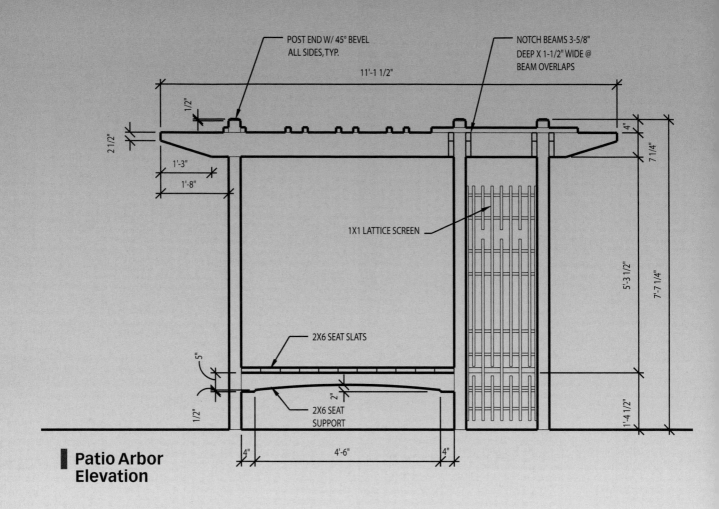

POST END W/ 45° BEVEL
ALL SIDES, TYP.

NOTCH BEAMS 3-5/8"
DEEP X 1-1/2" WIDE @
BEAM OVERLAPS

11'-1 1/2"

1/2"

2 1/2"

1'-3"

1'-8"

1X1 LATTICE SCREEN

5'-3 1/2"

7'-7 1/4"

4"

7 1/4"

2X6 SEAT SLATS

5"

2X6 SEAT
SUPPORT

2"

1/2"

1'-4 1/2"

4"

4'-6"

4"

Patio Arbor Elevation

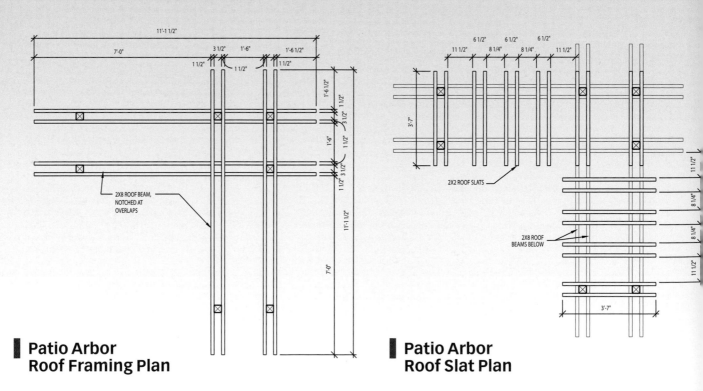

11'-1 1/2"

7'-0"

3 1/2"

1'-6"

1'-6 1/2"

1 1/2"

1 1/2"

1 1/2"

1'-6 1/2"

1 1/2"

3 1/2"

1'-6"

1 1/2"

1 1/2"

3 1/2"

11'-1 1/2"

7'-0"

2X8 ROOF BEAM,
NOTCHED AT
OVERLAPS

Patio Arbor Roof Framing Plan

6 1/2"

6 1/2"

6 1/2"

11 1/2"

8 1/4"

8 1/4"

11 1/2"

3'-7"

2X2 ROOF SLATS

2X8 ROOF
BEAMS BELOW

11 1/2"

8 1/4"

8 1/4"

11 1/2"

3'-7"

Patio Arbor Roof Slat Plan

Patio Arbor Screen Layout

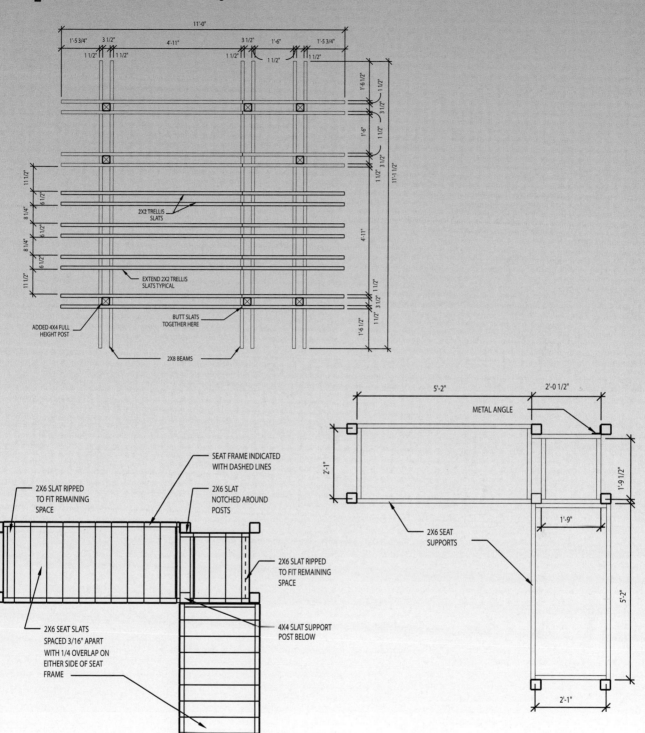

2X2 TRELLIS SLATS

EXTEND 2X2 TRELLIS SLATS TYPICAL

ADDED 4X4 FULL HEIGHT POST

BUTT SLATS TOGETHER HERE

2X8 BEAMS

SEAT FRAME INDICATED WITH DASHED LINES

2X6 SLAT RIPPED TO FIT REMAINING SPACE

2X6 SLAT NOTCHED AROUND POSTS

2X6 SLAT RIPPED TO FIT REMAINING SPACE

4X4 SLAT SUPPORT POST BELOW

2X6 SEAT SLATS SPACED 3/16" APART WITH 1/4 OVERLAP ON EITHER SIDE OF SEAT FRAME

2X6 SLAT RIPPED TO FIT REMAINING SPACE

METAL ANGLE

2X6 SEAT SUPPORTS

Patio Arbor Seat Slat Layout

Patio Arbor Seat Framing Plan

Concrete Slab Installation: Use post bases with metal standoff plates to protect the posts from surface moisture.

Ground Installation: Anchor the posts in concrete, overfilling the footings to create a rounded top.

How to Build the Patio Arbor

Step A—For Concrete Slab Installation

1. Lay out the post locations on your patio or deck, following the POST LAYOUT PLAN, on page 193.

2. Each post is anchored to the slab with a galvanized metal post base. Use a hammer drill to drill a hole for each post base anchor. Refer to the base manufacturer for the size and type of anchor to use. Secure the anchor to the concrete; then bolt the post base to the anchor, using the recommended hardware.

3. Cut the full-height posts to length so that they will stand 91¼" above the patio surface when they're installed on the post bases. Cut the seat support post so it will stand 16½" above the surface when installed on its base.

4. If desired, bevel the top ends of the full-height posts at 45°, as shown in the ELEVATION, on page 194.

5. Set each post on its base and support it with temporary braces so that it stands perfectly plumb. Fasten the post to the base using the fasteners recommended by the base manufacturer.

Step A—For Ground Installation

1. Lay out the post locations on the ground, following the POST LAYOUT PLAN, on page 193.

2. Protect the ends of the posts by soaking them overnight in a pan of wood preservative/sealer, or coat the underground portion of the posts with roofing tar (the tar should extend a few inches above the ground level when the posts are installed).

3. At each post location, dig a hole 12" in diameter and at a depth required by the local building code, plus 4". Building codes in cold winter regions require that post footings extend below the frost line.

4. Fill the holes with 4" of gravel, then compact the gravel with a hand tamper.

5. Set each post in a hole and support it with temporary cross bracing so it is perfectly plumb and square to the project layout. Fill the holes with concrete, creating a slight mound above the ground to shed water away from the posts. Let the concrete dry completely.

6. Mark one of the full-height posts for cutting at 91¼" above the ground. Using a mason's string and line level, transfer that height mark to the remaining full-height posts. Mark the seat support post at 16½" above the ground.

7. Cut the posts using a reciprocating saw or circular saw. If desired, bevel the top ends of the full-height posts at 45°, as shown in the ELEVATION, on page 194.

Step B: Cut & Shape the Roof Beams

1. Cut the eight 2 × 8 beams to length at 133½".

2. To shape the beam ends, make a mark 2½" down from the top corner at each end. Make another mark 15" in from the bottom corner. Draw a line connecting the two marks. Cut along this diagonal line.

3. At the corner of the arbor, the four sets of beam pairs intersect with half-lap joints, as shown in the ROOF FRAMING PLAN, along with the detail, on page 194. To mark the notches for the half-lap joints, measure the depth (width) and thickness of the beams. The width of the notches must match the thickness of the beams; the length of the notches must equal half the depth of the beams. Mark the layout of the notches, following the ROOF FRAMING PLAN.

4. Cut the notches. Tip: You can save time by clamping two or more beams together and cutting them at once. Using a circular saw or handsaw, cut the outside edges of the notches first. Then, make a series of interior cuts at ⅛" intervals. Use a chisel to remove the waste and smooth the seats of the notches.

5. Test-fit the notches on the ground and make any necessary adjustments for a good fit.

Step C: Install the Roof Beams

1. Mark the sides of the posts that will receive the beams 11¼" down from the top ends.

2. Starting with the beams with the top-down notches, sandwich one set of posts so the notches clear the posts on both sides and the bottom edges of the beams are on the reference marks made in the last step. Clamp the beams in place.

3. Drill two pilot holes for ¼ × 6 ½" carriage bolts through both beams and the post. On the less-visible beam sides, countersink the holes just enough to completely recess the washer and nut. Fasten the beams to the posts with the carriage bolts.

4. Repeat Steps 2 and 3 to install the other set of parallel beams.

5. Install the perpendicular beams, fitting the notches together so all the beams are flush at the top and bottom edges. Clamp the beams as before, then drill pilot holes and attach the beams with carriage bolts. Tip: Drill the through pilot holes from the outsides of the beam intersections, so you'll have enough room for the drill bit.

Test-fit the beam joints and make adjustments before installing the beams.

Counterbores help hide the bolt hardware. Locate them in the least conspicuous areas.

Drill pilot holes for the roof slats, and fasten them to the roof beams with deck screws.

A flexible wood strip helps you make a perfect curve for the long side seat supports.

Step D: Install the Roof Slats

1. Cut the 20 roof slats to length at 43".

2. Mark the slat layout on the tops of the roof beams, following the ROOF SLAT PLAN, on page 194.

3. Position each slat on its layout mark so it overhangs the outer roof beams by 6" on both sides. Fasten the slat to each intersecting beam with 2½" deck screws driven through pilot holes.

Step E: Build the Seat Frames

1. Look at the SEAT FRAMING PLAN, on page 195, to understand the seat frame layout. There are three, 4-sided seat frames. You can build them on a workbench, then install them—just make sure they will fit snugly between the sets of posts.

2. Measure between the posts for each seat frame. Cut the side seat supports to length so they extend from post to post. Cut the end seat supports to length so they will fit between the side supports.

3. Lay out the arched cutout on one of the side supports, following the ELEVATION, on page 194. Make the cut with a jigsaw or band saw, then sand the arch smooth. Use the support as a pattern to mark the three remaining long seat supports, then make the cuts.

4. Assemble the seat frames with 3½" deck screws driven through the side supports and into the end supports. Make sure the pieces are flush along their top edges.

5. Measure up from the patio surface, and mark the inside faces of the posts at 16½". Install the seat frames as shown in the SEAT FRAMING PLAN, on page 195, so their top edges are on the reference marks; fasten through the end seat supports and into the posts with two 3½" lag screws at each location. Fasten the frame at the outside corner of the Arbor using a metal angle and screws.

Step F: Add the Seat Slats

1. Measure between the outside faces of the seat frames to find the lengths of the seat slats. You can either make the slats flush to the frames or overhang the frames by ¼" on either side.

2. Notch the first slat to fit around the posts where the left-side frame meets the corner frame; see SEAT SLAT LAYOUT, on page 195. Fasten the slat to the seat frames with pairs of 2½" deck screws driven through pilot holes.

3. Cut and install the remaining slats, gapping them at 3⁄16". Rip the last slat in each section to fit the remaining space.

Step G: Build the Lattice Screens

How you use the lattice screening is your choice. You might want screens only on the ends of the seats, as shown in the plan drawings, or you might cover the entire back side of the project. The basic procedure for building screens is shown here.

1. Construct a jig for assembling the lattice screens: On a sheet of plywood, fasten two straight 2 × 4s in an "L" pattern, using a framing square to set the pieces at an exact 90° angle.

2. Cut several 2 × 6" spacers from ¾" plywood.

3. Cut the lattice pieces to length from ¾ × ¾" (actual dimensions) lumber, following the SCREEN LAYOUT, on page 195.

4. Using the jig and spacers, assemble the screens according to the drawing, or create your own pattern. Fasten the pieces with waterproof wood glue and 4d finish nails.

5. To install the screens, fasten a lattice backer strip to each post, as shown in the plan detail of the SCREEN LAYOUT, using 6d finish nails. Then, install the screens against the backer strips.

Notch the slats as needed to fit snugly around the posts. Gap the slats by ³⁄₁₆"

Construct a jig for assembling the lattice screens.

Plywood spacers help you keep the lattice screens square as you work.

Trees

Trees are great companions for any patio. Their full canopies offer much needed shade in the summer, while their branches provide structure for hanging lanterns, wind chimes, and other accents any time of the year. And there's nothing like the sound of rustling leaves to lull you into an afternoon nap. By planting several trees in formation, similar to a hedge, you can create a privacy screen that helps reduce noise and protects the patio from wind. Evergreens are most effective for a windbreak, while deciduous trees, when mature, form a graceful, natural ceiling at the side of a patio space.

Note: Never pave over exposed roots at the tree's base or cover them with soil. Even when kept at a safe distance from the roots, patio paving can deprive a tree of water and nutrients so you may need to water the tree yourself.

Tools & Materials
Shovel ▪ Garden hose ▪ Utility knife ▪ Tree ▪ Soil amendments, as needed.

Selecting Trees

First, decide what features you'd like your tree(s) to provide. For example, do you want the tree to provide shade on the patio? If so, when and where? What color do you want the leaves to be? Do you want flowers on the tree? Next, consider root growth. In general, it is best to avoid shallow-rooted trees. To ensure the tree is planted at a safe distance from your patio—and to prevent roots from coming up through your paving—divide the mature spread of the tree in half. Your tree should be at least that far from the patio, if not more. This means that the branches of the mature tree may reach to the edge of the patio but will not hang over it. Select a tree with a canopy size and trunk shape that you will enjoy year-round, and avoid trees that litter the ground beneath (and your patio) with berries, seeds, or nuts. Consult an arborist for specific advice about your type of tree and your patio plans.

Buying Trees

Nurseries and garden centers sell trees packaged in three different ways. Container-grown trees are packed in pots of soil and are available in many sizes. Bare-root trees are dug up during dormancy, so the branches and roots are bare. The roots are exposed and must be kept moist and protected from sun and wind damage during transport and before planting. Balled-and-burlapped (B&B) trees are established trees with a large compact root ball that's tightly secured in burlap. B&B trees are very heavy and require special care when transporting. The soil and roots must not dry out before planting.

Transporting Trees

All trees need protection during transport. Because this can be a difficult process, many people opt to pay the nursery a delivery fee to handle the job. But, if you have access to a pickup or trailer, you can save money by transporting the tree yourself. Branches, foliage, and roots must be protected from breakage, and wind and sun damage, during transport. To protect them, wrap them in burlap tied on with twine. Secure the tree inside the truck bed with straps or rope. Drive slowly and carefully, especially on corners, and unload the tree by lifting it only by the roots, not the trunk.

How to Prepare the Planting Hole

The planting hole is one of the greatest contributing factors to the health of a tree. To prepare the hole, start by digging a hole two to three times as wide as the root ball of the tree. If you're planting a bare-root tree, the hole should be two to three times wider than the spread of the branches. To help the roots develop horizontally, slope the sides of the hole toward the surface. When finished, the hole should resemble a wide, shallow basin. If you need a guide for where to dig, use a garden hose.

How to Plant Bare-root Trees

The roots of bare-root trees should be planted at a depth that is slightly higher than that at which they were originally grown. Start by slightly backfilling the planting hole with the soil you removed. Hold the tree in the hole. If the tops of the roots are still below the top of the hole, backfill more soil into the hole. Position the tree so that the largest branches are facing southwest, then spread out the roots. Backfill dirt into the hole to cover the roots. As you backfill, gently lift the tree up and down to prevent air pockets from forming. When the hole is ¾ full, tamp the soil and water generously to remove any remaining air pockets. Completely fill the hole with soil, and lightly tamp it.

How to Plant B&B Trees

Carefully set the plant in the hole. Add or remove soil until the root ball rests slightly above ground level. Cut and remove the twine at the top of the ball. Cut the burlap away from the top and sides of the root ball and remove as much of it as possible. Set the tree back down and backfill until the hole is ¾ full. Lightly tamp the soil down; then water it slowly to remove the air pockets. Finish backfilling the hole, and tamp the soil.

How to Care for New Trees

Trees require routine maintenance, especially during the first year. It takes almost a full year for a newly planted tree to establish a healthy root system. During the root development period, routine waterings are very important. The best method for watering trees is to place a garden hose at the base of the tree. Adjust the hose to release water in a slow trickle, and leave it on for several hours. With this method, you can easily water the soil around the tree to a depth of 6" to 8". Use this method to water new trees any time the moisture depth in the soil is less than 6". In addition to watering, encourage root development by applying a fertilizer formulated for trees. Apply the fertilizer according to the directions on the label.

Projects: Patio Lighting & Outdoor Kitchens

No patio is complete without lighting. Whether you're illuminating a water feature, spotlighting a grill, or brightening the mood with a string of twinkling decorative lights, a good lighting scheme is an invaluable patio feature. If your current lighting plan consists of a basic, bare-bulb fixture mounted next to your back door, you'll be amazed by the difference a few well-placed lights can make. Low-voltage fixtures are now the standard for outdoor lighting, offering do-it-yourself installation and a wide range of fixtures for patios and the surrounding landscape.

While the right lighting turns your patio into an inviting nighttime retreat, an outdoor kitchen might just double the time you spend outside. The outdoor kitchen is a natural evolution for those who want to take barbecuing to the next level: If you love to grill, why not make the whole meal outdoors? Don't worry if the dream kitchens featured on television aren't within your budget or even your sense of proportion. In the end, the best kitchens are the ones that get used. This chapter can help you decide what's right for your own patio plans.

In This Chapter

- Creating a Patio Lighting Plan
- Installing Low-voltage Lighting
- Planning an Outdoor Kitchen

Creating a Patio Lighting Plan

A thoughtful lighting plan not only makes your patio more useful at night, it gives the space a second life with a completely different feel from the daytime setting. Designing a plan and installing lighting takes some careful forethought, but the basic process is a reasonable project for any homeowner, especially if you're using low-voltage systems. The amount of lighting required might also surprise you. When you consider that a single lantern or a few votive candles can provide enough light for a dining table, you realize how little it takes to set the right mood and still create a comfortable, safe environment. It's all about using the appropriate light for specific purposes.

Tips for Effective Lighting

There are a few rules that apply to all outdoor lighting schemes:

Keep it subtle. With the exception of surprise-oriented security lights, outdoor lighting should be mellow and subdued—an intermingling of soft light and shadows, not a battle against the darkness.

Mix it up. The best lighting plans employ a combination of fixtures and levels of illumination. Use brighter or more direct lights to highlight a few features or patio areas; otherwise, stick to low, unobtrusive lighting. Variation helps emphasize key elements.

Illuminate surfaces, not people. Direct fixtures downward to light paths and patio surfaces or upward for indirect background lighting. As a general rule, viewers shouldn't see naked bulbs or even fixtures, whenever possible. Never direct beams of light into the viewer's line of sight, which creates an especially harsh glare at night.

Use the right fixture for the job. There's an outdoor light for virtually every application. Some are decorative and made to be visible; others are easy to hide under low plantings or tuck away into the shadows. Shopping carefully for the right fixtures is a critical step for an effective lighting plan.

An effective lighting design incorporates a customized plan of general illumination, safety and path lighting, decorative or landscape lighting, and security lighting.

Nothing sets the mood for late-night entertaining like a string of decorative lights.

Soft, indirect, or diffuse lights are key with background lighting. Avoid bare bulbs.

Types of Lighting & Outdoor Fixtures

General Illumination

Most patios need some atmospheric lighting for general nighttime use—so party guests can see one another (at least in dim light) and diners can see their food during late-evening meals. One option is to provide a soft wash of background light, with sconces mounted to the house wall. Another is to use globe fixtures placed on outer posts for an open-yet muted glow. Avoid relying on a single, bright bulb, such as the light from a standard entryway fixture. For entertaining, a sprinkling of small accent lights, one at each table or dotted along the patio's borders, can create enough light for socializing while maintaining a sense of mystery.

Decorative Lighting

Decorative lights can work in concert with general lighting or can be used in place of general lights when a darker atmosphere is desired. By nature, though, decorative lights are fun to look at, like stars or distant city lights. Fanciful lanterns or cafe lights strung along a wire create an especially festive mood.

Small Christmas lights, or twinkle lights, can be wrapped around tree branches, strung overhead, or festooned along walls or fences. For a cleaner twinkle light effect, use rope lights hidden under railings or tacked along an eave. In general, white is best for string or rope lights, as colored lights can be garish, and multicolored lights look as though you were too lazy to take down your holiday decorations.

Illuminated water features can be magical nighttime decorations. Lights can shine onto a fountain from the side, top, or rear, or from underneath the water. Lighting ground-level pools and ponds on or near a patio creates an ethereal focal point but also is an essential safety measure.

Safety & Path Lighting

Main traffic routes on and off a patio need lighting to make access safe and convenient. On patios, include lights at all changes in floor height and on any obstructions not easily seen at night. Recessed lights for step risers place a small amount of light precisely where it's needed. Paths are typically lighted with low-voltage pole fixtures, using a "path" effect for localized pools of light or a "spread" pattern for a broader wash. As mentioned above, open water features must be lighted at night to define the water's boundaries. Lighted pavers offer a novel way to illuminate paved patios and walkways.

Task Lighting

Outdoor cooking calls for bright, focused lighting that's easy to turn off when the work is done. Choose downlights that focus on the work areas only, much like under-cabinet lighting in an indoor kitchen.

Security Lighting

Floodlights are much too bright and glaring for a pleasant patio atmosphere. In fact, unless your patio is doubling as a used car lot, use floods only for security purposes. Direct floodlights to illuminate entrances and hidden windows, but include a switch so you can turn off the lights when you're out on the patio. Motion detectors are always a good idea. They save energy by operating the lights only when they're needed, and they'll help prevent complaints from the neighbors.

Underwater lights create a dazzling nighttime effect. Submersible spotlights shimmer at night. Placing lights in ponds and fountains creates beautiful effects, and at the same time increases visibility of the water for safety precautions.

Changes in surface level must be illuminated for safe nighttime patio use.

Outdoor cooking calls for bright, focused lighting that's easy to turn off when the work is done. Choose downlights that focus on the work areas only, much like under-cabinet lighting in an indoor kitchen.

Specialty pavers that use fiber optics, solar power, or conventional wiring, among other technologies, add subtle yet clever lighting to patio surfaces.

Floodlights should be used judiciously for security, not for general outdoor lighting.

Low-voltage & Line Voltage Lighting

Low-voltage systems offer the broadest range of fixtures and the easiest installation for most types of residential outdoor lighting. A typical low-voltage system plugs into a standard electrical outlet (must be GFCI-protected) and uses a transformer to convert, or "step down," your home's 110/120-volt current to a 12-volt current. The advantages of low-voltage are many. It's safe and quick to install and doesn't require a permit in most municipalities. The low-wattage lights save energy—for example, a standard 150-watt light uses more power than eight 18-watt low-voltage lights. And because outdoor lighting is all about placing small amounts of light over a large area, low-voltage offers just the right design flexibility and low-level illumination. See pages 210-211 for steps to installing a basic low-voltage system.

The alternative to low-voltage lighting is to connect fixtures to your home's 110/120-volt ("line voltage") circuitry. Line voltage makes sense for high-wattage security floodlights and other fixtures that are typically mounted to a house or garage wall, since there's likely a circuit or outlet already in the area. Bringing line voltage out onto the patio or yard requires protected underground wiring. The advantage of this type of system is the greater power supplied to fixtures, plus it allows you to install remote outlets for plugging in outdoor equipment or servicing a garden shed or other outbuilding. If your lighting needs exceed the capability of a low-voltage system or if you're planning an outdoor kitchen, consult an electrician about installing line voltage outdoor circuits.

Low-voltage fixtures come in a wide range of styles, both decorative and utilitarian.

Line voltage systems require the addition of full-voltage (110/120) outdoor circuits.

Landscape Lighting ▸

Low-level lighting dotted throughout a landscape can be its own form of decorative lighting, creating a special nighttime view from the patio. Just a few lights can add depth and interest and eliminate the "black hole" effect resulting from a lighted patio surrounded by darkness. Here are some common techniques used by professionals to set the nighttime stage:

Shadowing is created with uplights that shine into a plant or other object, casting its shadow onto a background surface.

Uplighting uses a lamp directed upward into a tree or other planting or to highlight statuary or walls.

Moonlighting mimics the effect of moonlight filtering through a tree's branches. Lights are placed high in the tree and pointed downward.

Backlighting accents gorgeous plants from behind, bringing out the silhouettes of plantings in front of the wall.

Installing Low-voltage Lighting

Low-voltage lighting systems are commonly available in complete kits that include a low-voltage transformer, low-voltage cable, and several light fixtures, each with a wire lead that links to the main cable via a special cable connector. A basic landscape kit typically has three or more fixtures for standard in-ground installation. To use specialty patio fixtures, such as step (or "brick") lights, pole- and wall-mount fixtures, and task lights for outdoor cooking, make sure your system is compatible with a full range of accessory lights.

Also consider these factors when shopping for a system:

- Transformer power—for best performance, the total wattage of the light fixtures should be at least ⅓ of the transformer's wattage rating but should not exceed the wattage rating. If necessary, use two systems to avoid overloading one system with too many fixtures.

- Transformer controls—including timers and photo-sensitive switches.
- Cable gauge (size)—12-amp UF cable is recommended to reduce voltage drop (thus reduced brightness in fixtures farthest down the line). Long runs of cable may require 8- or 10-gauge wire to prevent voltage drop.
- Fixture (and bulb) brightness—often rated in foot-candles: one foot-candle is equivalent to the brightness of a 12" square area lighted by a candle held 12" away.

All outdoor low-voltage systems must be plugged into a GFCI receptacle. For exposed outlets, install an in-use outlet cover to protect against moisture. In addition to standard wired systems, there are also solar-powered low-voltage fixtures available. These self-contained wireless units install anywhere and offer an easy way to supplement a wired system.

Tools & Materials
Power drill and bits ▪ Screwdrivers ▪ Trenching spade ▪ In-use outlet cover (optional) ▪ Low-voltage lighting kit ▪ Plastic wire staples ▪ Corrosion-resistant nails and screws, as needed.

Low-voltage outdoor light styles include well lights (A), garden lights (B), adjustable spotlights (C) and adjustable floodlights (D). You'll also need low-voltage cable (E), halogen bulbs (F), and a control box (G) containing a transformer, timer, and a light sensor to operate your light system.

System Layout Options

Transformer
Lights
Cable

Serial circuit

Split circuit

Tee circuits

Loop circuit

Note: Follow the system manufacturer's directions for cable layout and proper wiring connections (examples shown above).

How to Install Low-voltage Lighting

Step A: Mount the Transformer

1. Plan the system layout based on your patio design and the manufacturer's recommendations. See System Layout Options, on page 210, for various options available with some systems.

2. Mount the transformer to a house wall or other permanent structure near a GFCI outlet. If the outlet is not in a sheltered area, install an in-use receptacle cover. This type of cover allows you to keep the transformer plugged in while protecting the outlet from the elements.

3. If the transformer has a photo-sensitive switch, make sure the light sensor will be adequately exposed.

Step B: Lay Out the Cable & Fixtures

1. Starting at the transformer, roll out the main fixture cable along your planned layout, leaving plenty of slack at both ends for adjustments.

2. Set each fixture in place as desired, making sure the fixture leads will easily reach the main cable.

3. Make adjustments to the cable and fixture positions, keeping in mind how you will bury or hide the cable for the final installation.

Step C: Install the Fixtures

1. Mount the light fixtures, using corrosion-resistant fasteners on patio or wall surfaces. For yard or garden lights, plant the fixtures in the ground with the manufacturer's installation stakes.

2. Connect each fixture to the main cable using the system's cable connector. Some connectors snap onto the cable; others are secured with a screw.

Step D: Complete the Job

1. Connect the main cable to the transformer, following the manufacturer's instructions.

2. Plug in the transformer to test the lights. When you're sure all of the fixtures are working properly, unplug the transformer.

3. Starting near the transformer, permanently install the cable: Over ground, bury the cable in a narrow trench that's 6-8" deep. On patio surfaces, hide the cable where it will be out of view and protected from accidental damage. Where practical, attach the cable to wood or masonry surfaces using plastic wire staples and corrosion-resistant nails or screws.

4. Adjust the lighting controls or set the timer as desired.

Mount the transformer near a GFCI outlet, following the manufacturer's directions.

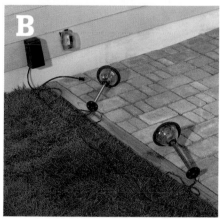

Position the cable and fixtures according to your plan, and make any necessary adjustments.

Mount the fixtures to the patio surface or into the ground as needed. Connect the fixture leads to the main cable, using the supplied connectors (inset).

(Below) Test the system, then bury the main cable in the ground or attach it to permanent structures, as needed.

Planning an Outdoor Kitchen

An outdoor kitchen combines the open-air, smoke-infused pleasure of barbecue cooking with the basic conveniences of an indoor kitchen. Starting with the essential components of a grill and some built-in counter space, many outdoor kitchens also include a sink, a small refrigerator, and cabinetry for storage. The popularity of outdoor kitchens in all regions of the country has led to a wealth of new products designed for alfresco cuisine—from commercial-grade stainless steel cooktops to weatherproof polymer cabinets. But for anyone who's used to grilling with the aid of a lawn chair for extra workspace or serving onto flimsy paper plates balanced on a cooler, even the most modest outdoor kitchen can be a major home improvement.

Planning an outdoor kitchen involves several factors. The primary considerations are discussed here. When it's time to get serious about plans, make your first stop the local building department to learn about code requirements for outdoor kitchens in your area. Also consult your utility providers, which may have legal control over how you install gas, electrical, and plumbing lines. Critical matters, such as grill setup, utility hookups, and zoning restrictions, can have a significant impact on your kitchen's layout and construction costs.

Choosing a Location

A kitchen's location affects many aspects of its design. Most kitchens naturally end up on a patio close to a main entry door to the house, and this offers several advantages: convenient access to the indoor kitchen, shorter utility runs, and partial shelter from the elements. Building directly against the house wall makes utility hookups even easier, and sometimes an existing window can be used as a pass-through between the two kitchens.

Conveniences aside, you should locate your kitchen where you most like to hang out. This might be in a remote part of the lot, because its the best place to take in a good view while cooking. Getting

Ceramic and porcelain outdoor tile makes an attractive kitchen counter surface that suits patio styling, but it must be sealed thoroughly.

utilities to a remote site is more difficult, but if any of the main hookups prove too daunting, you can always improvise with a propane grill, low-voltage lighting, and bottled water. Kitchens located away from the house should be as well equipped as possible to minimize trips to and from the house. Chances are, you're less likely to use a remote kitchen for everyday meals if you have to walk across your lot just to check your shish kebabs.

Another important consideration is cooking smoke. Vent hoods can capture smoke in a well-contained area, but out in the open the slightest breeze renders a vent useless. You can position a grill to take advantage of prevailing winds. However, wind is fickle, so it's advisable to place the grill far enough from the house entry and outdoor eating or sitting areas to allow smoke to dissipate sufficiently, no matter which way the wind is blowing.

Building for the Outdoors

Everything in an outdoor kitchen must be weather-resistant, period. Even if the area is sheltered under a solid roof or up against the house wall, the elements will take their toll. To protect against moisture and sun exposure, use only the toughest building materials. Starting with cabinet framing (for custom-built units), cedar, redwood, and pressure-treated lumber will resist rot for many years, while galvanized steel studs and concrete block (and brick) not only stand up to moisture but also are noncombustible and can be used to frame around grills. Several cabinet manufacturers now offer pre-built outdoor cabinets made with tough materials like PVC, polymers, and steel clad with cementboard.

For vertical surfaces, stucco, stone, tile, and cedar or redwood siding make attractive, durable finishes. Horizontal surfaces, like countertops, require more careful consideration. Concrete and tile are popular countertop and backsplash materials, but they must be thoroughly sealed to prevent food stains. Granite and stainless steel countertops are highly durable and stain-resistant but also among the most costly. In general, you can't go wrong with stainless steel—for surfaces, cooking equipment, sinks, refrigerators, even screws and other hardware used for construction.

To promote water drainage, slope countertops and other horizontal surfaces at least ⅛" per foot

The farther your kitchen is from the house, the more you'll appreciate having everything you need on your patio and close to your outdoor activities. Here a poolside bar is right next to the outdoor kitchen for convenience.

from back to front. Also consider drainage holes for base cabinets that could collect rainwater or snow in severe conditions. Pests are another common concern. Rubber gaskets can help keep bugs and dust from getting into drawers and cabinets; latches or strong catches deter hungry critters.

Matters of Style

When it comes to choosing the materials and decoration that will define the look of your outdoor kitchen, consider two different approaches to get ideas flowing. One is to take your cue from the interior kitchen or nearest indoor room. Using similar finishes and motifs creates continuity with the house, making the outdoor kitchen appear as an extension of the interior living space. The other approach is to follow the styling of your patio (if that's where the outdoor kitchen resides). For many patios, stainless steel and polished granite just don't fit the outdoor environment. Instead, you might find some rustic fixtures, an old reclaimed zinc tub or stone water basin, and weathered teak boards to embrace a garden-style theme, linking the house to the natural landscape. Note: Make sure any surface materials you use are safe for food contact.

A built-in grill can operate on refillable propane tanks or have a plumbed supply line.

▌ Appliances & Other Elements

Grill

The heart and hearth of the outdoor kitchen, many grills are now designed for built-in installation. Choose a grill that's big enough for the way you cook. Liquid propane grills run on refillable tanks, while natural gas models have a plumbed supply line stemming from the house source. Prices for grills are based primarily on BTU output, overall cooking area, and, of course, bells and whistles. Grills must be set into a noncombustible structure (such as masonry or steel stud and cementboard) or include a special jacket or surround (available from the manufacturer) for installing within a wood framework.

An elaborate remote outdoor kitchen may be defined by low walls, beams, and an overhead. These details set the basis for a truly luxurious outdoor kitchen.

To ease the process of running electricity and plumbing to your outdoor kitchen, consider placing it adjacent to a house wall.

Cabinets & Countertop

Outdoor kitchen cabinets can be built from scratch, using rot-resistant materials, or they can be purchased in pre-built units. Some cabinets can be customized for a variety of kitchen layouts. Base cabinets are standard in outdoor kitchens, while kitchens built against a house wall offer the option of upper cabinets, as well.

Surface materials for countertops are similar to many of those used in indoor kitchens. However, the supporting substrate for outdoor countertops must be weather-resistant—no particleboard or standard plywood. Suitable base materials include marine plywood, cement-board, and concrete. As with conventional kitchens, counter space is critical. If possible, provide at least 36" of countertop at one or both sides of the grill and 24" at one or both sides of a sink. Bar-style counters for eating or socializing require 24" of length for each person, with a legroom depth of 15" underneath the counter.

Refrigerator

Most outdoor kitchens are well served by a compact under-counter refrigerator or even a dorm-room-style mini-fridge. Keep in mind that refrigerators may not perform ideally in hot conditions and may need to be taken

inside during the coldest months. A built-in icemaker is a great feature for outdoor meals and entertaining.

Sink

A small bar sink might suit your needs for filling glasses and cleaning vegetables. Or, for washing dishes outdoors, look into full-size single or double units. Stainless steel is the most durable option and comes in a wide range of sizes and styles.

Lighting

In addition to low-level atmospheric lighting for eating and lounging areas adjacent to the kitchen, make sure to include plenty of task lighting for the grill and countertop work areas. The idea is to focus task lights where they're needed and to keep glare away from guests. A dimmer switch close by gives you easy control over task lighting. See pages 204 to 207 for a complete discussion of patio lighting.

Overheads

Shelter is a matter of convenience as well as design. An awning or solid roof lets you cook while it's raining (or snowing, for true grill fanatics). Pergolas, arbors, and other post-and-beam frameworks can define the kitchen area and provide structure for mounting lights, outdoor speakers, and racks for cooking tools. Lattice or other types of side screening adds privacy and creates a partial windbreak. With any overhead or shelter, make sure the grill area will be sufficiently ventilated and all combustibles are kept at a safe distance.

Specialty Appliances & Features

Given the steady rise in interest for outdoor kitchens, it's not surprising that appliance manufacturers have expanded their lines to accommodate this booming market. There's a piece of outdoor equipment for every kind of cuisine: wok burners, pizza ovens, deep fryers, rotisseries, griddles, vegetable cookers, to name a few, plus warming ovens for party food and to help in the preparation of complex meals. Outdoor appliances are available from many of the same manufacturers known for quality indoor kitchen equipment.

Modern appliances have their place in every kitchen, but for atmosphere and true outdoor-style cooking, you can't beat a traditional fireplace or wood-burning oven. Elevating the fire up to seating or table level makes the most of the fire's warmth and beauty and creates an authentic arrangement for traditional cooking techniques.

Adding Utilities

A fully equipped outdoor kitchen may require all three utility hookups—gas, electricity, and plumbing. Simpler designs might get by with no additional lines by using a propane grill, skipping the sink, and plugging appliances and low-voltage lighting systems into existing outdoor outlets. Running utility lines outdoors can get expensive, so it's important to address them early in the planning process.

As mentioned earlier, find out about installation requirements from your municipality's building department and the appropriate utility companies. Unless the runs are very short (such as when the kitchen is built against the house wall), most outdoor lines must be buried underground. Some codes allow burying multiple lines in the same trench, provided the lines are separated by 12" or more. Other regulations require separate trenches. If you're installing a sink, find out whether you can drain it into a dry well, which saves money, especially in remote kitchens.

Gas and water lines must include shutoff valves, usually located inside the house for easy access. Most kitchens need only a cold-water line, for rinsing vegetables and soaking dirty dishes. Add a hot-water line if you plan to wash dishes outside. Water lines must be shut off and drained for winter in cold climates. When it comes to electricity, a few countertop (backsplash) outlets are quite handy, as they are in standard kitchens. Grills and cooktops with electric starters also need a power supply. All outdoor outlets must be GFCI-protected to protect against shock hazards.

Woodfire ovens have a rustic design and allow for restaurant-style cooking.

U-shaped kitchens are inviting and set a dramatic stage for entertaining and great views.

Corridor kitchens allow you to multi-task between cooking and preparing plates and drinks.

(Above left) Wall or "galley" kitchens tuck away from the dining and entertaining area. They often consist of base cabinets for extra storage.

(Above right) This kitchen setup allows the cook to keep an eye on all the action and easily communicate with guests sitting at the adjacent counter.

(Left) L-shaped kitchens are yet another common design. To choose the best design for you, consider what appliances you use most, which setup is most efficient for you, and which layout fits your needs. For example, do you want a nice view while cooking or would you prefer to keep an eye on the kids or chat with party guests?

Projects: Cleaning & Maintaining Patio Surfaces

Your patio is outdoors and that means no matter where you live, it will need maintenance. In addition to rain, snow, and sunlight, a patio must endure hard use—from barbecue spills to furniture scrapes to spray paint straying from the kids' science projects. That's why cleaning and protecting the surfaces can be just as important as repairs for keeping a patio in good shape.

Each type of patio surface has its weaknesses. Sandset floors tend to sprout weeds over time, and they are vulnerable to shifting along with the ground below. Mortared materials often need work on the mortar, whether its fixing cracks or scrubbing out stubborn food stains. And concrete patios, despite their durability, can suffer from any of the standard concrete ailments—chipping, spalling, cracking, and pop-outs that create holes. This chapter can help you tackle all of these common patio problems.

It's important to keep in mind that outdoor maintenance is not only for appearances, it's also needed to protect the structures. If you neglect to paint your house, eventually water and sunlight start to destroy the siding and trim, leading to leaks, rot, and other problems. The same goes for patios. Cracks allow water beneath the surface, where it freezes and expands, causing more cracking. In the case of sandset materials, neglect can turn a limited problem area into a need for total replacement of the patio surface. Every homeowner knows how easy it is to put off outdoor projects, especially during winter, but seasonal upkeep will undoubtedly save you trouble in the long run.

In This Chapter

- Brick & Concrete Pavers
- Concrete Slab
- Tile
- Flagstone

Brick & Concrete Pavers

While the durable surfaces of brick and concrete pavers need very little maintenance, the joints between units often require regular (or at least annual) attention. Staying ahead of weeds, shifting pavers, and mortar cracks goes a long way to keeping your patio looking good and retaining a solid, flat patio floor.

For routine spruce-ups, remove weeds that have grown up between pavers. Sandset pavers may need to be repacked occasionally with sand to prevent loosening of the units. You can repack small sections by hand or repeat the original joint-filling process, sweeping sand across the entire patio, then wetting it to settle the sand. Cracked pavers are easily replaced with the same materials, and resetting sunken or heaved sections of paving helps keep your patio level.

Mortared pavers are much less susceptible to weed growth and shifting than sandset applications. More common fixes are replacing cracked or deteriorated mortar and replacing damaged pavers. Make these types of repairs as soon as possible to prevent water from getting beneath the surface and causing further damage.

As with all masonry, stains are a common problem with brick and concrete paver patios. To remove stains from brick, follow the tips below, or use a commercial cleaning agent. Always test any cleaning solution in an inconspicuous area before applying it to the general patio space. To clean concrete pavers, consult the manufacturer for specific recommendations.

Remove weeds from between pavers using a putty knife. Dig out as much of the roots as possible to kill the weeds and prevent regrowth.

▶ Cleaning Solutions for Brick Stains

- **Efflorescence:** (whitish, chalky discoloration caused by a natural process of salts in the brick rising to the surface): Scrub surface with a stiff-bristled brush. Use a household cleaning solution for heavy accumulation.
- **Iron stains:** Spray or brush a solution of oxalic acid crystals dissolved in water, following the manufacturer's directions. Apply directly to stains.
- **Oil:** Apply a paste made from mineral spirits and an inert material, such as sawdust.
- **Paint:** Remove new paint with a solution of trisodium phosphate (TSP) and water, following the manufacturer's mixing instructions. Old paint can usually be removed with heavy scrubbing or sandblasting.
- **Mildew:** Apply a solution of 1 part bleach to 3 parts water, plus a small amount of laundry detergent. Scrub with a brush, then let solution sit for 15 minutes. Rinse thoroughly.

Refill small sections of sandset joints as needed, using the edge of a board to pack the sand.

How to Reset/Replace Sandset Pavers

Step A: Remove the First Paver

1. Loosen the sand from around the paver, using a putty knife. As you work, pull the sand out of the joint with a shop vacuum. Remove as much of the sand as possible to loosen the paver.

2. Pry up the paver carefully, using two screwdrivers or other prying tools. It may help to have another person hold the paver in place to prevent it from slipping down while you reposition the tools. Pull the paver completely out of its slot.

Step B: Level the Sand Bed

1. Remove pavers over the entire affected area.

2. Build a screed board using a piece of plywood fastened to a straight 2 × 4; the plywood should

extend below the 2 × 4 a distance equal to the thickness of the pavers.

3. To bring a sunken area up to level, add sand, then spray with water and tamp as needed to raise the sand bed to the proper level. Use the screed board to level and smooth the sand bed throughout the area.

If the pavers were too high, remove sand as needed, then tamp and screed the bed to the proper level. Note: If a tree root caused the heaving, consult an arborist or nursery about dealing with the root. Simply cutting out the root could kill the tree.

Step C: Reset the Pavers

1. Return the pavers to their original positions on the sand bed, checking as you work to make sure the reset pavers are level with the surrounding surface. Tap high pavers with a rubber mallet as needed to bring them flush to the patio surface; add sand beneath low pavers.

2. Spread sand over the entire area, sweeping it into the paver joints with a broom.

3. Dampen the area with water to settle the joints, and then let the sand dry. Repeat as needed until the joints are full and the pavers firmly locked in place.

Tools & Materials Putty knife ▪ Shop vacuum ▪ Screwdrivers ▪ Hand tamper (or board for tamping sand bed) ▪ Level ▪ Rubber mallet ▪ Broom ▪ 2 × 4 ▪ Plywood ▪ Sand.

Pry up the first paver, being careful not to damage the surrounding units.

Add or remove sand as needed, then smooth and level the bed using a homemade screed board.

Reset the pavers flush with the patio surface, and then fill the joints with sand.

Chip out the damaged mortar joints, using a small cold chisel. A mortar raking tool is effective for removing mortar close to the surface (inset).

Use a grout bag or a tuck-pointer to fill the cleaned joints with fresh mortar.

Tool the new mortar so it blends perfectly with the old joints.

How to Repair Cracked Mortar Joints

Step A: Remove the Old Mortar

1. Carefully dig out the damaged mortar from between the pavers. Start with a mortar raking tool or a small cold chisel. Use a cold chisel to remove deeper portions of mortar.

2. Vacuum the joint with a shop vacuum to remove all loosened mortar, dirt, and dust.

Step B: Fill the Joints

1. Mix a batch of mortar, using the same type as the original mortar. Add concrete fortifier to the mix to increase the strength and bond of the repair. If necessary, also add tint to match the old mortar.

2. Load a grout bag with mortar and fill the empty joints, squeezing the mortar down into the joints as much as possible. Option: You can use a tuck-pointer instead of a grout bag to fill the joints. Apply the mortar in ¼"-thick layers, letting each layer dry for 30 minutes before applying another layer. Fill the joints until they are flush with the paver faces.

Step C: Tool the Joints

1. Let the top layer of mortar set until it holds a thumbprint, then tool the joints to match the profile of the surrounding joints, using a jointer. Complete the horizontal joints first, then tool the short vertical joints. Smooth the new mortar into the old so the repair is flush with the surrounding joints. If desired, shape the joints with burlap or a coarse rag.

2. Let the mortar dry until it is crumbly, then brush off excess mortar with a stiff-bristled brush.

Tools & Materials Mortar raking tool (optional)
▪ Cold chisel ▪ Hammer ▪ Shop vacuum ▪ Supplies for mixing mortar ▪ Concrete fortifier ▪ Grout bag or tuck-pointer ▪ Jointer ▪ Burlap or coarse rag (optional) ▪ Stiff-bristled brush.

How to Replace a Mortared Brick or Paver

Step A: Remove the Paver & Mortar

1. Using a small cold chisel or a mortar raking tool, begin chipping away the mortar surrounding the damaged paver. Avoid driving the chisel into neighboring pavers. Remove the mortar in the joints as deeply as possible, using smaller chisels as needed to prevent wedging the chisel against neighboring pavers.

2. Break the paver into small pieces and remove them, using cold chisels and a brick set. Tip: To break up the paver more easily, score the face with a drill and a masonry-cutting disc.

3. Remove the paver entirely, then clean out the underlying mortar bed, using chisels. If you don't have a spare paver, save fragments of the damaged paver to use for color reference when shopping for a replacement.

Step B: Set the New Paver

1. Clean out the cavity with a shop vacuum to remove all dust and debris. Rinse the surfaces of the repair area with water, then vacuum out any excess water.

2. Mix a batch of mortar, using the same type used to install the original pavers. Add concrete fortifier to the mix to increase the strength and bond of the repair. If necessary, also add tint to match the old mortar.

3. Add a ½"-thick layer of mortar over the bottom of the cavity, then rake the mortar with a notched trowel.

4. Dampen the replacement paver slightly, then set it into the mortar. Bed the paver with a slight twisting motion, or tap lightly with a rubber mallet. Check with a straightedge to make sure the paver is flush with the faces of the neighboring pavers. If necessary, bed the paver deeper or add mortar underneath to bring it flush with the patio surface.

Step C: Mortar the Joints

1. Load a grout bag with fresh mortar. Carefully fill the empty mortar joints so the mortar is flush with the tops of the pavers. Do not overfill the joints.

2. Allow the mortar to set until it is stiff enough to hold a thumbprint. Tool the joints with a jointer that matches the profile of the original joints. Make sure the new mortar creates a smooth transition into the old. If desired, smooth the joints further, using burlap or a coarse rag.

3. Let the mortar dry until it is crumbly, then brush away any excess mortar with a stiff-bristled brush.

Tools & Materials Masonry chisels
- Hammer ▪ Power drill and masonry-cutting disc (optional) ▪ Shop vacuum ▪ Supplies for mixing mortar (page 99) ▪ Concrete fortifier ▪ Notched trowel ▪ Replacement paver(s) ▪ Jointer ▪ Burlap or coarse rag (optional) ▪ Stiff-bristled brush.

Carefully break out the paver and surrounding mortar, using masonry chisels.

Set the new paver into the mortar so it is flush with the tops of the surrounding pavers.

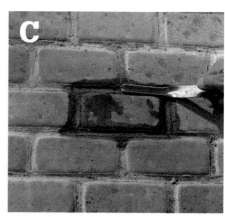

Mortar the new paver in place, then tool and smooth the mortar for a seamless repair.

Concrete Slab

Aside from cleaning and sealing the surface, concrete slab patios require very little regular maintenance. Stains are a common problem, due to the porous surface of concrete, as well as its light color that can't hide spills. A little elbow grease and the right cleaning solution eliminates most stains. Once the slab is clean, a concrete sealer will help prevent future stains and protect the surface from water intrusion that can lead to surface cracks.

More serious problems with concrete include holes, cracks, spalling (deterioration of the surface layer), and chipped corners and edges of the slab. For widespread spalling or other surface damage, consider resurfacing the slab. However, this is recommended only for structurally sound slabs, as resurfacing is essentially a cosmetic repair and will not solve structural problems.

Despite the effectiveness of control joints, cracking is quite common in concrete slabs. Widespread, deep cracks often indicate structural failure of the slab; surface repairs may hold for a while, but eventually the slab should be replaced. Isolated cracks often occur on structurally sound slabs and can be effectively repaired for the long run. You can fill small cracks (less than ¼" wide) with caulk for a temporary fix, while larger cracks require a cementitious patching material.

Patches and other repairs that call for new concrete or cement will last longer if they cure slowly. Unless directed otherwise, cover new repairs with plastic and let them cure for at least a week. In dry, hot weather, mist underneath the plastic periodically to keep the repair area damp during the curing process.

Tips for Repairing Concrete Patios ▶

Seal the edge of the slab where the patio meets the house's foundation wall, using a quality polyurethane or rubber silicone sealant. This keeps water and dirt from getting in between the two structures.

Add pigment to patching compounds to help blend repairs into the existing concrete. Experiment with different mixtures, allowing the samples to dry to reveal the final colors.

Masonry paint effectively covers repairs and unsightly discoloration on concrete slabs. High-traffic areas like patios need regular touch-ups or repainting to maintain a consistent finish.

Tips for Cleaning Concrete Patios ▶

Many stains on concrete can be removed with water and a stiff-bristle brush. Consult the solutions chart for specific solvents and detergents to use on common stains.

Never leave residue from a solvent or detergent on concrete. Rinse the surface with trisodium phosphate (TSP), then with water from a hose or pressure washer on a fan setting (not a stream setting).

Apply concrete sealer with a paint roller, squeegee, garden sprayer, or broom, following the manufacturer's directions. Allow new concrete to cure fully, and let old concrete dry before applying a concrete sealer.

▶ Cleaning Solutions for Poured Concrete Surfaces

Stain	Solution	Stain	Solution
Asphalt, tar, or pitch	Scrape off as much as possible. Scrub with scouring powder, water, and a stiff-bristle brush.	Efflorescence (salt deposits)	Remove as much as possible with a dry brush, then rinse with a pressure washer.
Blood	Wet the area with water. Wearing gloves and a mask, cover with a thin layer of sodium peroxide powder. Mist the powder with water to keep it from blowing away. CAUTION: Peroxide is highly caustic. After several minutes, sweep up as much of the powder as possible and dispose of it, then scrub with water and a stiff-bristle brush.	Oil, oil-based	As soon as possible, cover the area with a commercial oil-absorbent product. Portland cement, sawdust, talc, cat litter, cornmeal, and cornstarch also work well. Allow the product to soak up the oil. Remove as much as possible with a shovel, then wash the surface with a pressure washer.
Caulking, chewing gum	Scrape off as much as possible. Cover with a rag soaked in denatured alcohol and plastic to slow evaporation. After the alcohol has evaporated, brush off the remaining material with a stiff-bristle brush. Wash the surface with hot water and scouring powder.	Wet paint (water-based)	Soak up paint with paper towels or rags. Scrub the area with scouring powder, water, and a stiff-bristle brush.
Coffee, tea, soft drinks, alcohol	Soak a rag in a 1-to-4 solution of glycerin and water and place it on the surface for 15 minutes. Remove and clean the surface with water and a stiff-bristle brush.	Dry paint	Brush on a small amount of paint stripper. Allow the paint stripper to loosen the paint before scrubbing off the residue with scouring powder and a stiff-bristle brush.

Clean up the hole and cut a 15° keyed edge, using an abrasive wheel on a grinder.

Coat the area with a latex bonding agent to strengthen the repair.

Pack the patching compound firmly into the hole in ¼" to ½" layers.

How to Patch Small Holes in Concrete

Step A: Prepare the Area

1. Cut out around the damaged area with an abrasive wheel on a grinder or a hammer and stone chisel or cold chisel. Bevel the cuts at about 15° down and away from the center of the hole. The objective is to remove all loose pieces of concrete and aggregate and to create a firm, beveled edge for the patch to "key" into.

2. Clean the area thoroughly with a shop vacuum to remove all dust and debris.

Step B: Apply Bonding Agent

1. Apply a thin layer of latex bonding agent over the entire hole, overlapping the top surface where the patch will feather in to the old concrete. Use a paintbrush or other applicator, and follow the manufacturer's directions. The agent is an adhesive that creates a strong bond between the damaged surface and the patching compound.

2. Wait until the bonding agent is tacky (typically no more than 30 minutes) before proceeding to the next step.

Step C: Fill the Hole

1. Mix a batch of vinyl-reinforced concrete patching compound, following the manufacturer's directions.

2. Using a small mason's trowel, fill the hole with compound, applying it in ¼"-thick to ½"-thick layers. Wait about 30 minutes (or as directed) between applications. Add layers until the compound is packed to just above surface level.

3. Smooth the patch with the trowel, feathering the edges so it is level with the surrounding surface. Cover the area with plastic, and protect it from foot traffic for at least 1 week.

Tools & Materials Power drill and masonry-grinding disc ▪ Hammer and stone chisel or cold chisel (optional) ▪ Shop vacuum ▪ Paintbrush ▪ Mason's trowel ▪ Latex bonding agent ▪ Vinyl-reinforced concrete patching compound ▪ Plastic sheeting.

How to Patch Large Areas of Concrete

Cut around the damaged area to create a 15° keyed edge for the patch material.

Step A: Prepare the Area

1. Mark straight cutting lines around the damaged area.

2. Outfit a circular saw with a masonry-cutting blade, then set the saw to cut at a 15° angle. Using a thin, flat board to protect the foot of the saw, cut the concrete along the lines so the bevel points down and away from the center of the area. Make the cuts approximately as deep as the surface damage.

3. Chisel out the surface layer and any loose pieces within the cut area, using a hammer and stone chisel or cold chisel. Also use a wire brush to help loosen the material.

Step B: Apply the Concrete Patch

1. Clean the repair area thoroughly with a shop vacuum to remove all dust and debris.

2. Apply a thin layer of latex bonding agent over the entire area, overlapping the top surface where the patch will feather in to the old concrete. Use a paintbrush or other applicator, and follow the manufacturer's directions. The agent is an adhesive that creates a strong bond between the damaged surface and the patching compound. Wait for the bonding agent to become tacky (typically no more than 30 minutes).

3. Mix sand-mix concrete with concrete acrylic fortifier, following the manufacturer's directions. Fill the damaged area with concrete, packing it into all holes and crevices. The patch should rise just above the surrounding surface.

Apply a bonding agent, then fill the area with sand-mix concrete.

Step C: Float the Patch

1. Smooth and feather the area with a concrete float until the patch is level with the surrounding surface.

2. When the patch has dried sufficiently, recreate any surface texture, such as brooming, that was used on the original surface, if desired.

3. Cover the repair with plastic, and protect it from foot traffic for at least 1 week.

> **Tools & Materials** Circular saw and masonry-cutting blade ▪ Board ▪ Hammer and stone chisel or cold chisel ▪ Wire brush ▪ Shop vacuum ▪ Paintbrush ▪ Mason's trowel ▪ Concrete float ▪ Latex bonding agent ▪ Sand-mix concrete ▪ Concrete acrylic fortifier ▪ Plastic sheeting.

Smooth the patch with a concrete float to blend it into the surrounding surface.

Chisel out the crack to form a key that is wider at the bottom than the top.

Shown cutaway

Brush inside the crack and along the surface edges with latex bonding agent.

Patch the crack with compound, and smooth the surface with a trowel.

How to Repair Large Cracks in Concrete

Step A: Key the Crack

1. Chisel out the crack to create a backward-angled cut that is wider at the base than at the surface. This forms a "key" that helps lock the repair material in place. Use a stone chisel and hammer, and angle the chisel at about 15° to make the key.

Option: You can cut the upper portion of the key using a circular saw and masonry-cutting blade or a grinder and masonry disc.

2. Clean the crack thoroughly, using a wire brush to remove loose material and a shop vacuum to pull out all dust and debris.

Step B: Apply Bonding Agent

1. Apply a thin layer of latex bonding agent to the entire repair area, using a paintbrush. The bonding agent helps keep the patching compound from loosening or popping out of the crack.

Option: For larger cracks, fill the crack with sand up to ½" below the surface, providing a base for the patching compound. Apply bonding agent after the sand.

Step C: Fill the Crack

1. Mix vinyl-reinforced concrete patching compound, following the manufacturer's directions.

2. Fill the crack with compound, forcing it deep into the recesses with a trowel. Smooth and feather the patch so it is flush with the surrounding surface.

3. Cover the repair with plastic, and protect it from foot traffic for at least a week.

Tools & Materials Hammer and stone chisel ▪ Wire brush ▪ Shop vacuum ▪ Paintbrush ▪ Mason's trowel ▪ Latex bonding agent ▪ Vinyl-reinforced concrete patching compound ▪ Plastic sheeting.

How to Repair Concrete Slab Edges

Step A: Prepare the Area

1. Make a cut in the top of the slab, just outside of the damaged area, using a circular saw with a masonry-cutting blade; set the saw to cut at a 15° angle. Tip: Place a thin, flat board on the slab to protect the foot of the saw.

2. Make a second cut on the outside edge of the slab. The cut should angle down and in toward the core of the slab, to create a "key" that holds the patching material in place. Use the circular saw if it will fit, or cut the keyed edge with a hammer and stone chisel or a drill with a masonry-grinding disc.

3. Chisel the damaged area between the two cut edges to remove any loose concrete and aggregate. Vacuum the area thoroughly with a shop vacuum to remove all dust and debris.

Step B: Set the Form & Apply the Patch

1. Cut plywood form boards to match the height of the slab. To patch a corner, fasten two boards together with screws to form a 90° angle.

2. Coat the insides of the form boards with vegetable oil or a commercial release agent to prevent a bond with the patching cement.

3. Position the form against the slab and brace it with concrete blocks. Make sure the top of the form is level with the top of the slab.

4. Apply a thin layer of latex bonding agent to the repair area, using a paintbrush. Wait until the bonding agent is tacky (typically no more than 30 minutes), and then press a stiff mixture of quick-setting cement into the damaged area with a trowel.

Step C: Finish the Patch

1. Smooth the patch with a concrete float so it is flush with the slab surface.

2. Let the new cement stiffen for a few minutes, and then shape the edges of the patch with a concrete edger. Use a trowel to slice off the sides of the patch, so it is flush with the vertical faces of the slab. If desired, texture the patch to match the original slab surface.

3. Cover the repair with plastic, and protect it from foot traffic for at least 1 week.

Tools & Materials Circular saw and masonry-cutting blade ▪ Hammer and stone chisel ▪ Shop vacuum ▪ Paintbrush ▪ Mason's trowel ▪ Concrete float ▪ Concrete edger ▪ Plywood ▪ Vegetable oil or commercial release agent ▪ Concrete blocks ▪ Latex bonding agent ▪ Quick-setting cement ▪ Plastic sheeting.

Cut into the slab at a 15° angle to create a clean keyed edge for the patching material.

Set the form flush with the slab surface, then apply bonding agent and patching cement.

Smooth the patch with a concrete float. Round-over the top edges of the patch with a concrete edger (inset).

Tile

Like concrete, many types of tile can stain easily if not properly sealed. But even sealer can't keep spilled food and liquid from sticking to the rough surface of grout or getting into crevices of naturally textured stone tiles. Therefore, the best maintenance approach is to keep the tile clean, removing stains when they first appear and sealing the tile regularly, as recommended by the tile and sealer manufacturers.

What works best for removing stains depends on the tile type. A mild household detergent and synthetic scrub brush should remove many common stains. Beyond that, it's best to consult the dealer who sold you the tile, or the tile manufacturer, for recommendations. Strong cleaning solutions may strip away the tile's sealer, resulting in spotty coverage, and some agents can stain stone tiles. Ask your dealer to recommend a sealer, as well, if you haven't already found one you're happy with. Not all sealers are the same. Some soak into the tile and do a better job of retaining the tile's natural color, while others form a glossy film on top of the tile.

Outdoor tile is strong, but dropped objects and heavy patio furniture can often result in one or two tiles getting cracked. This calls for a simple, if somewhat labor-intensive, repair (see opposite page). A long crack that cuts across many tiles often is caused by a crack in the concrete slab below. The solution for this is uncertain. If the concrete hasn't finished moving, any tiles you replace will crack again. To protect against minor future movement, however, you can install new tiles over an isolation membrane (see sidebar, below).

Isolation Membranes

An isolation membrane can help protect tile from movement in the supporting base—the concrete slab, in the case of patios. Use a membrane only when the crack in the concrete is less than ⅛" wide and the surfaces on opposite sides of the crack are level with each other. Wider cracks, and especially uneven slab sections, usually indicate structural failure in the slab, and a membrane won't work for long.

To install a membrane, remove the affected tiles—at least one full tile away from the concrete crack, following the same technique used to remove a single tile. Apply the membrane to the slab according to the manufacturer's directions. Install new tiles, filling the grout joints on both sides of the affected area with caulk to create expansion joints. Grout between tiles within the area.

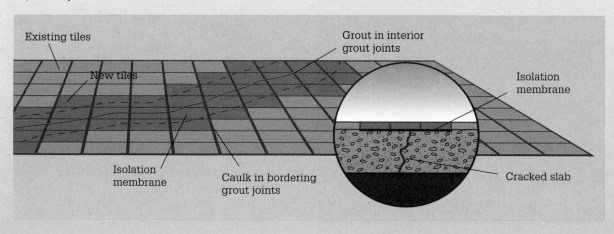

How to Replace a Damaged Tile

Step A: Remove the Tile

1. Carefully scrape away the grout around the perimeter of the damaged tile, using a utility knife, a grout saw, or a section of hacksaw blade. If you're using a utility knife, replace the blade as soon as it slips along the grout without grabbing.

Note: This is an important step; without all of the grout removed, you risk damaging neighboring tiles while chiseling out the bad one.

2. Break up the damaged tile by striking its center with a hammer or with a hammer and cold chisel. Strike the tile sharply, but avoid heavy blows that shock the surrounding area.

3. Chisel out the tile in pieces, working carefully to prevent damage to neighboring tiles.

4. Use a putty knife or chisel to remove the mortar underneath the tile. Make sure the slab surface is smooth and free of all mortar and that all grout is removed from the tile edges surrounding the cavity.

Step B: Set the New Tile

1. Vacuum the cavity thoroughly with a shop vacuum to remove all dust and debris.

2. Mix a small batch of thinset mortar (preferably the same mortar used on the existing tile). Spread a layer of mortar over the slab in the cavity and on the back of the replacement tile, using a notched trowel.

3. Set the tile into the cavity, and press down firmly until the tile is level with the surrounding tile surfaces. Make sure the grout joints are even all the way around the new tile.

Step C: Complete the Repair

1. Remove all wet mortar that has oozed into the grout joints, using a small screwdriver. Wipe the top of the tile clean, and then let the mortar dry for 24 hours.

2. Mist the empty grout joints with water, then grout the joints using the same grout used on the existing tile.

3. After the grout has fully cured, apply a tile sealer as desired.

Tools & Materials Utility knife and replacement blades ▪ Hammer ▪ Cold chisel ▪ Putty knife ▪ Shop vacuum ▪ Notched trowel ▪ Flathead screwdriver ▪ Rubber grout float ▪ Sponge ▪ Supplies for mixing thinset mortar and tile grout ▪ Tile sealer (optional).

Cut out the grout, then break up and remove the damaged tile in pieces.

Apply adhesive to the slab surface and the new tile, using a notched trowel.

Clean out the grout joints and wipe off the tiles before letting the mortar dry.

Flagstone

General maintenance on stone floors can be a little trickier than with other patio surfaces. Because stone is a natural material, and often porous, it can be difficult to clean and can also react adversely to many common cleaning agents.

Replacing a damaged stone presents the challenges of finding a new piece that matches the look of the patio, as well as cutting the replacement to fit. Extra care taken when working with stone is always well rewarded by the uncommon beauty of the material.

When it comes to cleaning stone, start with the gentlest treatment—water and a natural or synthetic fiber brush (never metal). If that won't do the job, consult your stone supplier for cleaning recommendations. All stone is different, and the people who work with your particular species should know it best. Be warned that some cleaners can stain some stones. Never use acid-based solutions on any stone. After your patio has been thoroughly cleaned,

consider sealing the surface to protect against stains and water intrusion, using a sealer recommended by your supplier.

Replacing a damaged flagstone in a sandset patio is an easy project that just takes some patience. If you're replacing a large stone that has split in two, you may be able to reuse it by shaping the edges of the broken pieces to look like individual stones. To keep a mortared stone floor in top condition, replace any loose, cracked, or deteriorated mortar joints (follow Step A, below, and Step C on page 233). To replace a damaged mortared stone, complete all of the steps shown here.

How to Replace a Mortared Flagstone

Step A: Remove the Mortar

1. Using a cold chisel or stone chisel and hammer, carefully chip out the mortar surrounding the damaged stone. Point the chisel away from neighboring stones to prevent damaging them.

Note: If you're simply removing damaged mortar, direct the chisel into the mortar only. Stop chiseling once all loose mortar is removed.

Step B: Remove the Damaged Stone

1. Working carefully to avoid cracking neighboring stones or mortar, break up the damaged stone with a hammer and chisel. Direct the chisel into the damaged stone and away from healthy areas. Strike sharply, but avoid heavy blows that shake the general patio surface.

2. Once the stone is removed, chisel out the remaining mortar bed, using the same care to prevent further damage.

Tools & Materials Cold chisels ■ Stone chisel ■ Hammer ■ Shop vacuum ■ Replacement stone ■ Supplies for mixing mortar ■ Mason's trowel ■ Straightedge or level ■ Grout bag.

Replace a sandset flagstone by lifting out the damaged stone, leveling and tamping the sand bed, and setting in a new stone and repacking the sand joints. Trim and dress the new stone as needed (see page 233).

Step C: Fit the New Stone

1. Position the replacement stone over the cavity, and mark any cuts needed to fit it. When the new stone is installed, the size of the mortar joints should roughly match the surrounding joints for an inconspicuous repair.

2. Trim and/or dress the new stone as needed.

3. Test-fit the new stone in the cavity. Make sure the cavity is deep enough to accommodate a new ½"-thick mortar bed so the replacement stone will sit level with the surrounding stones.

Step D: Set the New Stone

1. Vacuum the cavity thoroughly with a shop vacuum to remove all dust and debris.

2. Mix a batch of mortar, using the same type used on the original installation. Mist the cavity with water, then spread an even layer of mortar, about ½" thick, using a small mason's trowel.

3. Set the replacement stone and press down firmly to bed it into the mortar. Check with a straightedge to make sure the stone is roughly level with the neighboring surfaces. Make any necessary adjustments to level the stone. Let the mortar dry for at least 24 hours.

4. Mix a batch of mortar for the new mortar joints. If desired, add tint to match the old mortar. (Experiment with small sample batches of mortar and tint and let them dry to determine the best formula.) Mist the empty joints around the replacement stone, then fill and shape the joints, following Steps pages 135 and 136.

Chisel out the mortar around the damaged stone, being careful not to strike surrounding stones.

Break up and remove the damaged stone in pieces, then clean out the old mortar bed.

Mark the replacement stone so it will fit into the cavity with the proper spacing for mortar joints.

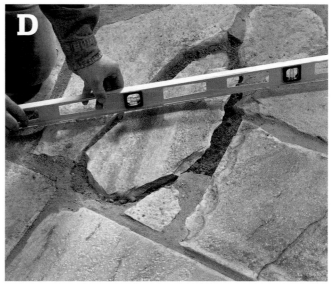

Set a straightedge across the top of the new stone to make sure it is even with the neighboring stones.

Photo Credits

PHOTOGRAPHERS

Alamy
www.alamy.com
© Beateworks, Inc./ Alamy: pages 14 (top), 209 (bottom left)
© Linda Burgess / Alamy: page 26 (top)
© Bob Elam/ Alamy: page 36
© Dynamic Graphics Group/ Creatas/ Alamy: page 200
© Piotr & Irena Kolasa/ Alamy: page 205B
© Steven Langerman/ Alamy: page 208

Ed Badham
© Ed Badhams: page 11, 17 (bottom),

Corbis
© Corbis/ royalty-free: page 49 (top)

Derek Fell's Horticultural Library
© Derek Fell: pages 27 (bottom), 28,

David Livingston
© www.davidduncanlivingston.com: pages 10 (bottom left, bottom right), 13 (bottom right), 22 (top)

Charles Mann
© Charles Mann: pages 20, 56 (bottom left), 192

Karen Melvin
© Karen Melvin: page 49 (top right)

Clive Nichols Garden Pictures
© Clive Nichols: page 21 for designer Amir Schlezinger/ My Landscapes; page 22 (bottom) for Charlotte Rowe; page 26 (top) and 57 (right) for Wynniatt-Husey Clarke.

Garden Picture Library/ Photo Library.com
© Susan Bell/ Garden Picture Library: page 12
© Rob Casey/ Garden Picture Library: page 154
© David Cavagnaro/ Garden Picture Library: page 59 (bottom)
© Jennifer Cheung/ Botanica/ Garden Picture Library: pages 11 (bottom), 33 (center)
© David Dixon/ Garden Picture Library: page 23 (top)
© Gil Hanley/ Garden Picture Library: page 23 (bottom)
© Sunniva Harte/ Garden Picture Library: page 73
© Jean-Claude Hurni/ Garden Picture Library: page 56 (top)
© Marc Laurin-Image Du Sud/ Garden Picture Library: page 9 (bottom)
© Clive Nichols/ Garden Picture Library: pages 8, 62
© Allan Pollok-Morris/ Garden Picture Library: page 140
© Lisa Romerein/ Botanica/ Garden Picture Library: page 9 (top)
© Kathryn Russel/ Botanica/ Garden Picture Library: page 25 (top)
© Jeremy Samuelson, Workbook, Inc./ Garden Picture Library: pages 18, 205 (top)
© Gunnar Smolianski/ Garden Picture Library: page 10 (top)
© Allan Pollok-Morris/ Garden Picture Library: page 24
© Tim Street-Porter/ Botanica/ Garden Picture Library: page 13 (bottom left)
© Ron Sutherland/ Garden Picture Library: pages 15 (top) , 48
© Dominique Vorillon/ Garden Picture Library: page 29 (center)
© Juliette Wade/ Garden Picture Library: page 63 (bottom)
© Matthew Wakem/ Garden Picture Library: page 15 (bottom)
© Stephen Wooster/ Garden Picture Library: page 53 (top)

The Interior Archive
© Fritz Von Der Schulenburg/ The Interior Archive: page 30 (both).

Jerry Pavia
© Jerry Pavia: page 52

Brian Vanden Brink Photography
© Brian Vanden Brink: page 5

Jessie Walker
© Jessie Walker: page 32, 34 (bottom), 35 (top)

Elizabeth Whiting and Associates:
© Tim Street-Porter/ Elizabeth Whiting and Associates: page 14 (bottom)

PHOTOGRAPHY CONTRIBUTORS

Anchor Wall Systems
www.anchorwall.com
page 112 (bottom)

Becker Concrete
www.beckerconcrete.com
651-554-0346
Page 144 (both), 146 (top right)

Belgard
www.belgard.biz
800-899-8455
Pages 6, 17 (top), 19, 29 (bottom), 34 (top), 50 (left), 51 (top), 55 (top and bottom left), 63 (top), 72 (left)

Brown Jordan International
www.brownjordan.com
page 72 (right)

Buddy Rhodes Concrete
www.buddyrhodes.com
page 53 (bottom)

California Redwood Association
www.calredwood.org
Page 49 (bottom)

Bob's Casa/ Bob Pearsall
www.bobscasa.com
Cabo San Lucas, Mexico
Page 29 (top)

Crossville Porcelain Stone
www.crossvilleinc.com
page 60, 148

Earthstone Ovens, Inc.
www.earthstoneovens.com
pages 214, 216, 217 (top left)

Ezydeck™ modular decking system
www.ezydeck.com
www.floorings.com
pages 33 (top), 47 (top left), 160

Exotic Flames, courtesy of Carl Herkes
www.exoticflames.com
page 44

Fire Stone Home Products
www.firestonehp.com
page 54

Intermatic Malibu Lighting
www.intermatic.com
page 206, 208 (left), 209 (top left, top right)

Kemiko Concrete Stains
www.kemiko.com
page 143 (top)

Kerr Lighting
www.kerrlighting.com
page 207 (bottom left)

Lewis Landscapes
www.lewislandscapes.com
page 132

Luxurious Mexico
www.luxuriousmexico.com
page 26 (bottom)

Portland Cement Company
www.cement.com
page 21 (bottom)

SOJOE FIREPITS
www.sojoe.com
page 55 (bottom right)

Southview Design, Kevin Johnson
www.southviewdesign.com
651-203-3010
page 16

Telescope Casual Furniture
www.telescopecasual.com
page 13 (top), 212

Tom Ralston Concrete
www.tomralstonconcrete.com
page 51 (bottom left)

U-Line
www.u-line.com
page 217 (top right)

Vermont Castings/ CFM Corporation
www.cfmcorp.com
page 25 (bottom)

VERSA-LOK® retaining wall systems
www.versa-lok.com
pages 31 (both), 35 (bottom), 50 (right), 51 (bottom right),
59 (top), page 62, 112 (top), 204

Wer/Ever Products, Inc.
www.werever.com
pages 213, 217 (center left, right, and bottom)

Wynniatt-Husey Clarke, Ltd.
www.whcgardendesign.com
page 57 (top left)

ADDITIONAL CONTRIBUTORS
Special thanks to:

Cover photo location courtesy of
Chris Becker
Becker Architectural Concrete
Saint Paul, MN
www.beckerconcrete.com

Tile samples contributed by
Rubble Tile
Minnetonka, MN 55345
www.rubbletile.com

Cover photo outdoor furnishings provided by
Tom Parsons
Seasonal Concepts
Bloomington, MN
www.seasonalconcepts.com

Index

A

Access considerations, 65, 68, 212–213

Acid staining concrete, 143

Adobe block, 41

Alcohol, cleaning, 225

Appliances for outdoor kitchens, 214–215, 216

Arbors
 building, 192–199
 design ideas for, 52

Asphalt, cleaning, 225

B

Backlighting, 209

Balance, 73

Balled-and-burlapped (B&B) trees, planting, 200, 201

Bare-root trees, planting, 200, 201

Basketweave brick pattern, 127

Bathing areas, 15

Beach patio ideas, 14

Bleed water, 95

Blood stains, removing, 225

Bricks
 building walls with, 184–187
 buttering, 100
 cleaning, 220
 creating island in loose material surface with, 155
 installing for edging, 163–164
 installing sandset surfaces, 122–125
 maintenance, 39
 marking and cutting, 97–98
 overview of, 83
 patterns, 126–127
 simulating with stamping, 145–146
 splitting, 98
 working with, 96–100

Building codes
 brick walls and, 184
 concrete slabs and, 140
 drainage and, 108
 fire pits and, 172
 planning and, 65

Bulb brightness, 210

Buttering bricks, 100

C

Cable gauges (sizes), 210

Caulking, removing excess, 225

Chewing gum, removing, 225

Chiminea ideas, 56, 57

Cinder blocks. See concrete blocks

Climate control. See overheads

Cobblestone fountains, building, 180–183

Coffee stains, removing, 225

Coloring concrete surfaces, 144

Concrete, 43–44
 acid staining, 143
 building basic slab, 140–142
 for building seeded concrete and wood surfaces, 137–139
 building wood forms for, 93
 cleaning, 220, 225
 coloring, 144
 creating curves with, 92
 delivery preparations, 89
 disadvantages of, 219
 estimating, 87
 footings, 90–92
 installing curb edging, 165
 mixing, 88–89
 overview of working with, 86
 patching holes, 226–227
 placing, 94–95
 ready-mix, 88
 reinforcing materials for, 87
 repairing, 224
 repairing cracks in, 228
 repairing edging, 229
 simulating flagstone with, 147
 stamping surfaces, 145–146

Concrete blocks
 mortared projects
  cutting blocks, 98
  mixing and throwing mortar, 99–100
  planning, 96
  overview of, 83

Concrete pads, 155

Concrete pavers
 installing, 128–129
 stamping, 145–146

Cost
 of brick, 39
 of stone, 42

Courtyards
 design ideas for, 12, 20–23
 landscaping with container plants, 33
 as welcoming patios, 34

Crushed stone surfaces, creating, 154–155

Curves
 creating with concrete, 92
 plotting, 118

D

Decks, 31

Decorative lighting, 205–206

Design considerations
 basic principles, 73
 blending with house, 72
 climate control, 70–71
 overview of, 61
 privacy, 12–15, 20–23, 27
 remote patios, 24
 site selection, 64–67
 size and layout, 68–69
 uses, 62–63
 wind, 71

Design elements
 fences, 20, 48–49
 gates, 32
 lattice screens, 199
 overheads, 52–53
 paths, walkways & steps, 50–51
 utilities, 58–59
 walls
  brick, 184–187
  climate considerations and, 71
  mortarless brick, 188–191
  overview of, 48–49
  for remote patios, 26–27
  retaining, 113–114
  see also surfaces

Design themes
 courtyards, 20–23
 dining & entertainment, 8–11
 multipurpose patios, 28–31
 openness, 16–19
 outdoor kitchens, 217
 overview of, 7
 privacy, 12–15, 20–23, 27
 remote patios, 24–27
 welcoming patios, 32–35

Detached patio ideas, 24–27

Dining area ideas, 8–11

Double-wythe construction, 184

Drainage, 66–67, 108–110

Drain tiles, 110

Dressing stones, 103

Dry paint, cleaning, 225

Dry wells, 66, 67, 111–112

E

Edging
- with concrete paver surfaces, 128
- installing brick paver, 163–164
- installing concrete curb, 165
- installing invisible plastic, 162
- installing lumber/board, 167
- Installing timber, 166
- with loose material surfaces, 155
- with mortared brick surfaces, 130
- with mortared flagstone surfaces, 134
- repairing concrete slab edges, 229
- with sandset brick surfaces, 122

Efflorescence, cleaning, 220, 225

Embedding concrete, 43

Entertainment area ideas, 8–11

F

Fences, 20, 48–49

Firebrick, 39

Fire pits
- building, 172–175
- design ideas for, 56–57

Fireplaces
- design ideas for, 56–57
- for outdoor kitchens, 216
- at remote patios, 25

Fixture brightness, 210

Flagstone
- cutting, 102
- installing mortared, 134–136
- installing sandset, 132–133
- overview of, 41
- replacing damaged, 232–233
- simulating with concrete, 147

Floodlights, 206

Footings, concrete, 90–92

Fountains
- building cobblestone, 180–183
- building wall, 176–179
- design ideas for, 20, 56
- privacy and, 12

Framed wood patios, building, 156–158

Freestanding patio ideas, 24–27

Freestanding walls, building, 184

G

Gates
- glass, 14
- for privacy, 32

Gravel
- creating surfaces with, 154–155
- for patio subbase, 115–118

types of, 110

Grills, 207, 214

H

Hardware, 83

Height changes
- lighting, 206, 207
- in multipurpose patios, 29
- in welcoming patios, 35

Herringbone brick patterns, 126

I

Invisible plastic edging, installing, 162

Iron stains, cleaning, 220

Isolation joints, 87

Isolation membranes, 230

L

Landscaping
- building raised garden beds, 170–171
- with container plants, 33
- courtyards/urban patios, 12, 22
- to increase openness, 16, 18–19
- lighting, 209
- for multipurpose patios, 29
- planting trees, 200–201
- plants for joints in sandset surfaces, 133
- for privacy, 27
- with retaining walls and terracing, 114
- tools for, 80
- walls & fences, 48–49

Lattice screens, building, 199

Levels
- lighting, 206, 207
- in multipurpose patios, 29
- in welcoming patios, 35

Lighting
- creating plan for, 204
- design ideas for, 59, 204–207
- line-voltage, 208
- low-voltage
  - installing, 210–211
  - overview of, 208
- for outdoor kitchens, 215
- overview of, 58
- types of, 205–206

Line-voltage lighting, 208

Loose surface materials, 46

Low-voltage lighting
- installing, 210–211
- overview of, 208

Lumber. See wood

Lumber/board edging, installing, 167

M

Masonry tools, 78–79

Materials for projects
- for adding railings to platform patios, 159
- for building arbors, 192, 193
- for building basic concrete slabs, 140
- for building brick walls, 184
- for building cobblestone fountains, 180
- for building drainage swales, 108
- for building dry wells, 111
- for building fire pits, 172
- for building footings, 91
- for building framed wood surfaces, 156
- for building mortarless brick walls, 188
- for building raised garden beds, 170
- for building seeded concrete and wood surfaces, 137
- for building wall fountains, 176
- for building wood forms, 93
- for creating loose material surfaces, 154
- estimating amount needed
  - brick, 39
  - loose materials, 46
  - lumber, 47
- for grading soil, 107
- for installing brick paver edging, 163
- for installing concrete curb edging, 165
- for installing concrete pavers, 128
- for installing invisible plastic edging, 162
- for installing low-voltage lighting, 210
- for installing lumber/board edging, 167
- for installing mortared brick, 130
- for installing mortared flagstone, 134
- for installing sandset brick surfaces, 122
- for installing sandset flagstone, 132
- for installing tiles, 148
- for installing timber edging, 166
- for installing wood tiles, 160
- lumber, 83
- mortar, 82
- for outdoor kitchens, 213–214, 215
- for patching holes in concrete, 226, 227
- for planting trees, 200
- for preparing patio subbase, 115
- for reinforcing concrete, 87
- for repairing cracked mortar joints, 220
- for repairing cracks in concrete, 228
- for repairing slab concrete edges, 229
- for replacing damaged flagstone, 232
- for replacing damaged tiles, 231
- for replacing mortared bricks or pavers, 223
- for resetting/replacing sandset pavers, 221

Mildew, removing, 220

Mock-ups for planning, 74

Moonlighting, 209

Mortar

mixing & throwing, 99–100

overview of, 82

repairing cracked joints, 220

Mortared brick projects

building walls, 184–187

installing, 130–131

marking and cutting bricks, 97–98

planning, 96

replacing bricks, 223

Mortared concrete block projects

cutting blocks, 98

mixing and throwing mortar, 99–100

planning, 96

Mortared flagstone, installing, 134–136

Mortared pavers, replacing, 223

Mortared surfaces, disadvantages, 219

Mortarless brick walls, building, 188–191

Multipurpose patios

design considerations, 62

design ideas for, 28–31

N

Natural gas, 58

Noise reduction, 12

O

Oil stains, cleaning, 220, 225

Open patios

advantages of, 11

design ideas for, 16–19

Outdoor kitchens

appliances, 214–215, 216

design ideas for, 217

planning, 212–214

utilities for, 58, 59

Outdoor rooms, 4

Overheads

building arbors, 192–199

climate considerations and, 70, 71

design ideas for, 52–53

for outdoor kitchens, 213, 215–216

privacy and, 13

P

Paint, removing, 220, 225

Partially enclosed patios, 10

Paths

design ideas for, 50–51

lighting, 206

Pavers

brick, 39

cleaning, 220

concrete, 43

creating island in loose material surface with, 155

installing brick for edging, 163–164

for lighting, 207

stamping concrete, 145–146

Pavilion ideas, 52, 53

Pergola ideas, 35, 52, 53

Perimeter trenches, 66, 67

Pinwheel brick pattern, 127

Pitch, cleaning, 225

Plans, making, 74–75

Platform patios, building, 156–158

Play areas, 62–63

Pond and pool ideas, 57

Porcelain tiles, 45

Poured concrete, 43

Power tools, 81

Premixed concrete, 88

Privacy

building lattice screens, 199

design ideas for, 12–15, 20–23, 27

remote patios, 24

using gates for, 32

Project drawings, 74

Proportion, 73

Q

Quarry tiles, 45

R

Railings, adding, 159

Raised garden beds, building, 170–171

Refractory mortar, 82

Remote patio ideas, 24–27

Retaining walls, 113–114

Right angles, plotting, 118

River rock surfaces, creating, 154–155

S

Safety lighting, 206

Salt deposits, cleaning, 220, 225

Saltillo tiles, 45

Salvaged brick, 39

Sand beds, 119

Sandset surfaces

brick, installing, 122–125

disadvantages of, 219

flagstone

installing, 132–133

replacing damaged, 232–233

pavers, resetting/replacing, 221

Security lighting, 206

Seeded concrete, 43, 137–139

Shadowing with lighting, 209

Shadows. See overheads

Sheltered areas

for multipurpose patios, 30

pavilion & pergola ideas, 35, 52–53

for remote patios, 26

see also overheads

Showers, 14

Site maps, 74

Site preparation

building drainage swales, 108–110

building dry wells, 111–112

building retaining walls and terracing, 113–114

grading soil, 106–107

laying out site and adding subbase, 115–

overview of, 105

preparing for sandset paving, 119

Slopes

building retaining walls and terracing, 113–114

grading soil, 106–107

Soft drinks, cleaning, 225

Staining concrete, 43

Stains, cleaning, 220, 225, 230

Stamping concrete, 43, 145–146

Steps

design ideas for, 50–51

lighting, 206, 207

Stone

creating surfaces with crushed, 154–155

overview of, 41

stamping to simulate, 145–146

tiles, 42

working with, 101–103

Sunlight and shadows. See overheads

Surfaces

adobe block, 41

brick, 39–40

cleaning, 220

installing mortared, 130–131

installing sandset, 122–125

replacing mortared, 223

climate considerations and, 71

concrete, 43–44

acid staining, 143

building basic slab, 140–142

building seeded concrete and wood, 137–139

cleaning, 225

coloring, 144

patching holes in, 226–227

repairing, 224

repairing cracks in, 228

repairing slab edges, 229

simulating flagstone with, 147

stamping, 145–146

creating loose material, 46, 154–155

flagstone

installing mortared, 134–136

installing sandset, 132–133

replacing damaged, 232–233

pavers

cleaning, 220

installing concrete, 128–129

replacing mortared, 223

resetting/replacing, 221

stone, 41–42

tile, 45

installing, 148–153

replacing damaged, 231

wood, 47

building framed, 156–158

decking tiles, 33

installing wood tile, 160–161

overview of, 38

Surface slope of patio, 66, 67

Swales for drainage, 66, 108–110

T

Tamping, 128

Tar, cleaning, 225

Task lighting, 206

Tea stains, removing, 225

Terracing, 113–114

Terra-cotta tiles, 45

Tiles

installing, 148–153

overview of, 45

replacing damaged, 231

stone, 42

topping mortarless brick walls with, 188, 191

wood, 47, 160–161

wood decking, 33

Timber edging, installing, 166

Tinting concrete, 43

Tools for projects

for adding railings to platform patios, 159

for building arbors, 192

for building basic concrete slabs, 140

for building brick walls, 184

for building cobblestone fountains, 180

for building drainage swales, 108

for building dry wells, 111

for building fire pits, 172

for building footings, 91

for building framed wood surfaces, 156

for building mortarless brick walls, 188

for building raised garden beds, 170

for building seeded concrete and wood surfaces, 137

for building wall fountains, 176

for building wood forms, 93

for creating loose material surfaces, 154

for cutting stone, 103

for grading soil, 107

for installing brick paver edging, 163

for installing concrete curb edging, 165

for installing concrete pavers, 128

for installing invisible plastic edging, 162

for installing low-voltage lighting, 210

for installing lumber/board edging, 167

for installing mortared brick, 130

for installing mortared flagstone, 134

for installing sandset brick surfaces, 122

for installing sandset flagstone, 132

for installing tiles, 148, 149

for installing timber edging, 166

for installing wood tiles, 160

landscaping, 80

masonry, 78–79

for patching holes in concrete, 226, 227

for planting trees, 200

power, 81

for preparing patio subbase, 115

for repairing cracked mortar joints, 220

for repairing cracks in concrete, 228

for repairing slab concrete edges, 229

for replacing damaged flagstone, 232

for replacing damaged tiles, 231

for replacing mortared bricks or pavers, 223

for resetting/replacing sandset pavers, 221

specialty, 80

Traffic flow, planning for, 68

Transformer power and controls, 210

Trees, planting, 200–201

Tumbled brick, 39

U

Uplighting, 209

Urban patios

design ideas for, 12, 20–23

landscaping with container plants, 33

as welcoming patios, 34

Utilities

marking lines, 65

for outdoor kitchens, 58, 59

safety, 58

W

Walkways

design ideas for, 50–51

lighting, 206

Wall fountains, building, 176–179

Walls

building brick, 184–187

building retaining, 113–114

climate considerations and, 71

ideas for remote patios, 26–27

mortarless brick, 188–191

overview of, 48–49

Water features

bathing areas, 15

for courtyards, 20

design ideas for, 56–57

privacy and, 12

showers for beach patios, 14

underwater lighting, 206

Welcoming patios

design ideas for, 32–35

see also courtyards

Wet paint (water-based), cleaning, 225

Wind, 71

Wood

building framed wood patios, 156–158

building seeded concrete and wood surfaces, 137–139

installing lumber/board edging, 167

installing timber edging, 166

overview of, 47

purchasing, 83

Wood chip surfaces, creating, 154–155

Wood decking tiles, 33

Wood forms, building, 93

Wood platforms, 47

Wood tiles, 47

Wood tile surfaces, installing, 160–161

Z

Zoning laws, 65, 172

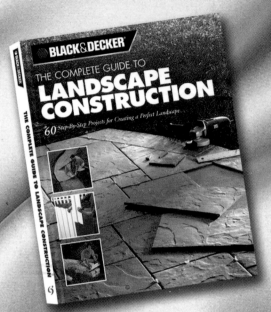